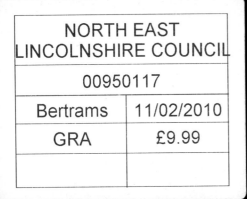
NEMI

ISBN-10: 1 84576 586 9
ISBN-13: 9781845765866

Published by
Titan Books
A division of
Titan Publishing Group Ltd
144 Southwark Street
London
SE1 0UP

First edition October 2007
4 6 8 10 9 7 5 3

Distributed by Strand Comics www.strandcomics.no
haakon@strandcomics.no, tel: +47 22 71 40 49

Visit our website:
www.titanbooks.com

Titan Books would like to thank Lise Myhre for giving us Nemi and for her invaluable input,
Håkon Strand and Lasse Espe at Strand Comics for their help in producing this book,
Deborah Dawkin and Erik Skuggevik for their translations, and Comicraft for lettering.

Did you enjoy this book? We love to hear from our readers. Please email us at:
readerfeedback@titanemail.com or write to Reader Feedback at the above address.
To receive advance information, news, competitions, and exclusive Titan offers online, please register as
a member by clicking the "sign up" button on our website: **www.titanbooks.com**

A CIP catalogue record for this title is available from the British Library.

Printed and bound in Spain.

BY
LISE MYHRE

TITAN BOOKS

FOREWORD

Nemi. Nearly ten years have passed since she first appeared on paper. Dark haired and pale, with a head full of dreams, a fistful of knuckles — and the enthusiasm of an eight year old. She was to turn my life upside down.

I was twenty-one years old and working as barmaid, illustrator, cleaner, graphic designer and cartoonist. In one page a month for the magazine *The Far Side* I had begun exploring ideas for cartoons, with mixed feelings. Although I adored drawing these, the figures (always men or animal characters) seemed alien to me and lacking in substance. I was about to shelve the cartoons, when Nemi popped up. A wild young girl in a goth setting: a figure I had more in common with than my previous crocodiles in ties — a girl I could illustrate with credibility.

Some children who go to the movies to see *Peter Pan*, are entertained for an hour or so, and go on with their lives just as before — while others sit on the car journey home thinking ecstatic thoughts until their heads ache, because they think perhaps — just perhaps — this was not a story at all and they really might be able to fly to Neverland when it is dark and everybody else is asleep. And none of these children will ever be heard saying they don't believe in elves — not even when they are nearing thirty (since every time anybody says this, an elf somewhere dies). The undersigned is just such a child, and I hated turning adult. I hated it so much that I now refuse to have a thirty–, forty–, or fifty–year crisis, because turning twenty was so traumatic.

Nemi was born of my enormous love of stories, of fairy tales, music and magic —

4

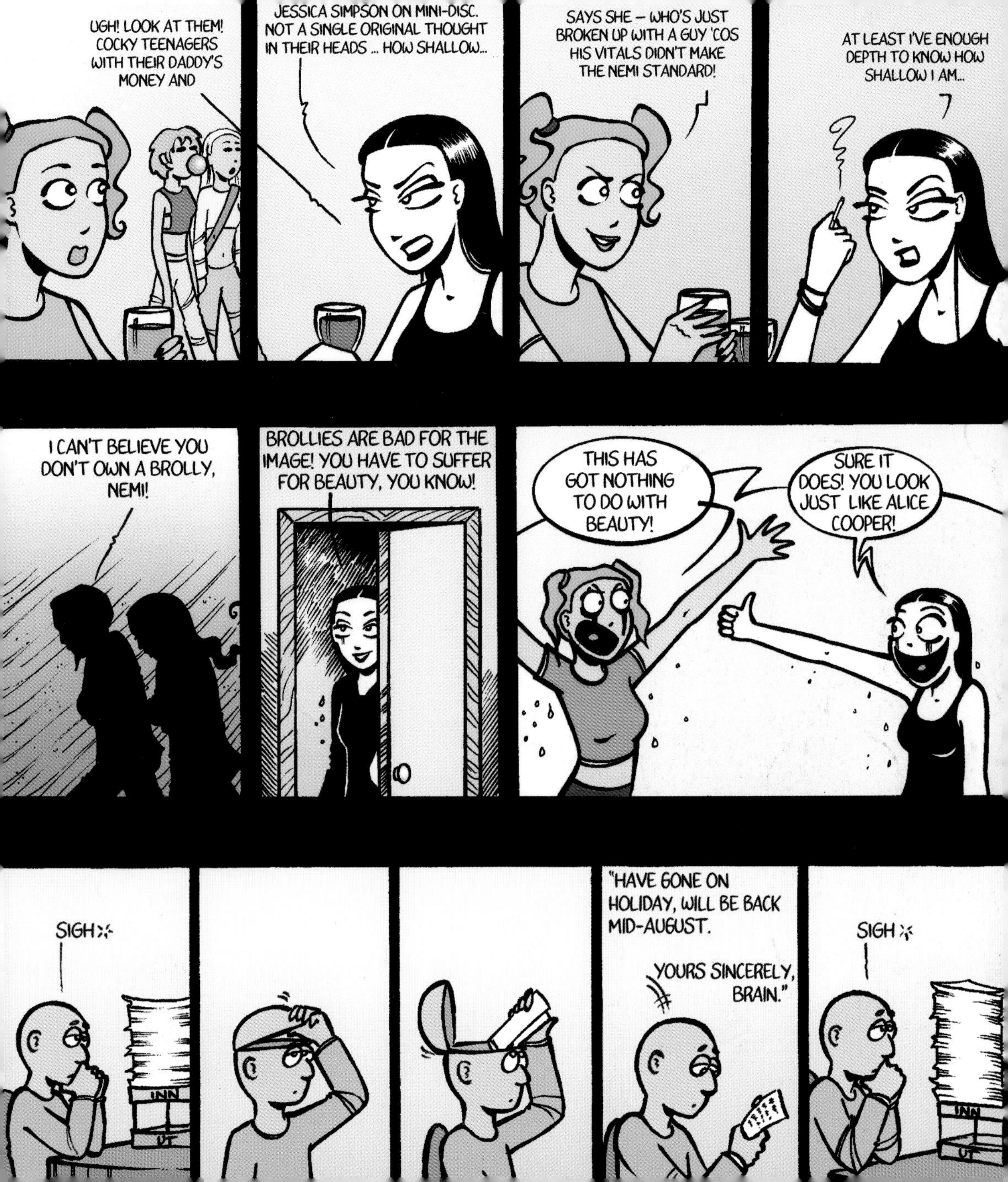

UGH! LOOK AT THEM! COCKY TEENAGERS WITH THEIR DADDY'S MONEY AND
JESSICA SIMPSON ON MINI-DISC. NOT A SINGLE ORIGINAL THOUGHT IN THEIR HEADS ... HOW SHALLOW...
SAYS SHE – WHO'S JUST BROKEN UP WITH A GUY 'COS HIS VITALS DIDN'T MAKE THE NEMI STANDARD!
AT LEAST I'VE ENOUGH DEPTH TO KNOW HOW SHALLOW I AM...
I CAN'T BELIEVE YOU DON'T OWN A BROLLY, NEMI!
BROLLIES ARE BAD FOR THE IMAGE! YOU HAVE TO SUFFER FOR BEAUTY, YOU KNOW!
THIS HAS GOT NOTHING TO DO WITH BEAUTY!
SURE IT DOES! YOU LOOK JUST LIKE ALICE COOPER!
SIGH
INN
UT
"HAVE GONE ON HOLIDAY, WILL BE BACK MID-AUGUST.
YOURS SINCERELY, BRAIN."
SIGH
INN
UT

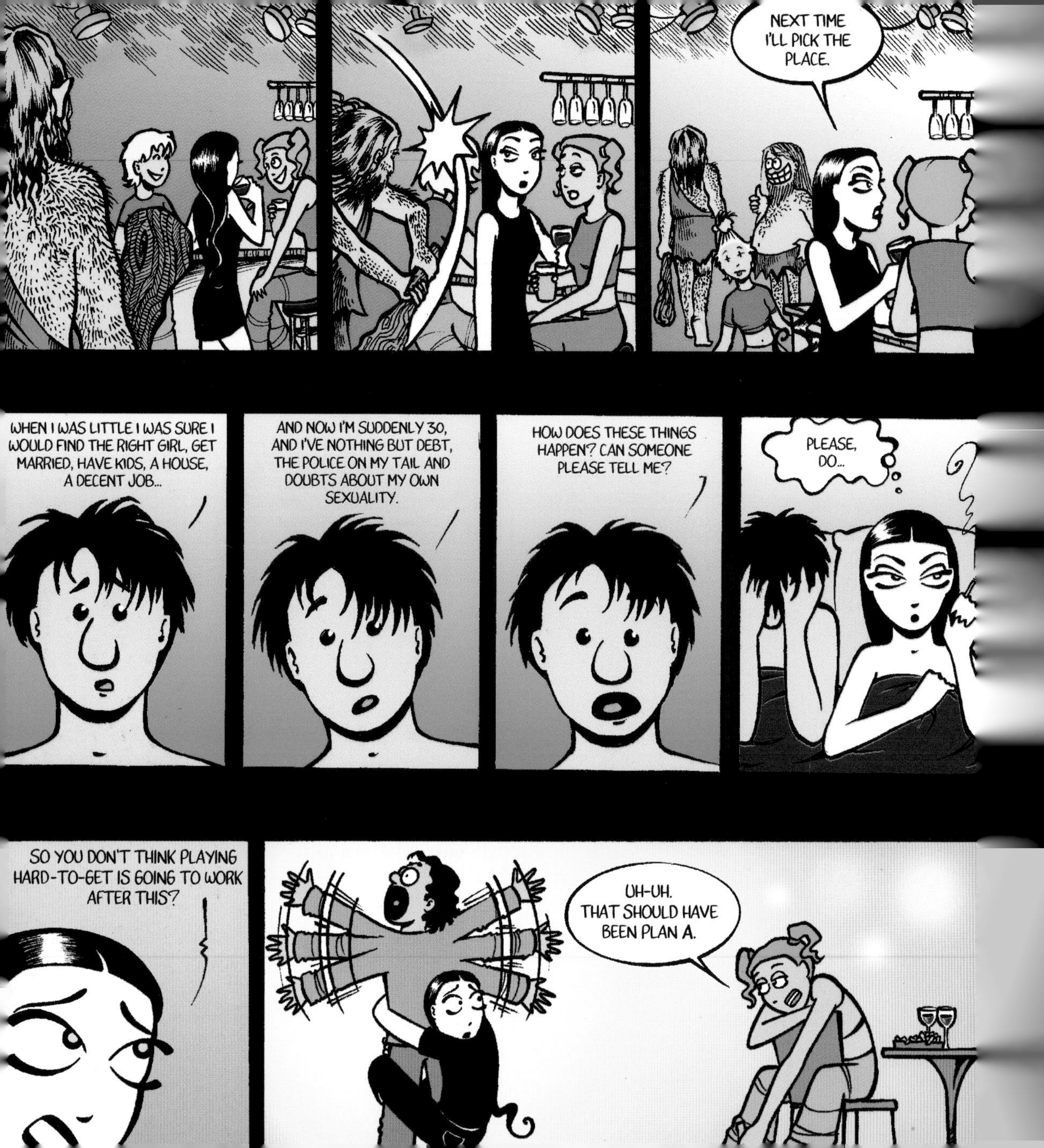
NEXT TIME I'LL PICK THE PLACE.
WHEN I WAS LITTLE I WAS SURE I WOULD FIND THE RIGHT GIRL, GET MARRIED, HAVE KIDS, A HOUSE, A DECENT JOB...
AND NOW I'M SUDDENLY 30, AND I'VE NOTHING BUT DEBT, THE POLICE ON MY TAIL AND DOUBTS ABOUT MY OWN SEXUALITY.
HOW DOES THESE THINGS HAPPEN? CAN SOMEONE PLEASE TELL ME?
PLEASE, DO...
SO YOU DON'T THINK PLAYING HARD-TO-GET IS GOING TO WORK AFTER THIS?
UH-UH. THAT SHOULD HAVE BEEN PLAN A.

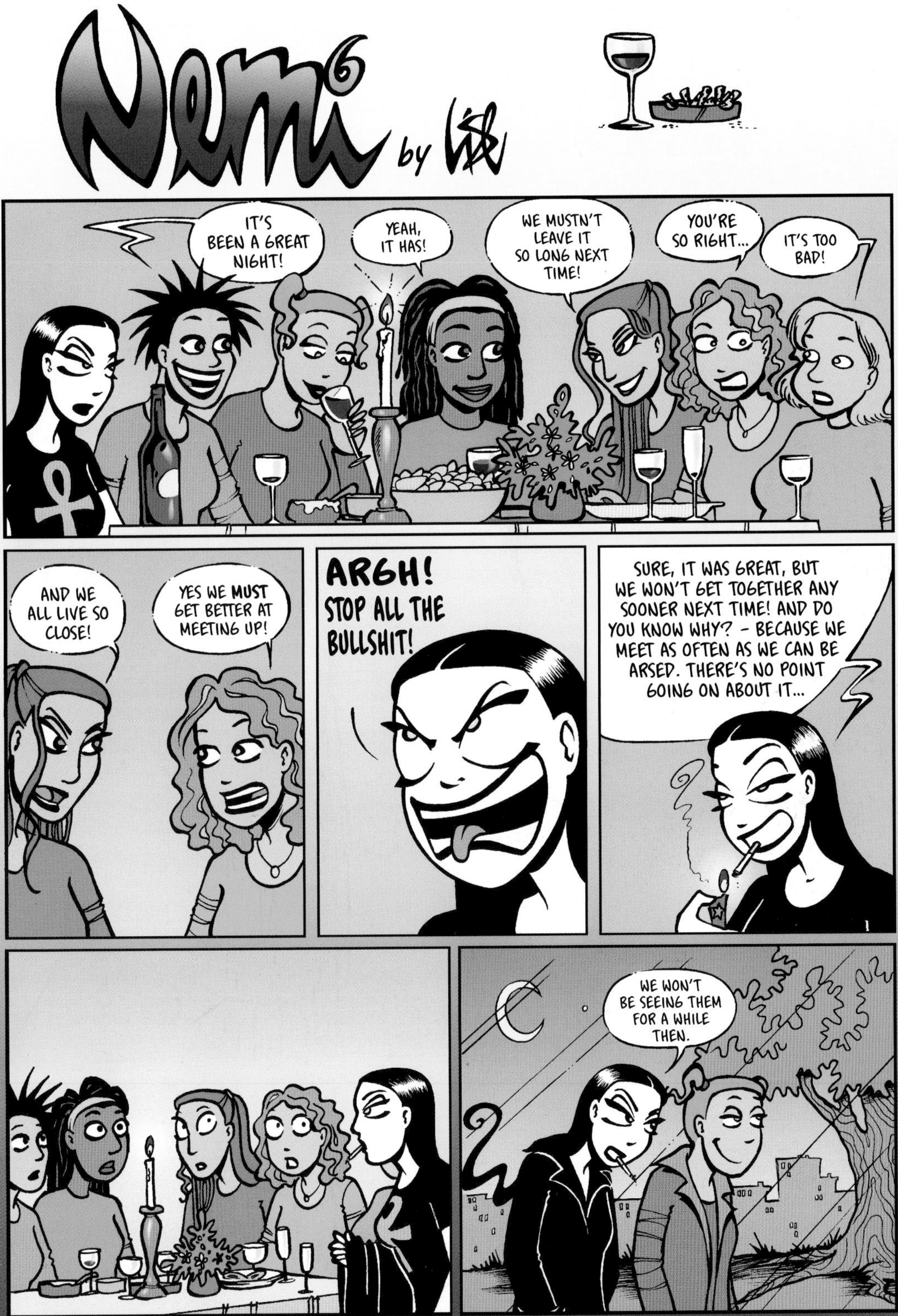
Nemi by Lise
IT'S BEEN A GREAT NIGHT!
YEAH, IT HAS!
WE MUSTN'T LEAVE IT SO LONG NEXT TIME!
YOU'RE SO RIGHT...
IT'S TOO BAD!
AND WE ALL LIVE SO CLOSE!
YES WE MUST GET BETTER AT MEETING UP!
ARGH! STOP ALL THE BULLSHIT!
SURE, IT WAS GREAT, BUT WE WON'T GET TOGETHER ANY SOONER NEXT TIME! AND DO YOU KNOW WHY? - BECAUSE WE MEET AS OFTEN AS WE CAN BE ARSED. THERE'S NO POINT GOING ON ABOUT IT...
WE WON'T BE SEEING THEM FOR A WHILE THEN.

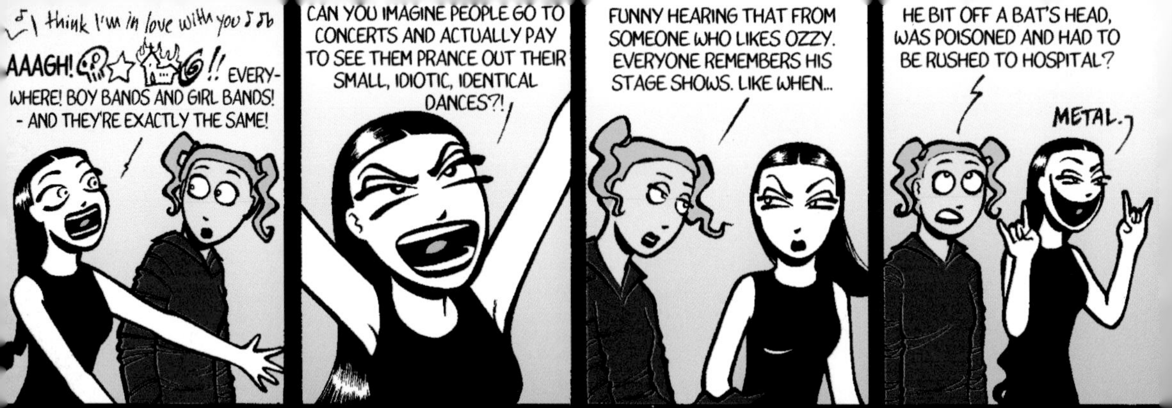
I think I'm in love with you
AAAGH! !! EVERY-WHERE! BOY BANDS AND GIRL BANDS! - AND THEY'RE EXACTLY THE SAME!
CAN YOU IMAGINE PEOPLE GO TO CONCERTS AND ACTUALLY PAY TO SEE THEM PRANCE OUT THEIR SMALL, IDIOTIC, IDENTICAL DANCES?!
FUNNY HEARING THAT FROM SOMEONE WHO LIKES OZZY. EVERYONE REMEMBERS HIS STAGE SHOWS. LIKE WHEN...
HE BIT OFF A BAT'S HEAD, WAS POISONED AND HAD TO BE RUSHED TO HOSPITAL?
METAL.

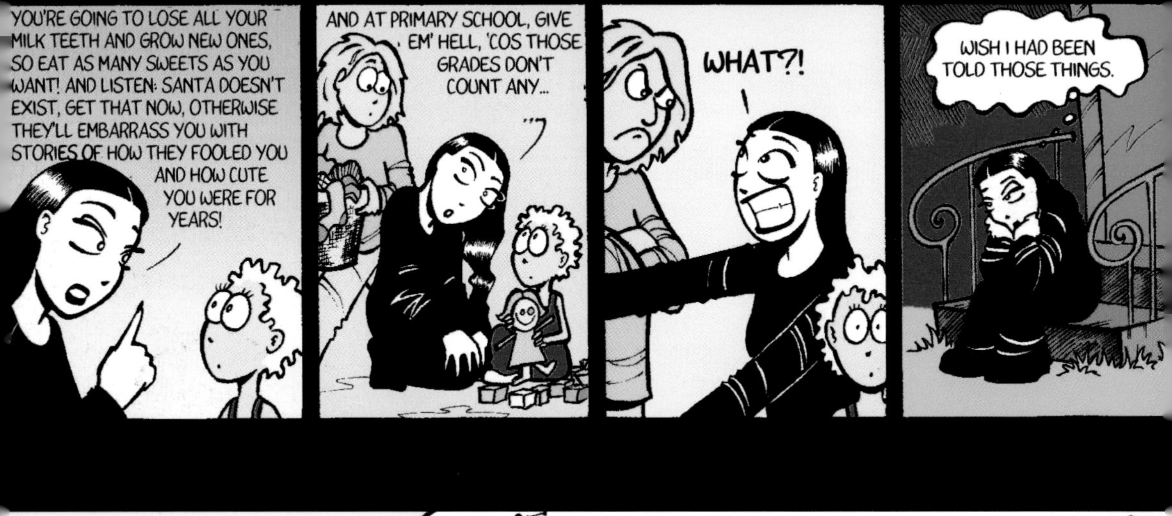
YOU'RE GOING TO LOSE ALL YOUR MILK TEETH AND GROW NEW ONES, SO EAT AS MANY SWEETS AS YOU WANT! AND LISTEN: SANTA DOESN'T EXIST, GET THAT NOW, OTHERWISE THEY'LL EMBARRASS YOU WITH STORIES OF HOW THEY FOOLED YOU AND HOW CUTE YOU WERE FOR YEARS!
AND AT PRIMARY SCHOOL, GIVE EM' HELL, 'COS THOSE GRADES DON'T COUNT ANY...
WHAT?!
WISH I HAD BEEN TOLD THOSE THINGS.

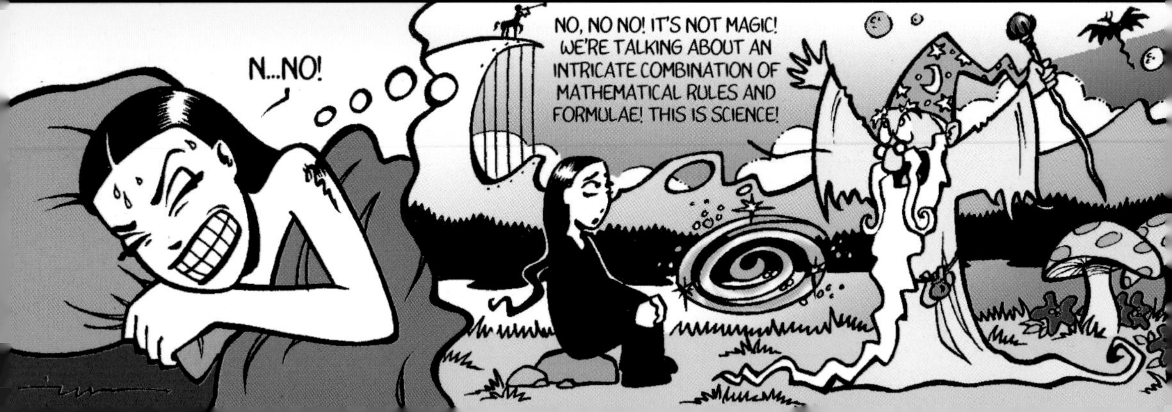
N...NO!
NO, NO NO! IT'S NOT MAGIC! WE'RE TALKING ABOUT AN INTRICATE COMBINATION OF MATHEMATICAL RULES AND FORMULAE! THIS IS SCIENCE!

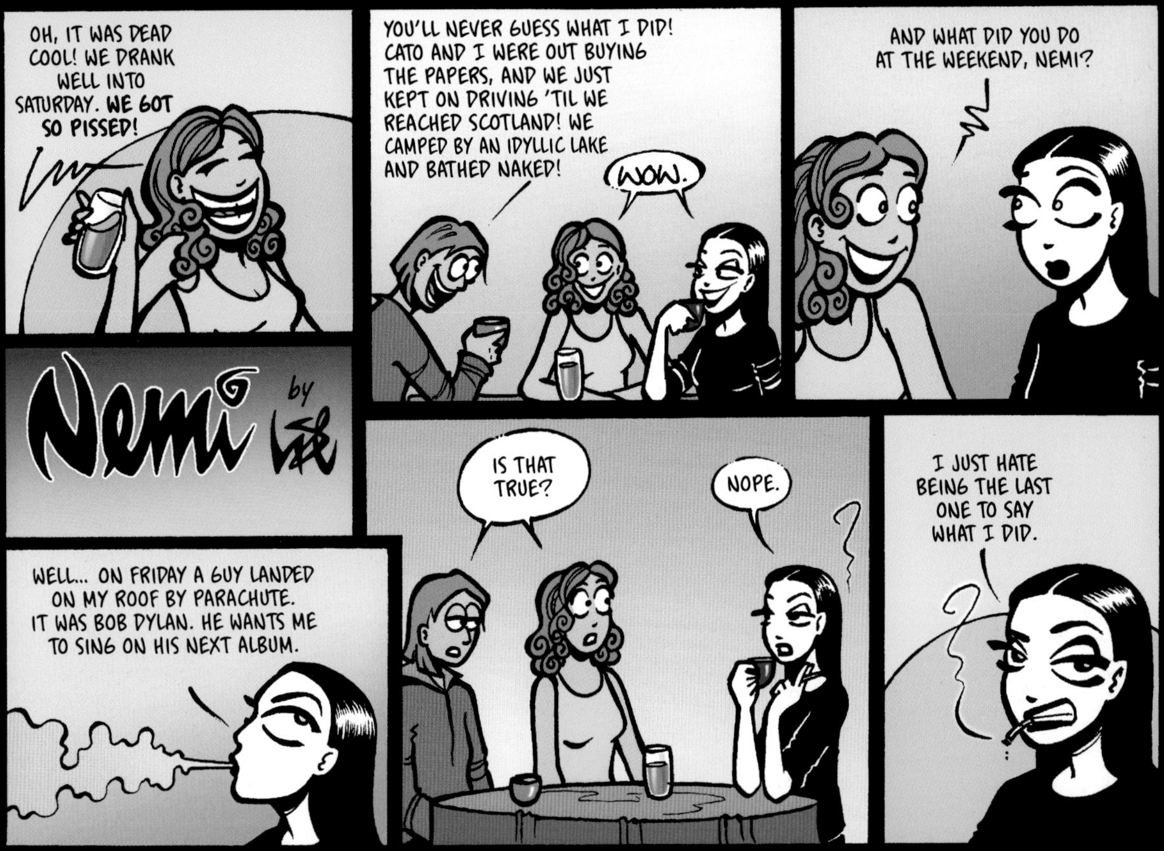
OH, IT WAS DEAD COOL! WE DRANK WELL INTO SATURDAY. WE GOT SO PISSED!
YOU'LL NEVER GUESS WHAT I DID! CATO AND I WERE OUT BUYING THE PAPERS, AND WE JUST KEPT ON DRIVING 'TIL WE REACHED SCOTLAND! WE CAMPED BY AN IDYLLIC LAKE AND BATHED NAKED!
WOW.
AND WHAT DID YOU DO AT THE WEEKEND, NEMI?
Nemi by Lise
WELL... ON FRIDAY A GUY LANDED ON MY ROOF BY PARACHUTE. IT WAS BOB DYLAN. HE WANTS ME TO SING ON HIS NEXT ALBUM.
IS THAT TRUE?
NOPE.
I JUST HATE BEING THE LAST ONE TO SAY WHAT I DID.

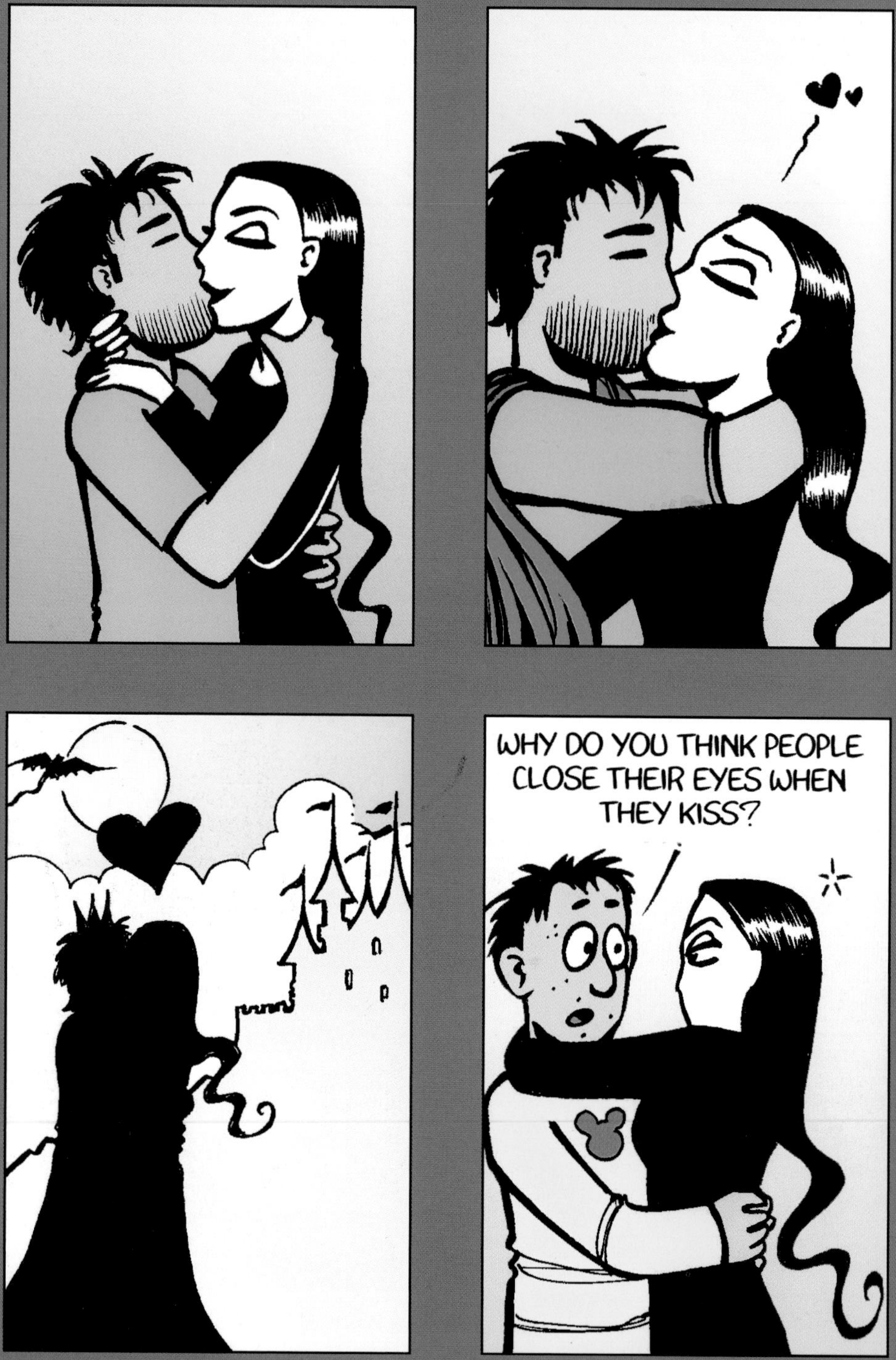
WHY DO YOU THINK PEOPLE CLOSE THEIR EYES WHEN THEY KISS?

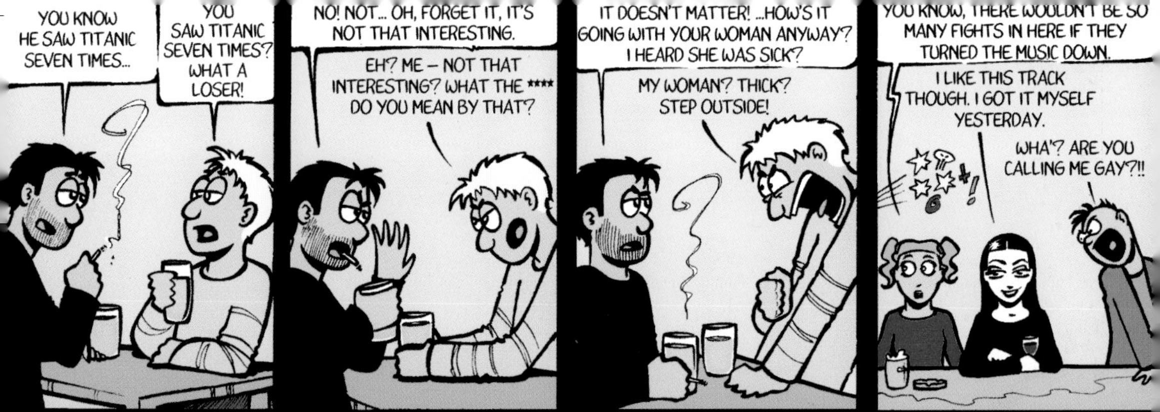
YOU KNOW HE SAW TITANIC SEVEN TIMES...
YOU SAW TITANIC SEVEN TIMES? WHAT A LOSER!
NO! NOT... OH, FORGET IT, IT'S NOT THAT INTERESTING.
EH? ME – NOT THAT INTERESTING? WHAT THE **** DO YOU MEAN BY THAT?
IT DOESN'T MATTER! ...HOW'S IT GOING WITH YOUR WOMAN ANYWAY? I HEARD SHE WAS SICK?
MY WOMAN? THICK? STEP OUTSIDE!
YOU KNOW, THERE WOULDN'T BE SO MANY FIGHTS IN HERE IF THEY TURNED THE MUSIC DOWN.
I LIKE THIS TRACK THOUGH. I GOT IT MYSELF YESTERDAY.
WHA'? ARE YOU CALLING ME GAY?!!

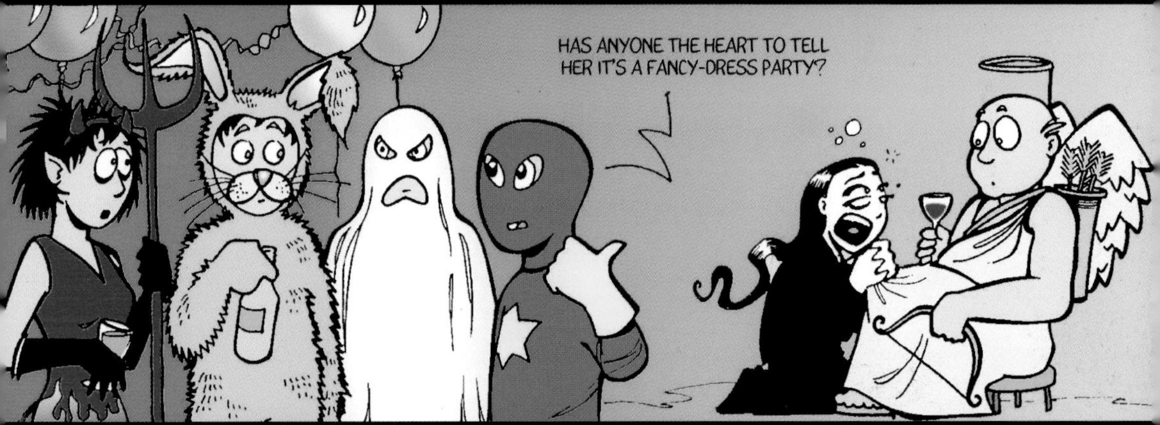
HAS ANYONE THE HEART TO TELL HER IT'S A FANCY-DRESS PARTY?

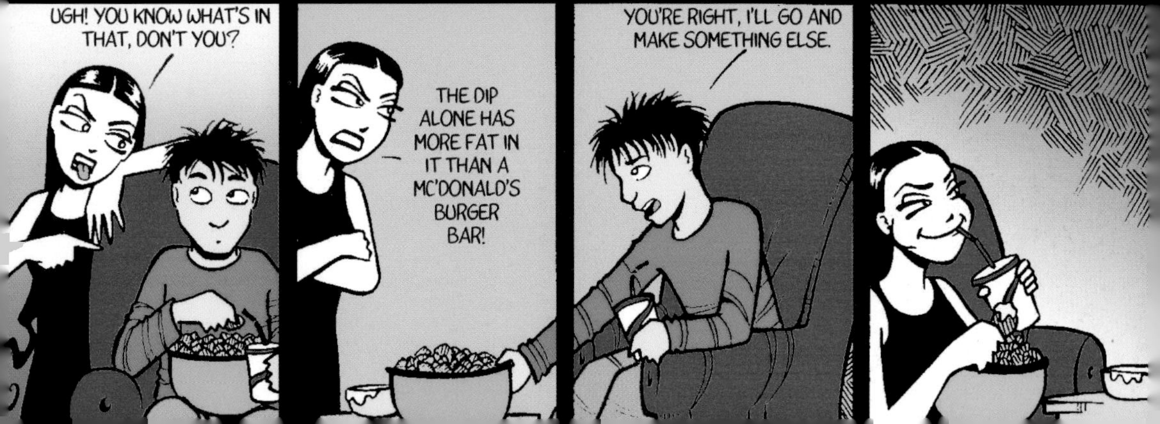
UGH! YOU KNOW WHAT'S IN THAT, DON'T YOU?
THE DIP ALONE HAS MORE FAT IN IT THAN A MC'DONALD'S BURGER BAR!
YOU'RE RIGHT, I'LL GO AND MAKE SOMETHING ELSE.

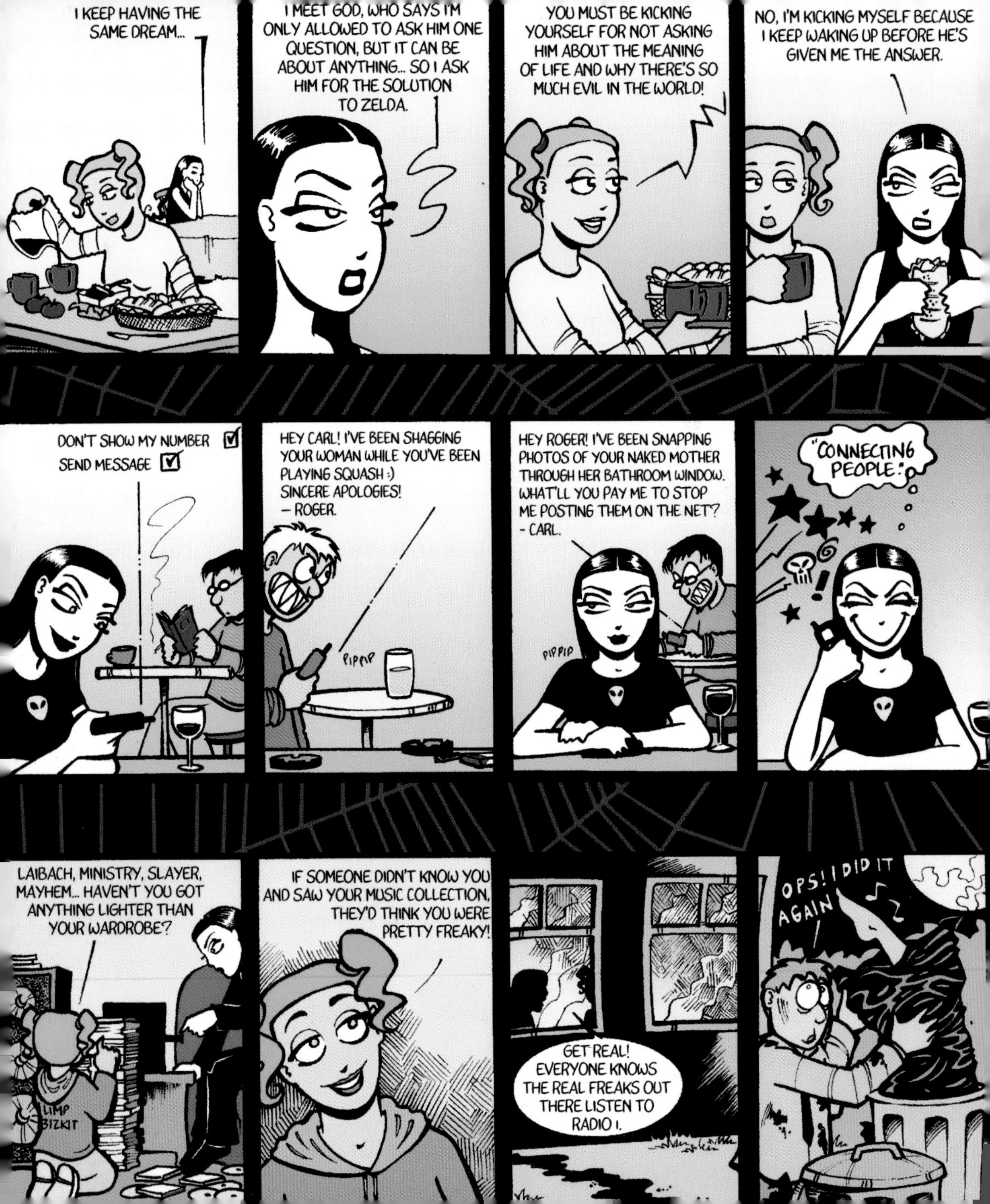
I KEEP HAVING THE SAME DREAM...
I MEET GOD, WHO SAYS I'M ONLY ALLOWED TO ASK HIM ONE QUESTION, BUT IT CAN BE ABOUT ANYTHING... SO I ASK HIM FOR THE SOLUTION TO ZELDA.
YOU MUST BE KICKING YOURSELF FOR NOT ASKING HIM ABOUT THE MEANING OF LIFE AND WHY THERE'S SO MUCH EVIL IN THE WORLD!
NO, I'M KICKING MYSELF BECAUSE I KEEP WAKING UP BEFORE HE'S GIVEN ME THE ANSWER.
DON'T SHOW MY NUMBER
SEND MESSAGE
HEY CARL! I'VE BEEN SHAGGING YOUR WOMAN WHILE YOU'VE BEEN PLAYING SQUASH :) SINCERE APOLOGIES! – ROGER.
PIPPIP
HEY ROGER! I'VE BEEN SNAPPING PHOTOS OF YOUR NAKED MOTHER THROUGH HER BATHROOM WINDOW. WHAT'LL YOU PAY ME TO STOP ME POSTING THEM ON THE NET? - CARL.
PIPPIP
"CONNECTING PEOPLE."
LAIBACH, MINISTRY, SLAYER, MAYHEM... HAVEN'T YOU GOT ANYTHING LIGHTER THAN YOUR WARDROBE?
LIMP BIZKIT
IF SOMEONE DIDN'T KNOW YOU AND SAW YOUR MUSIC COLLECTION, THEY'D THINK YOU WERE PRETTY FREAKY!
GET REAL! EVERYONE KNOWS THE REAL FREAKS OUT THERE LISTEN TO RADIO 1.
OPS! I DID IT AGAIN

JUST A BIT LONGER ... INDULGE A LITTLE MORE...
BIP BIP BIP BIP BIP BIP BIP BIP BIP BIP
!
GUESS WHAT? I MANAGED TO WAKE UP AFTER THOSE LEGENDARY TEN MINUTES! AND I AM WIDE AWAKE – ON A MONDAY!
IT'S TUESDAY.
WHOA THERE...
GOING OUT TONIGHT?
NO, I'M STAYING IN AND WATCHING A VIDEO.
YOU'VE GOT TO LIVE A BIT MORE, NEMI. WE'RE NOT YOUNG FOREVER YOU KNOW!
THE DOORS THAT ARE OPEN TODAY CAN BE CLOSED TOMORROW; DOESN'T THAT WORRY YOU?
THANKS, NOW I'VE GONE FROM BEING DULL TO APATHETIC.

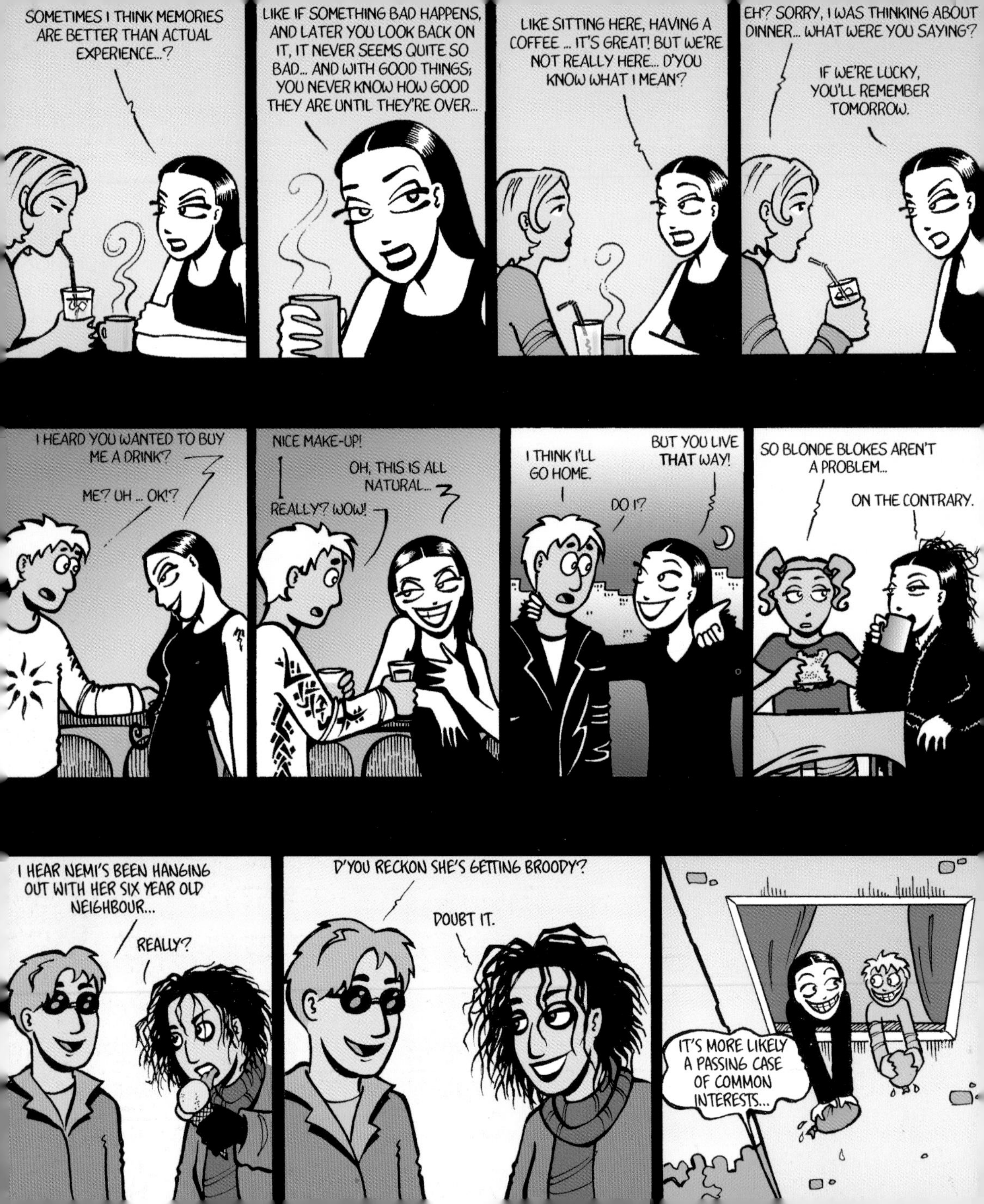
SOMETIMES I THINK MEMORIES ARE BETTER THAN ACTUAL EXPERIENCE...?
LIKE IF SOMETHING BAD HAPPENS, AND LATER YOU LOOK BACK ON IT, IT NEVER SEEMS QUITE SO BAD... AND WITH GOOD THINGS; YOU NEVER KNOW HOW GOOD THEY ARE UNTIL THEY'RE OVER...
LIKE SITTING HERE, HAVING A COFFEE ... IT'S GREAT! BUT WE'RE NOT REALLY HERE... D'YOU KNOW WHAT I MEAN?
EH? SORRY, I WAS THINKING ABOUT DINNER... WHAT WERE YOU SAYING?
IF WE'RE LUCKY, YOU'LL REMEMBER TOMORROW.
I HEARD YOU WANTED TO BUY ME A DRINK?
ME? UH ... OK!?
NICE MAKE-UP!
OH, THIS IS ALL NATURAL...
REALLY? WOW!
I THINK I'LL GO HOME.
BUT YOU LIVE **THAT** WAY!
DO I?
SO BLONDE BLOKES AREN'T A PROBLEM...
ON THE CONTRARY.
I HEAR NEMI'S BEEN HANGING OUT WITH HER SIX YEAR OLD NEIGHBOUR...
REALLY?
D'YOU RECKON SHE'S GETTING BROODY?
DOUBT IT.
IT'S MORE LIKELY A PASSING CASE OF COMMON INTERESTS...

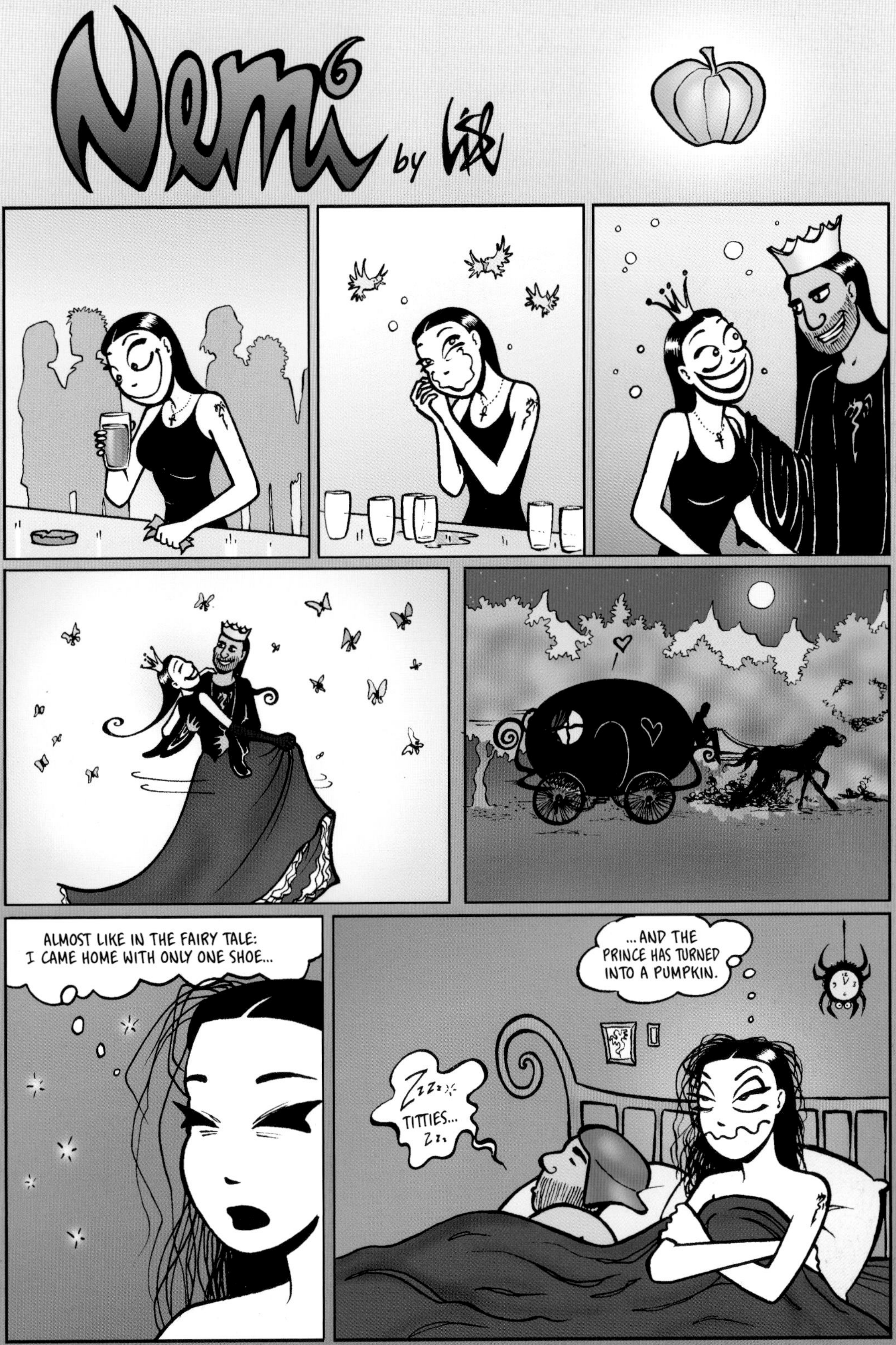
Nemi by Lise
ALMOST LIKE IN THE FAIRY TALE: I CAME HOME WITH ONLY ONE SHOE...
...AND THE PRINCE HAS TURNED INTO A PUMPKIN.
Zzzz TITTIES... Zzz

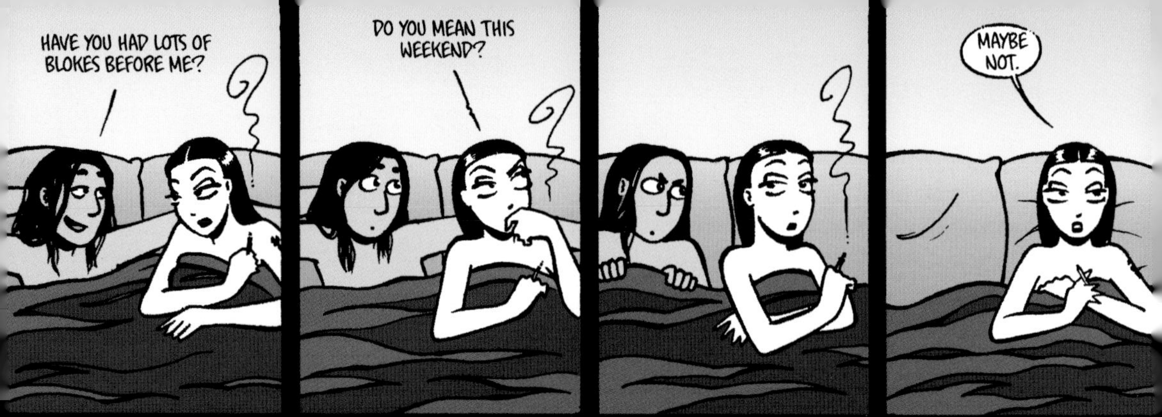

HAVE YOU HAD LOTS OF BLOKES BEFORE ME?
DO YOU MEAN THIS WEEKEND?
MAYBE NOT.

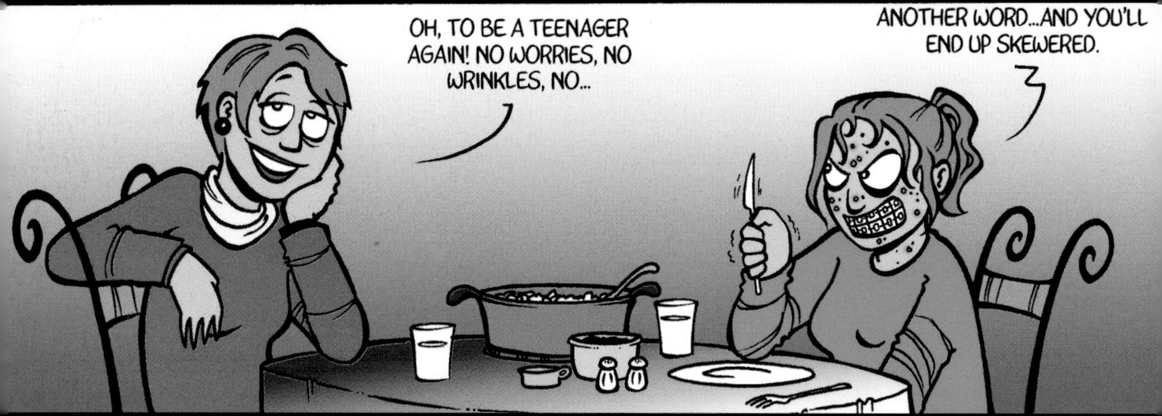

OH, TO BE A TEENAGER AGAIN! NO WORRIES, NO WRINKLES, NO...
ANOTHER WORD...AND YOU'LL END UP SKEWERED.

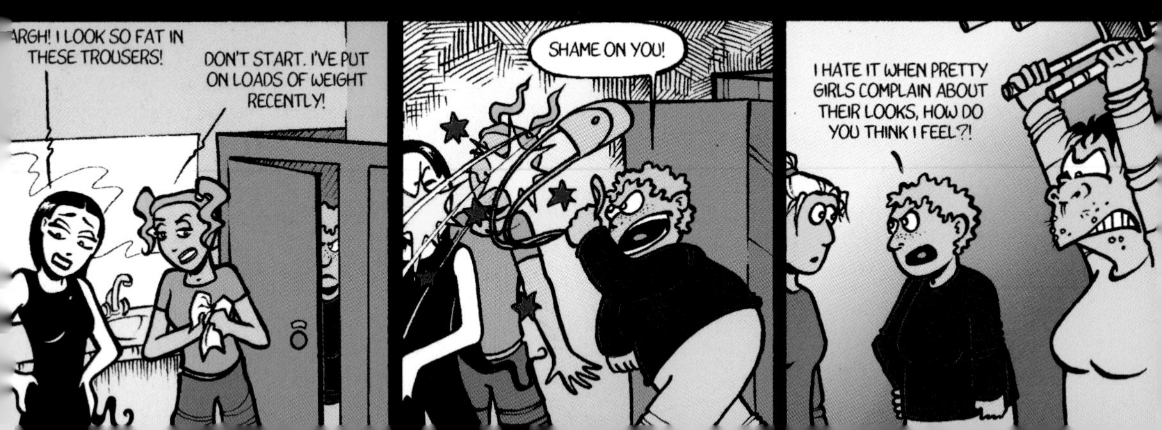

RGH! I LOOK SO FAT IN THESE TROUSERS!
DON'T START. I'VE PUT ON LOADS OF WEIGHT RECENTLY!
SHAME ON YOU!
I HATE IT WHEN PRETTY GIRLS COMPLAIN ABOUT THEIR LOOKS, HOW DO YOU THINK I FEEL?!

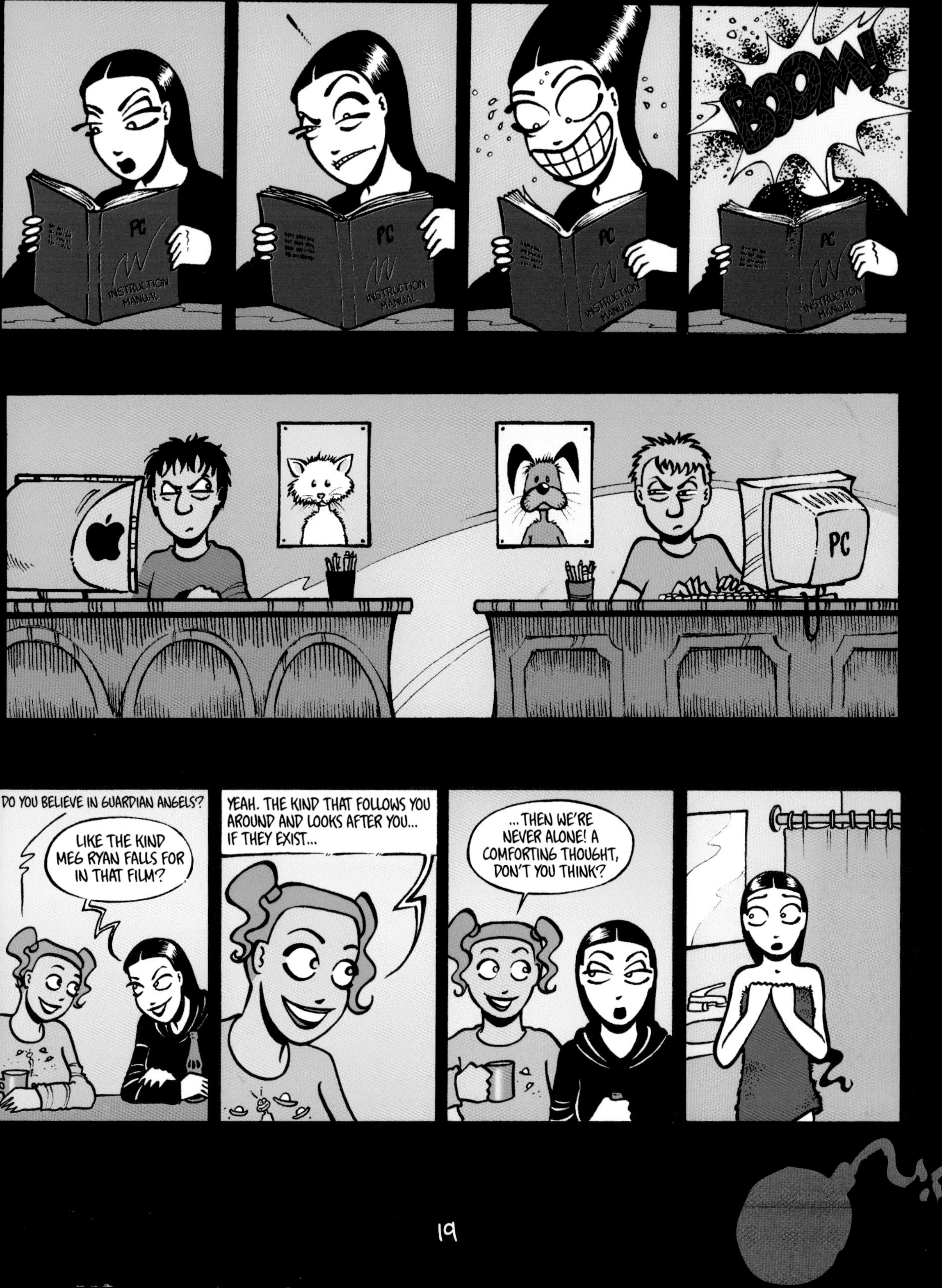
PC
INSTRUCTION MANUAL
BOOM!
PC
DO YOU BELIEVE IN GUARDIAN ANGELS?
LIKE THE KIND MEG RYAN FALLS FOR IN THAT FILM?
YEAH. THE KIND THAT FOLLOWS YOU AROUND AND LOOKS AFTER YOU... IF THEY EXIST...
... THEN WE'RE NEVER ALONE! A COMFORTING THOUGHT, DON'T YOU THINK?

THE RAIN WILL CONTINUE TODAY ACROSS THE COUNTRY...

IF THIS RAIN HAD BEEN SNOW, WE WOULD HAVE BEEN UNDER TEN-TWELVE FOOT BY NOW!

AND TALKING OF SNOW, BY THE END OF THE WEEK SNOW AND SLEET IS EXPECTED ACROSS MOST OF...

I LIVE IN MORDOR.

AND HERE THE DESERT TRIPPER IS FLARING OUT HIS COLOURFUL COLLAR IN HOPE OF ATTRACTING A FEMALE.

WHAT A DAFT, LITTLE CREATURE.

ARGH! WHERE DID I PUT THAT ****** PHONE NUMBER?! I WROTE IT ON A PIECE OF PAPER, BUT I MUST HAVE THROWN IT AWAY!

WHY DON'T YOU USE ...

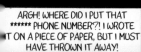

THE FILOFAX YOU GAVE ME? I CAN'T FIND THAT EITHER, AND THE LAST THING I NEED IS ADVICE FROM LITTLE MISS. ORGANISED! IT REALLY BUGS ME THE WAY YOU ALWAYS KNOW EXACTLY WHERE EVERYTHING IS...

MAYBE I SAVED THE NUMBER ON MY MOBILE? NOW WHERE'S THAT? I'LL HAVE TO PHONE IT, SO I CAN HEAR IT! UH... D'YOU KNOW MY NUMBER?

FOR GOODNESS'... I HOPE WE'RE NO LONGER FRIENDS WHEN YOU GET OLD.

NO CHANCE.

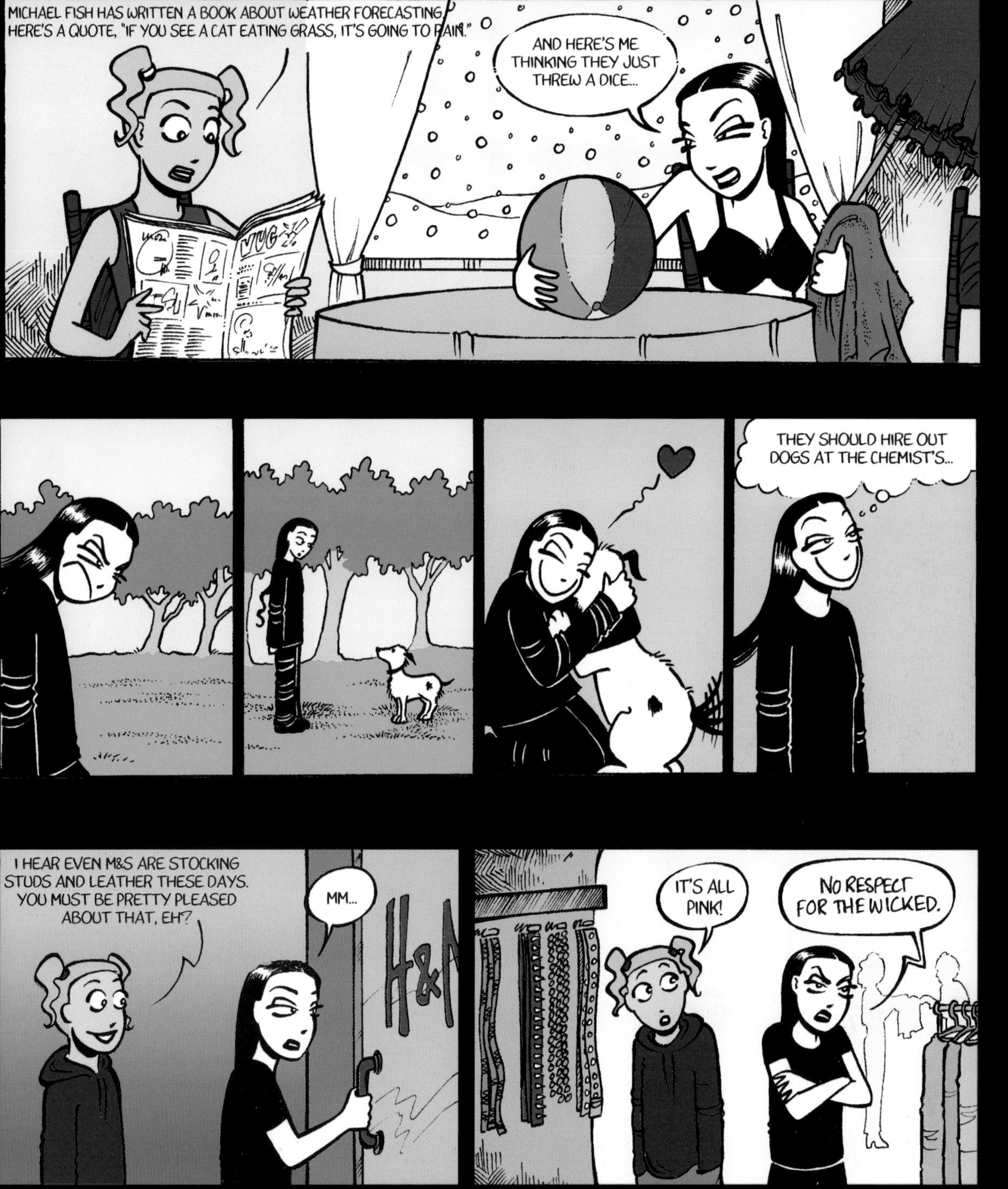
MICHAEL FISH HAS WRITTEN A BOOK ABOUT WEATHER FORECASTING. HERE'S A QUOTE, "IF YOU SEE A CAT EATING GRASS, IT'S GOING TO RAIN."
AND HERE'S ME THINKING THEY JUST THREW A DICE...
THEY SHOULD HIRE OUT DOGS AT THE CHEMIST'S...
I HEAR EVEN M&S ARE STOCKING STUDS AND LEATHER THESE DAYS. YOU MUST BE PRETTY PLEASED ABOUT THAT, EH?
MM...
IT'S ALL PINK!
NO RESPECT FOR THE WICKED.

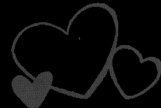

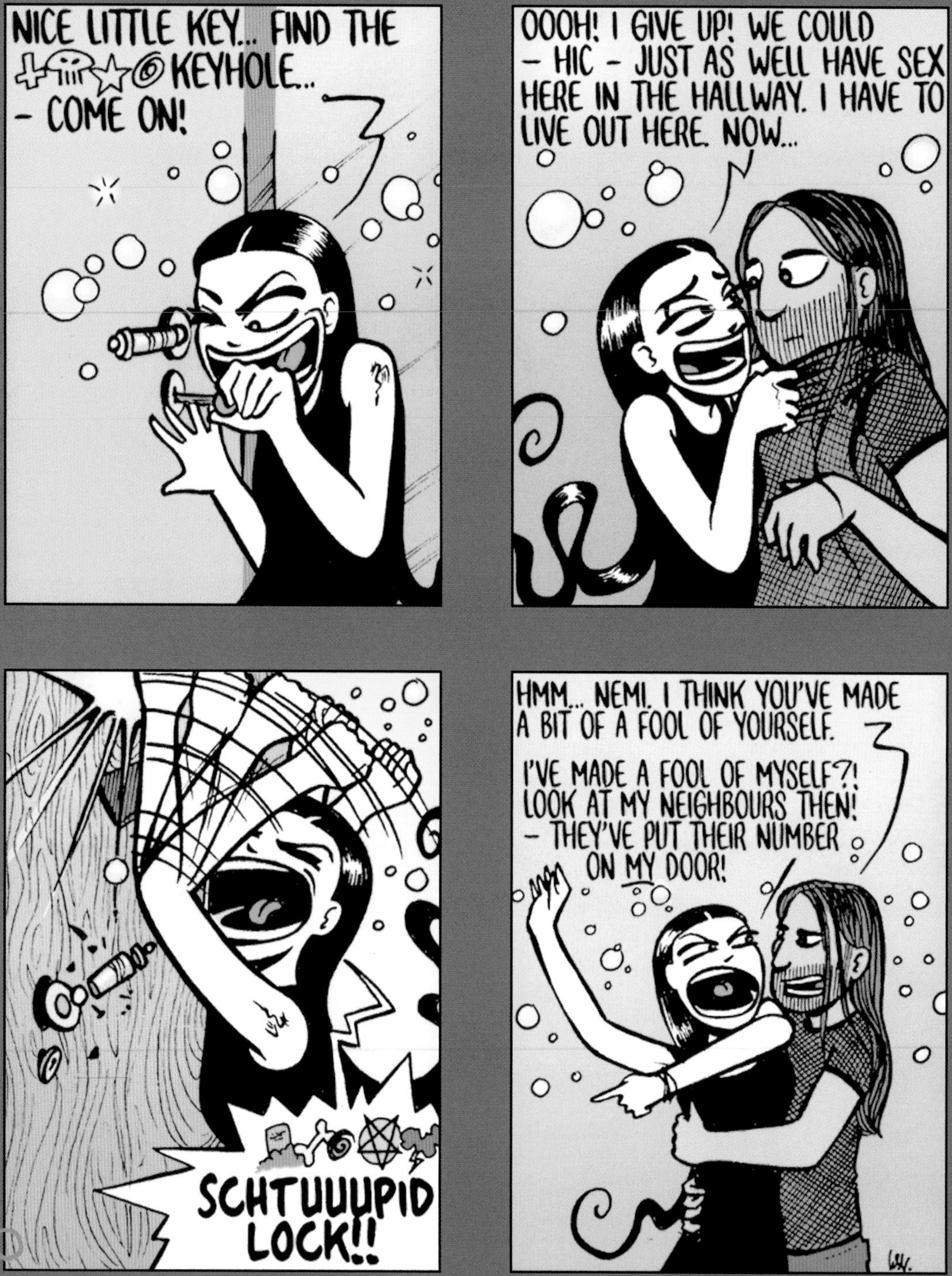

NICE LITTLE KEY... FIND THE KEYHOLE... – COME ON!
OOOH! I GIVE UP! WE COULD – HIC – JUST AS WELL HAVE SEX HERE IN THE HALLWAY. I HAVE TO LIVE OUT HERE. NOW...
SCHTUUUPID LOCK!!
HMM... NEMI. I THINK YOU'VE MADE A BIT OF A FOOL OF YOURSELF.
I'VE MADE A FOOL OF MYSELF?! LOOK AT MY NEIGHBOURS THEN! – THEY'VE PUT THEIR NUMBER ON MY DOOR!

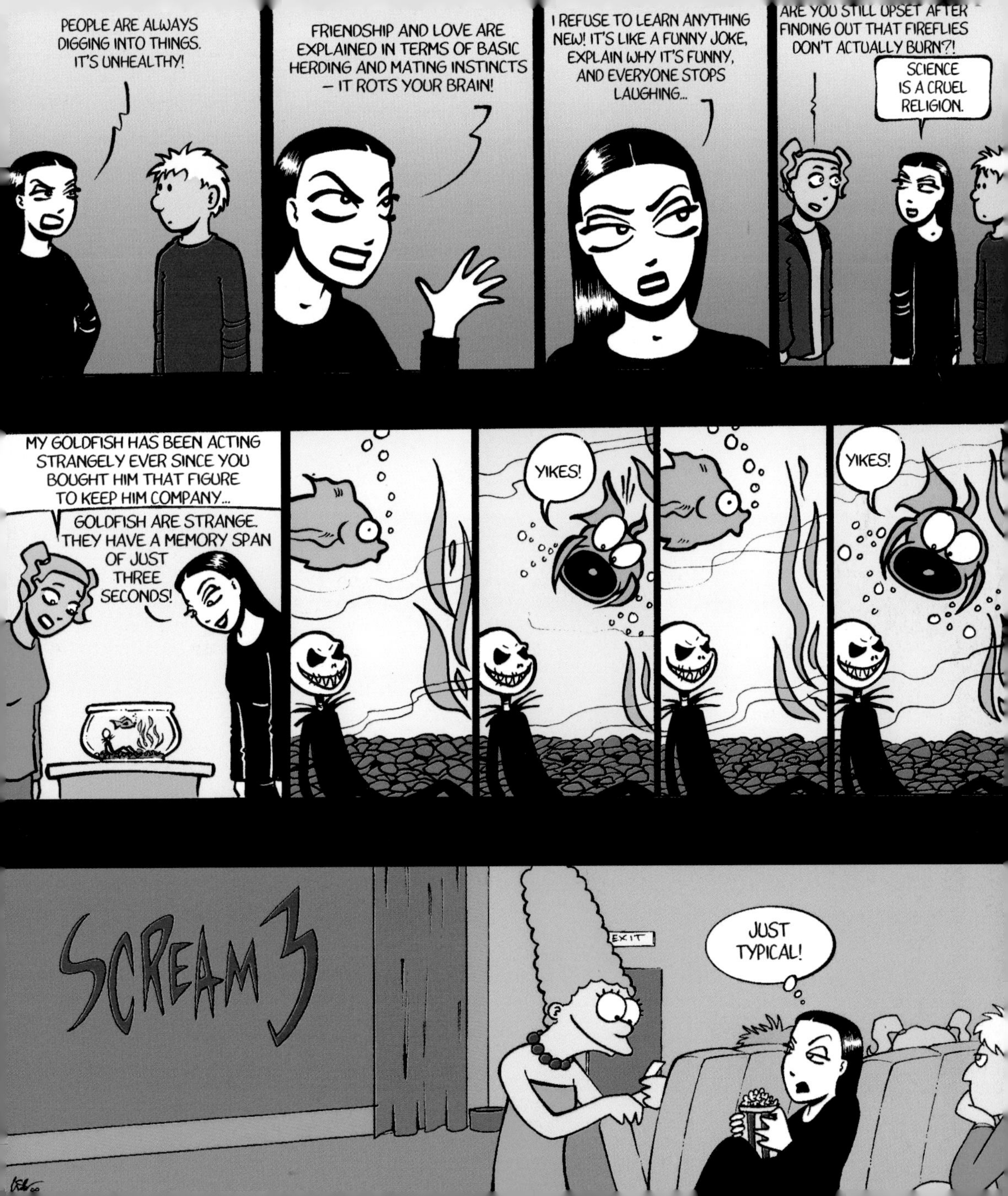
PEOPLE ARE ALWAYS DIGGING INTO THINGS. IT'S UNHEALTHY!
FRIENDSHIP AND LOVE ARE EXPLAINED IN TERMS OF BASIC HERDING AND MATING INSTINCTS – IT ROTS YOUR BRAIN!
I REFUSE TO LEARN ANYTHING NEW! IT'S LIKE A FUNNY JOKE, EXPLAIN WHY IT'S FUNNY, AND EVERYONE STOPS LAUGHING...
ARE YOU STILL UPSET AFTER FINDING OUT THAT FIREFLIES DON'T ACTUALLY BURN?!
SCIENCE IS A CRUEL RELIGION.
MY GOLDFISH HAS BEEN ACTING STRANGELY EVER SINCE YOU BOUGHT HIM THAT FIGURE TO KEEP HIM COMPANY...
GOLDFISH ARE STRANGE. THEY HAVE A MEMORY SPAN OF JUST THREE SECONDS!
YIKES!
YIKES!
SCREAM 3
EXIT
JUST TYPICAL!

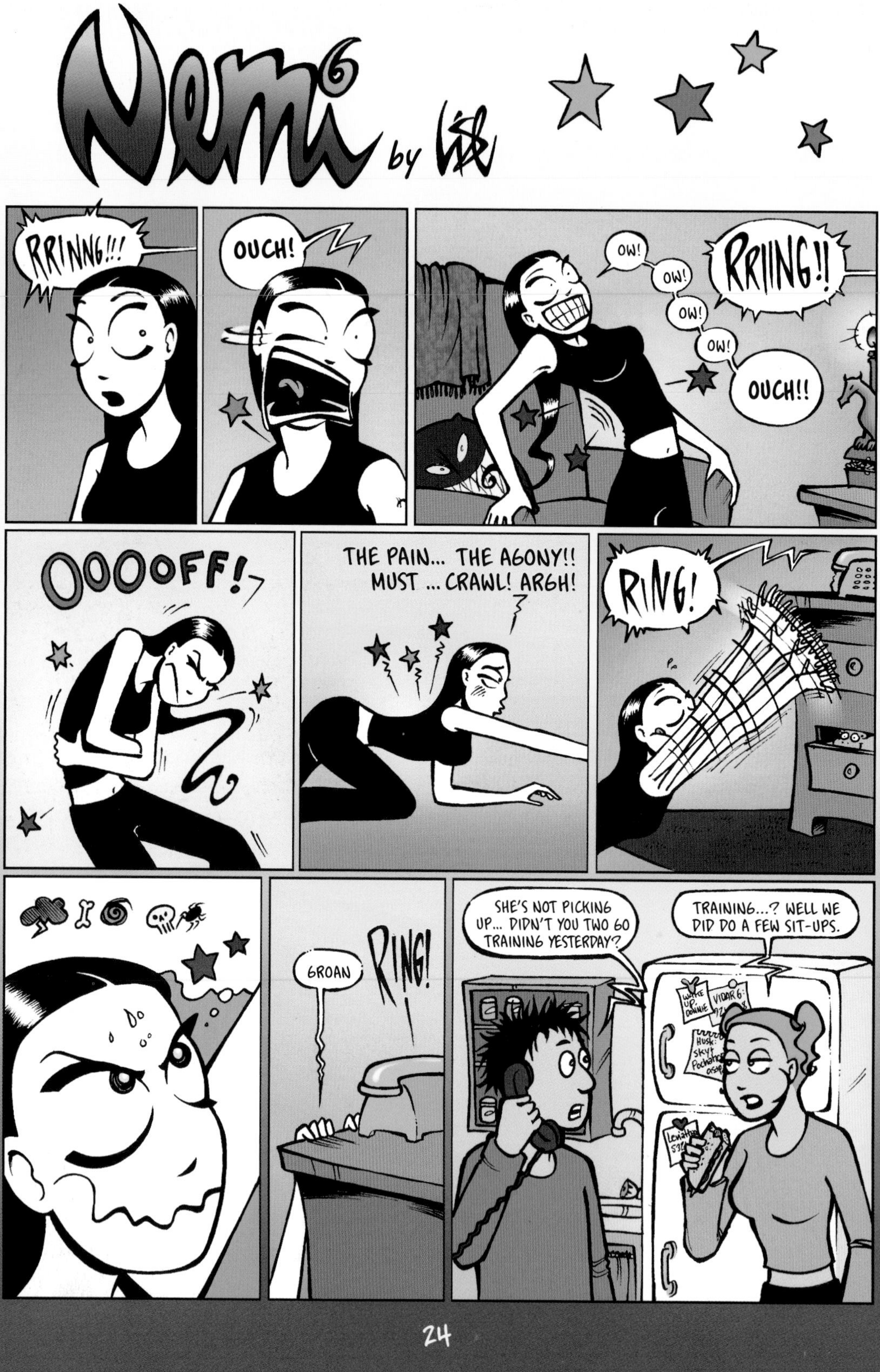
Nemi by Lise
RRINNG!!!
OUCH!
OW!
OW!
OW!
OW!
RRIING!!
OUCH!!
OOOOFF!
THE PAIN... THE AGONY!!
MUST ... CRAWL! ARGH!
RING!
GROAN
RING!
SHE'S NOT PICKING UP... DIDN'T YOU TWO GO TRAINING YESTERDAY?
TRAINING...? WELL WE DID DO A FEW SIT-UPS.

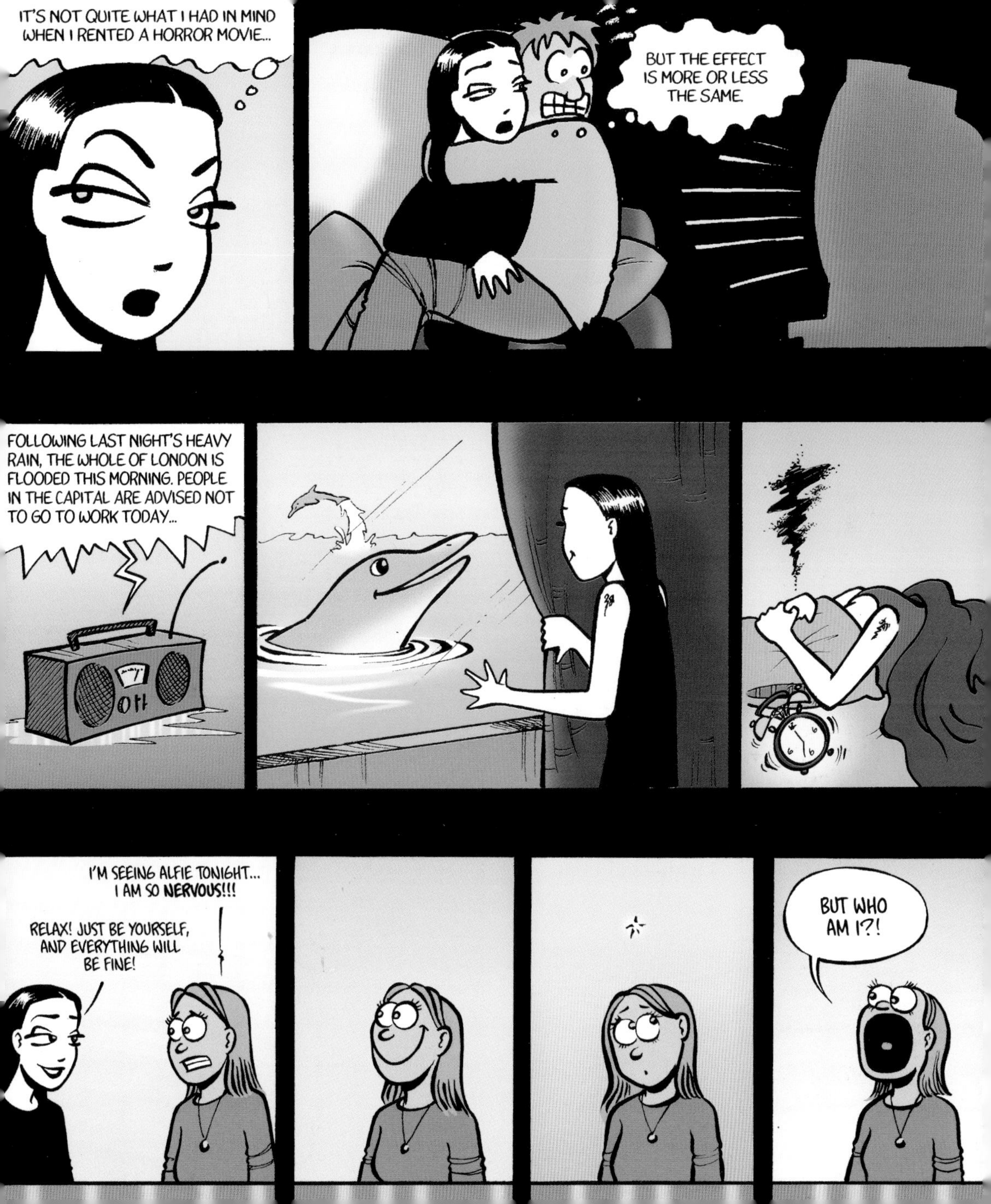
IT'S NOT QUITE WHAT I HAD IN MIND WHEN I RENTED A HORROR MOVIE...
BUT THE EFFECT IS MORE OR LESS THE SAME.
FOLLOWING LAST NIGHT'S HEAVY RAIN, THE WHOLE OF LONDON IS FLOODED THIS MORNING. PEOPLE IN THE CAPITAL ARE ADVISED NOT TO GO TO WORK TODAY...
I'M SEEING ALFIE TONIGHT... I AM SO **NERVOUS**!!!
RELAX! JUST BE YOURSELF, AND EVERYTHING WILL BE FINE!
BUT WHO AM I?!

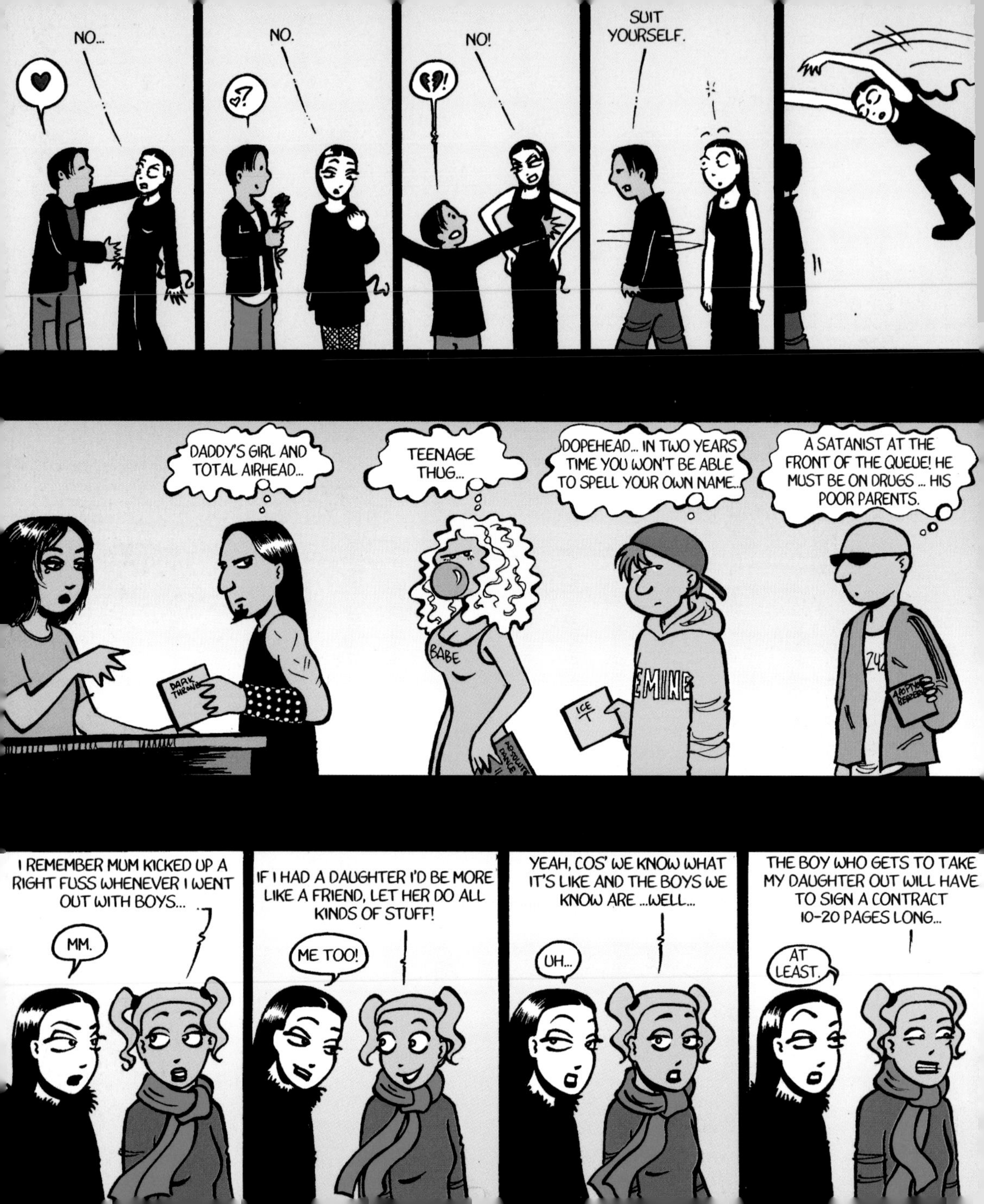

NO...
NO.
NO!
SUIT YOURSELF.
DADDY'S GIRL AND TOTAL AIRHEAD...
DARK THRONE
TEENAGE THUG...
BABE
DOPEHEAD... IN TWO YEARS TIME YOU WON'T BE ABLE TO SPELL YOUR OWN NAME...
ICE T
A SATANIST AT THE FRONT OF THE QUEUE! HE MUST BE ON DRUGS ... HIS POOR PARENTS.
I REMEMBER MUM KICKED UP A RIGHT FUSS WHENEVER I WENT OUT WITH BOYS...
MM.
IF I HAD A DAUGHTER I'D BE MORE LIKE A FRIEND, LET HER DO ALL KINDS OF STUFF!
ME TOO!
YEAH, COS' WE KNOW WHAT IT'S LIKE AND THE BOYS WE KNOW ARE ...WELL...
UH...
THE BOY WHO GETS TO TAKE MY DAUGHTER OUT WILL HAVE TO SIGN A CONTRACT 10-20 PAGES LONG...
AT LEAST.

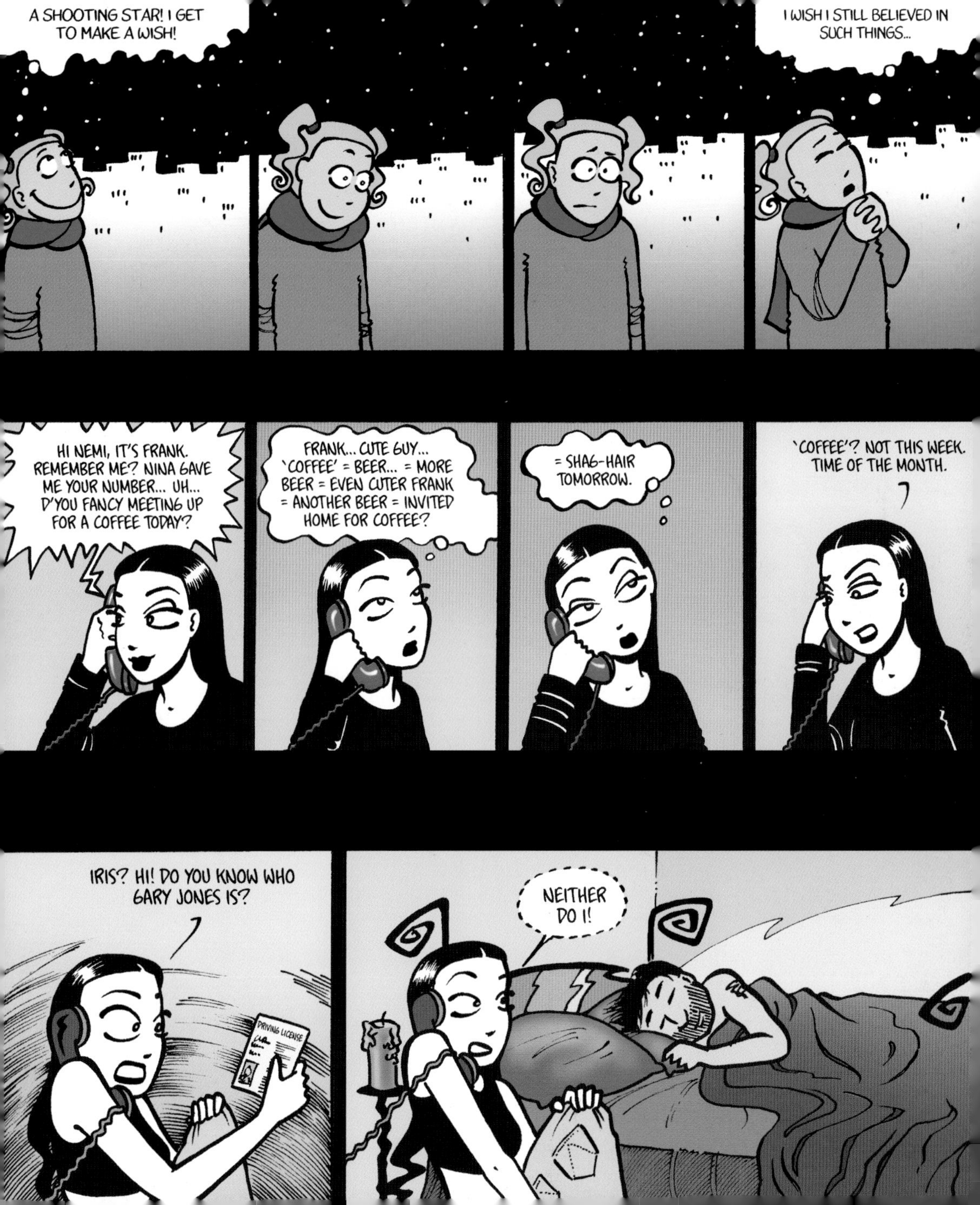
A SHOOTING STAR! I GET TO MAKE A WISH!
I WISH I STILL BELIEVED IN SUCH THINGS...
HI NEMI, IT'S FRANK. REMEMBER ME? NINA GAVE ME YOUR NUMBER... UH... D'YOU FANCY MEETING UP FOR A COFFEE TODAY?
FRANK... CUTE GUY... 'COFFEE' = BEER... = MORE BEER = EVEN CUTER FRANK = ANOTHER BEER = INVITED HOME FOR COFFEE?
= SHAG-HAIR TOMORROW.
'COFFEE'? NOT THIS WEEK. TIME OF THE MONTH.
IRIS? HI! DO YOU KNOW WHO GARY JONES IS?
DRIVING LICENSE
NEITHER DO I!

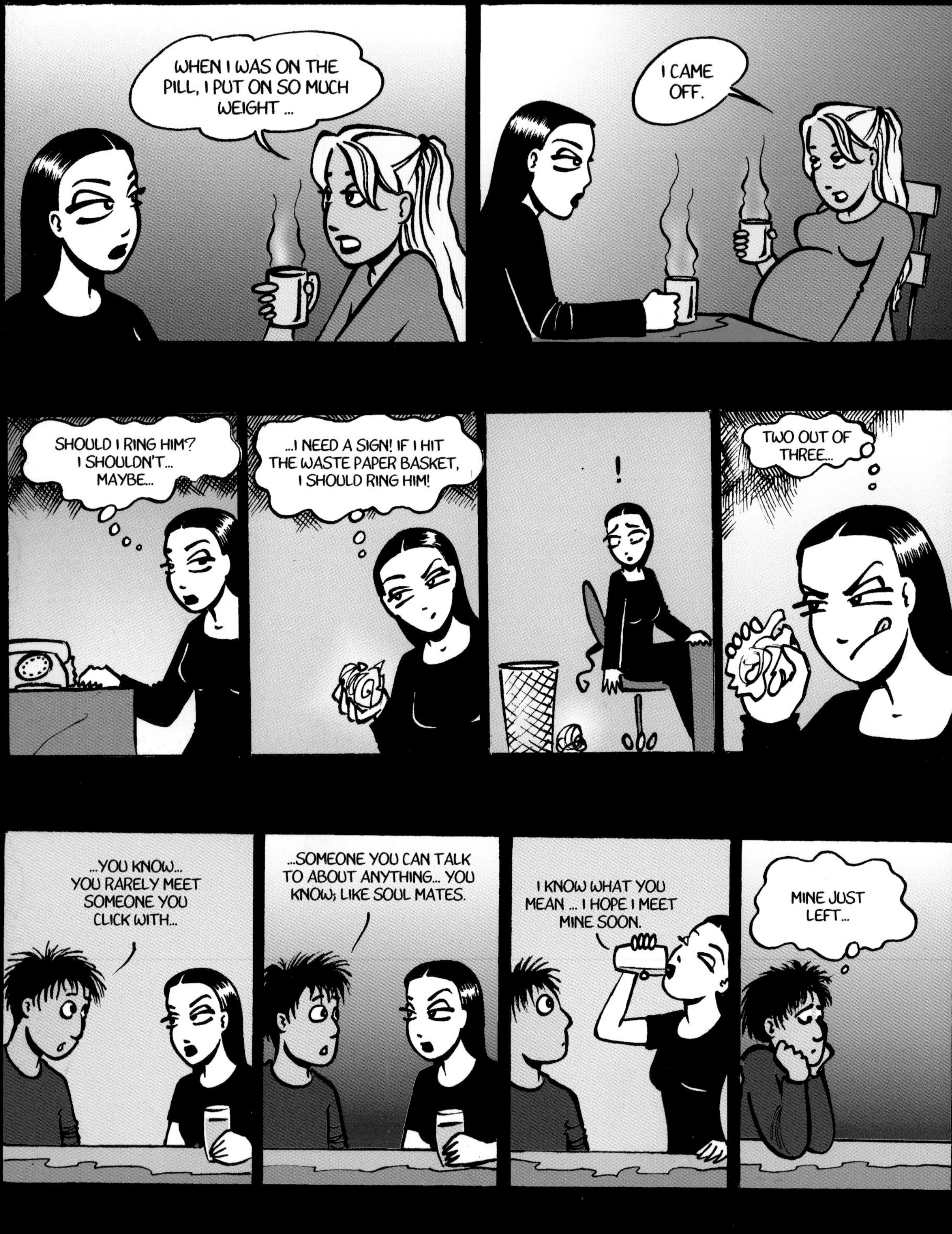
WHEN I WAS ON THE PILL, I PUT ON SO MUCH WEIGHT ...
I CAME OFF.
SHOULD I RING HIM? I SHOULDN'T... MAYBE...
...I NEED A SIGN! IF I HIT THE WASTE PAPER BASKET, I SHOULD RING HIM!
!
TWO OUT OF THREE...
...YOU KNOW... YOU RARELY MEET SOMEONE YOU CLICK WITH...
...SOMEONE YOU CAN TALK TO ABOUT ANYTHING... YOU KNOW; LIKE SOUL MATES.
I KNOW WHAT YOU MEAN ... I HOPE I MEET MINE SOON.
MINE JUST LEFT...

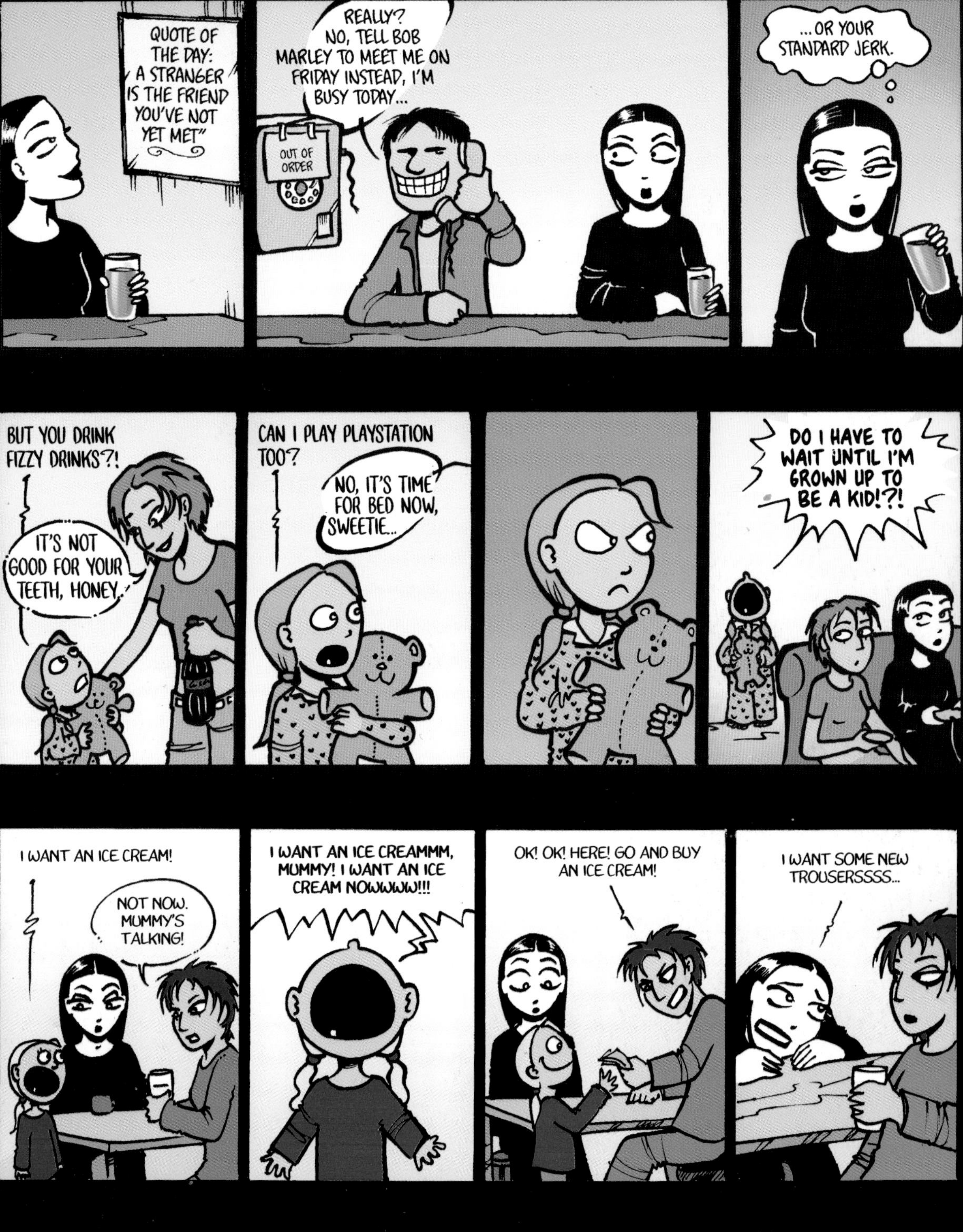
QUOTE OF THE DAY: A STRANGER IS THE FRIEND YOU'VE NOT YET MET"
OUT OF ORDER
REALLY? NO, TELL BOB MARLEY TO MEET ME ON FRIDAY INSTEAD, I'M BUSY TODAY...
...OR YOUR STANDARD JERK.
BUT YOU DRINK FIZZY DRINKS?!
IT'S NOT GOOD FOR YOUR TEETH, HONEY.
CAN I PLAY PLAYSTATION TOO?
NO, IT'S TIME FOR BED NOW, SWEETIE...
DO I HAVE TO WAIT UNTIL I'M GROWN UP TO BE A KID!?!
I WANT AN ICE CREAM!
NOT NOW. MUMMY'S TALKING!
I WANT AN ICE CREAMMM, MUMMY! I WANT AN ICE CREAM NOWWWW!!!
OK! OK! HERE! GO AND BUY AN ICE CREAM!
I WANT SOME NEW TROUSERSSSS...

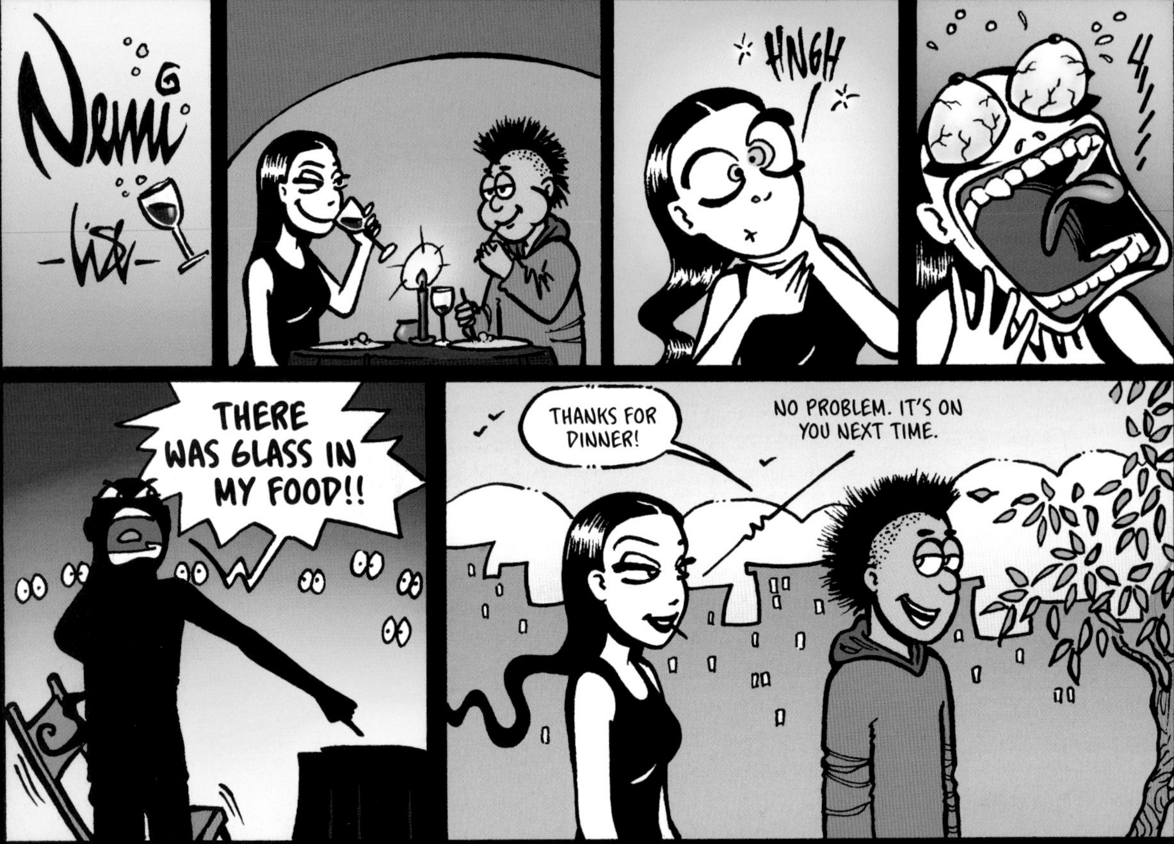
Nemi
Lise
HNGH
THERE WAS GLASS IN MY FOOD!!
THANKS FOR DINNER!
NO PROBLEM. IT'S ON YOU NEXT TIME.

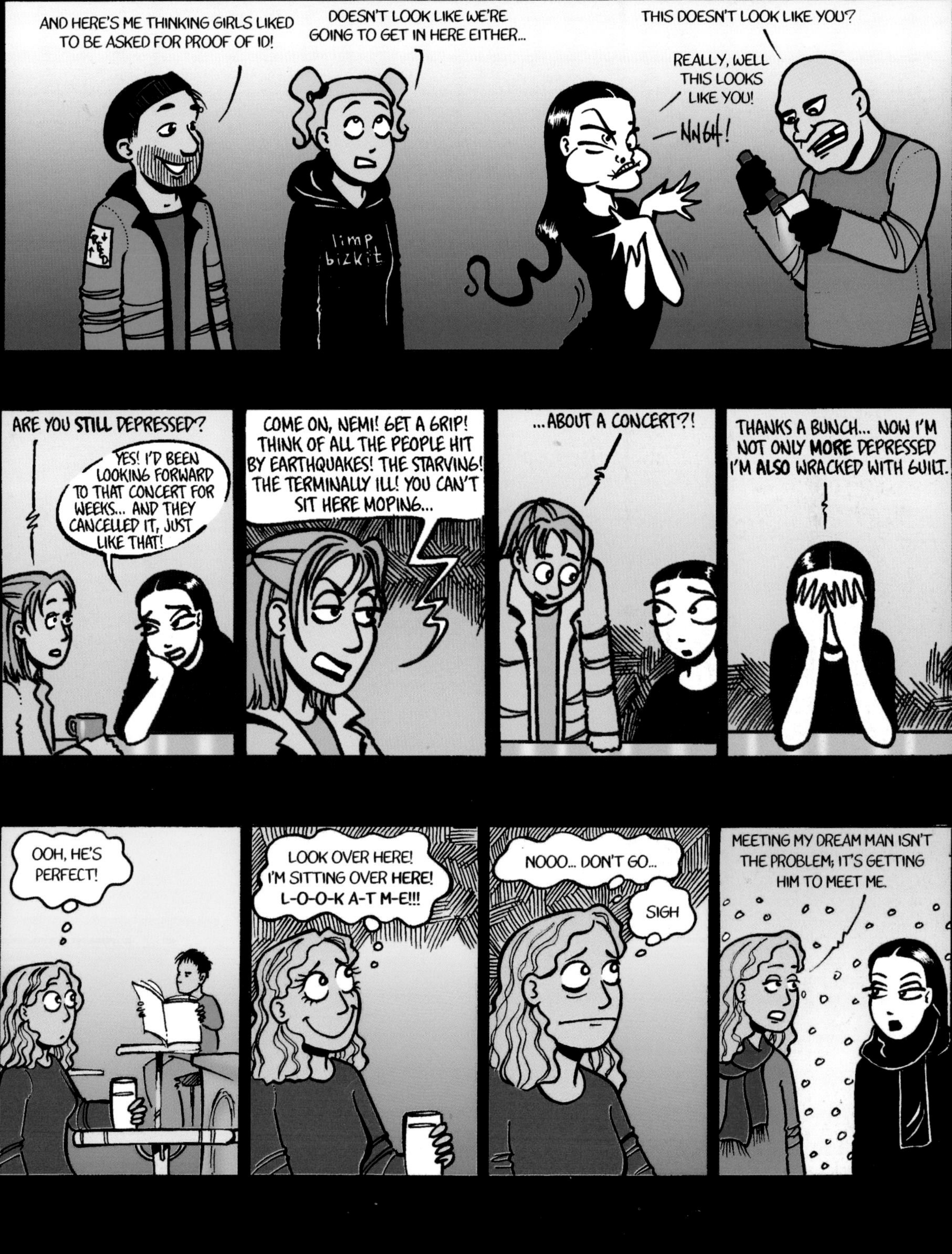
AND HERE'S ME THINKING GIRLS LIKED TO BE ASKED FOR PROOF OF ID!
DOESN'T LOOK LIKE WE'RE GOING TO GET IN HERE EITHER...
THIS DOESN'T LOOK LIKE YOU?
REALLY, WELL THIS LOOKS LIKE YOU!
NNGH!
ARE YOU STILL DEPRESSED?
YES! I'D BEEN LOOKING FORWARD TO THAT CONCERT FOR WEEKS... AND THEY CANCELLED IT, JUST LIKE THAT!
COME ON, NEMI! GET A GRIP! THINK OF ALL THE PEOPLE HIT BY EARTHQUAKES! THE STARVING! THE TERMINALLY ILL! YOU CAN'T SIT HERE MOPING...
...ABOUT A CONCERT?!
THANKS A BUNCH... NOW I'M NOT ONLY MORE DEPRESSED I'M ALSO WRACKED WITH GUILT.
OOH, HE'S PERFECT!
LOOK OVER HERE! I'M SITTING OVER HERE! L-O-O-K A-T M-E!!!
NOOO... DON'T GO...
SIGH
MEETING MY DREAM MAN ISN'T THE PROBLEM; IT'S GETTING HIM TO MEET ME.

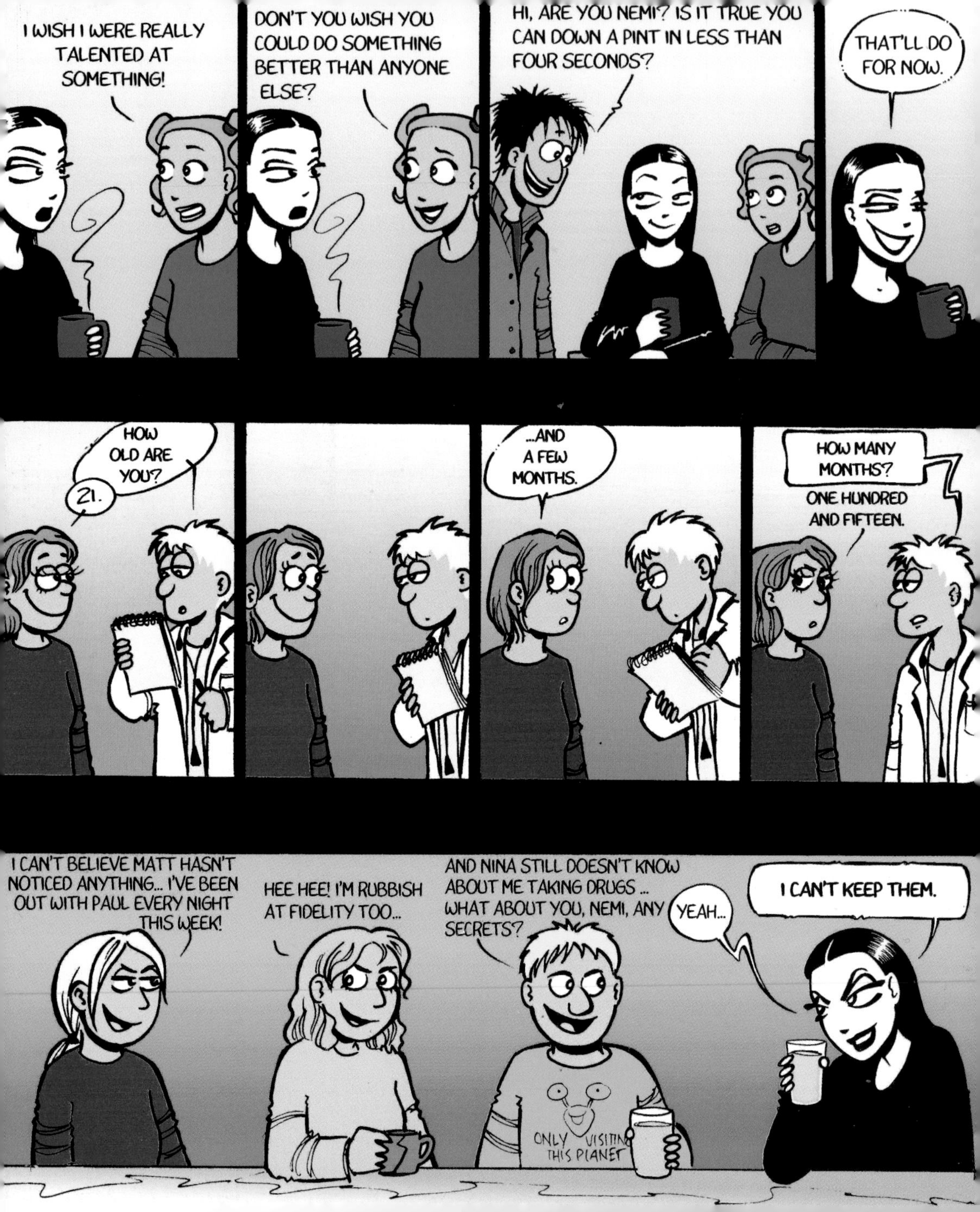
I WISH I WERE REALLY TALENTED AT SOMETHING!
DON'T YOU WISH YOU COULD DO SOMETHING BETTER THAN ANYONE ELSE?
HI, ARE YOU NEMI? IS IT TRUE YOU CAN DOWN A PINT IN LESS THAN FOUR SECONDS?
THAT'LL DO FOR NOW.
HOW OLD ARE YOU?
21.
...AND A FEW MONTHS.
HOW MANY MONTHS?
ONE HUNDRED AND FIFTEEN.
I CAN'T BELIEVE MATT HASN'T NOTICED ANYTHING... I'VE BEEN OUT WITH PAUL EVERY NIGHT THIS WEEK!
HEE HEE! I'M RUBBISH AT FIDELITY TOO...
AND NINA STILL DOESN'T KNOW ABOUT ME TAKING DRUGS ... WHAT ABOUT YOU, NEMI, ANY SECRETS?
YEAH...
I CAN'T KEEP THEM.
ONLY VISITING THIS PLANET

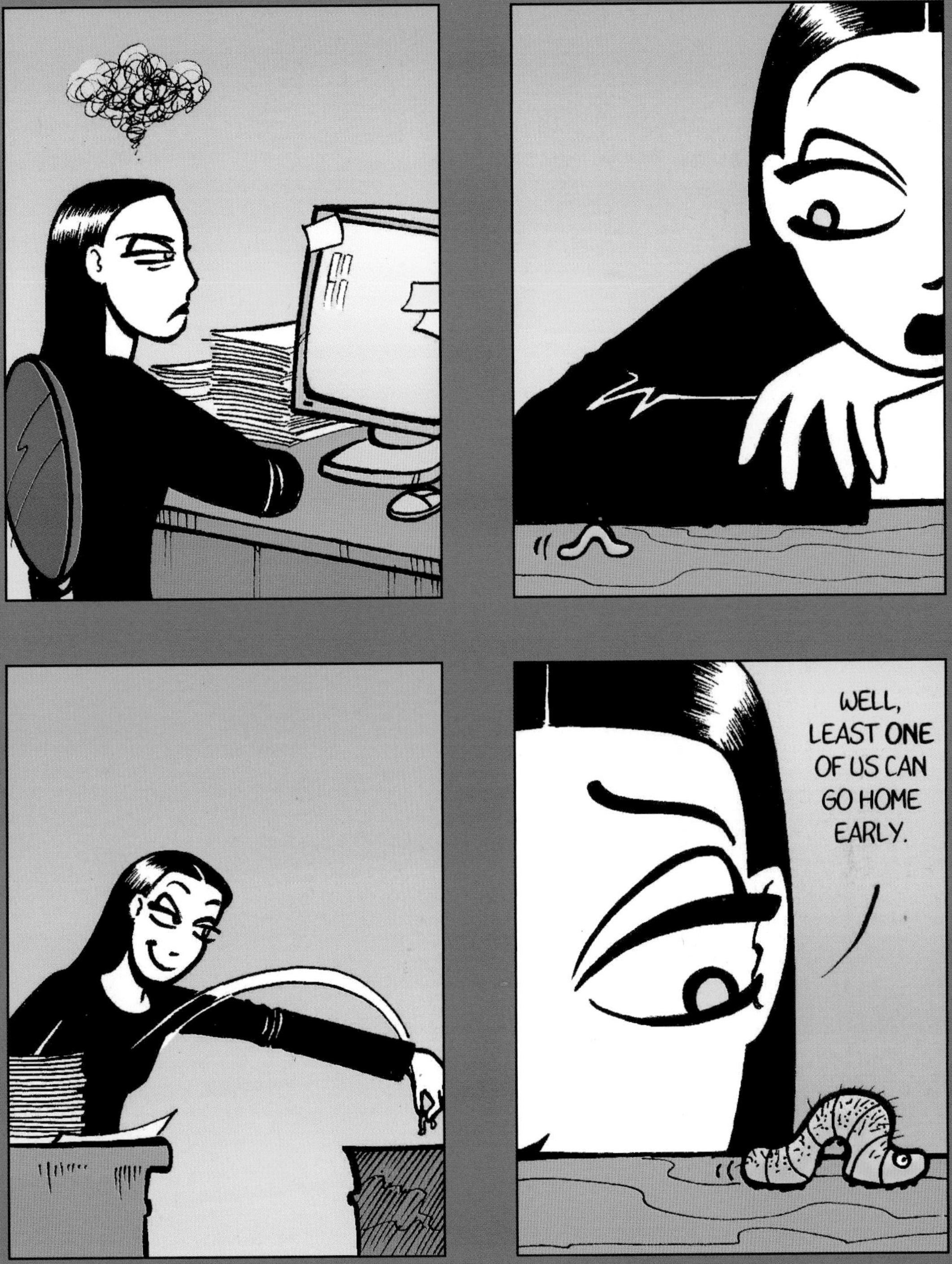
WELL, LEAST ONE OF US CAN GO HOME EARLY.

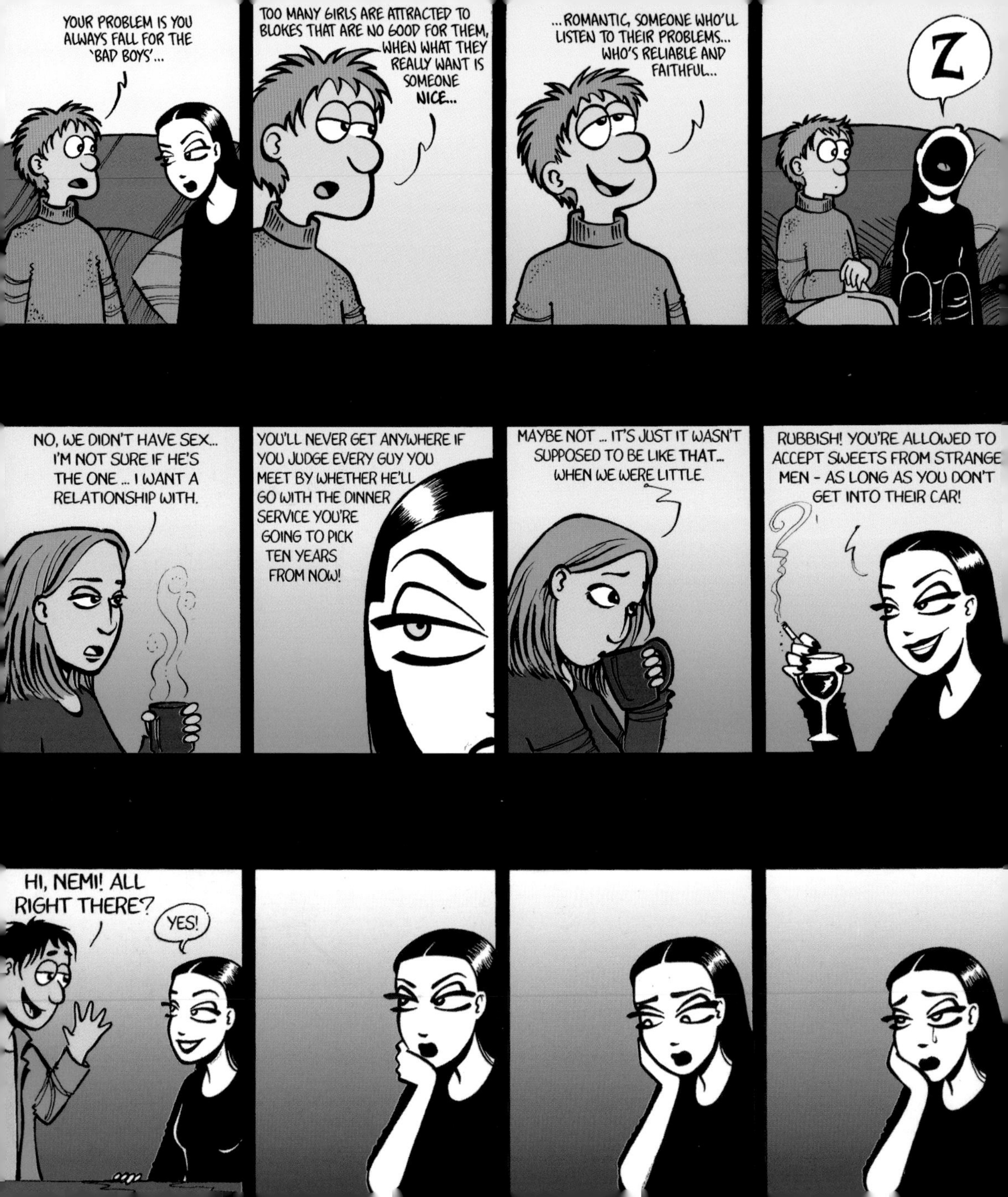

YOUR PROBLEM IS YOU ALWAYS FALL FOR THE 'BAD BOYS'...
TOO MANY GIRLS ARE ATTRACTED TO BLOKES THAT ARE NO GOOD FOR THEM, WHEN WHAT THEY REALLY WANT IS SOMEONE NICE...
...ROMANTIC, SOMEONE WHO'LL LISTEN TO THEIR PROBLEMS... WHO'S RELIABLE AND FAITHFUL...
Z
NO, WE DIDN'T HAVE SEX... I'M NOT SURE IF HE'S THE ONE ... I WANT A RELATIONSHIP WITH.
YOU'LL NEVER GET ANYWHERE IF YOU JUDGE EVERY GUY YOU MEET BY WHETHER HE'LL GO WITH THE DINNER SERVICE YOU'RE GOING TO PICK TEN YEARS FROM NOW!
MAYBE NOT ... IT'S JUST IT WASN'T SUPPOSED TO BE LIKE THAT... WHEN WE WERE LITTLE.
RUBBISH! YOU'RE ALLOWED TO ACCEPT SWEETS FROM STRANGE MEN - AS LONG AS YOU DON'T GET INTO THEIR CAR!
HI, NEMI! ALL RIGHT THERE?
YES!

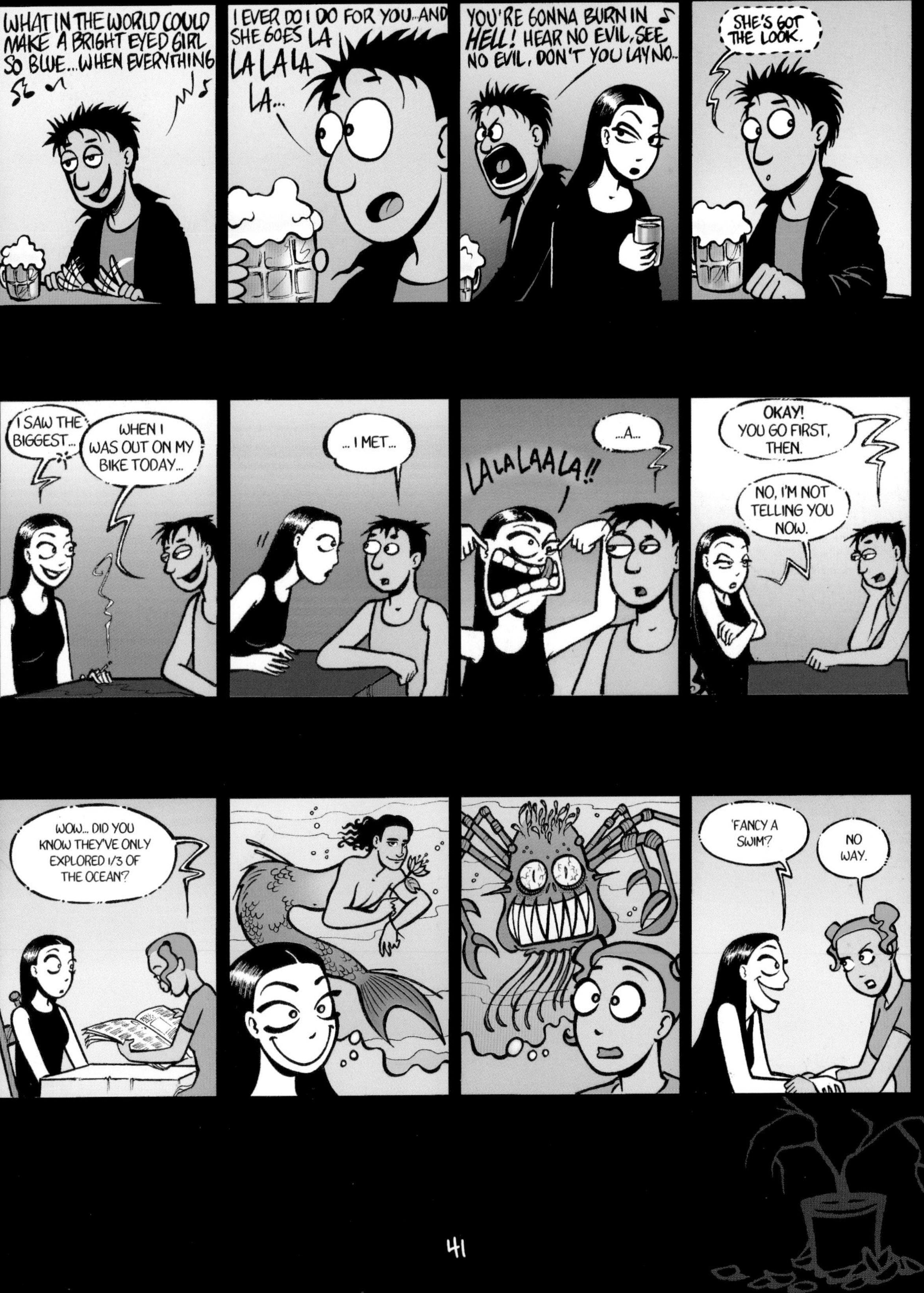

WHAT IN THE WORLD COULD MAKE A BRIGHT EYED GIRL SO BLUE... WHEN EVERYTHING
I EVER DO I DO FOR YOU... AND SHE GOES LA LA LA LA LA...
YOU'RE GONNA BURN IN HELL! HEAR NO EVIL, SEE NO EVIL, DON'T YOU LAY NO...
SHE'S GOT THE LOOK.
I SAW THE BIGGEST...
WHEN I WAS OUT ON MY BIKE TODAY...
... I MET...
LA LA LAA LA!!
...A...
OKAY! YOU GO FIRST, THEN.
NO, I'M NOT TELLING YOU NOW.
WOW... DID YOU KNOW THEY'VE ONLY EXPLORED 1/3 OF THE OCEAN?
'FANCY A SWIM'?
NO WAY.

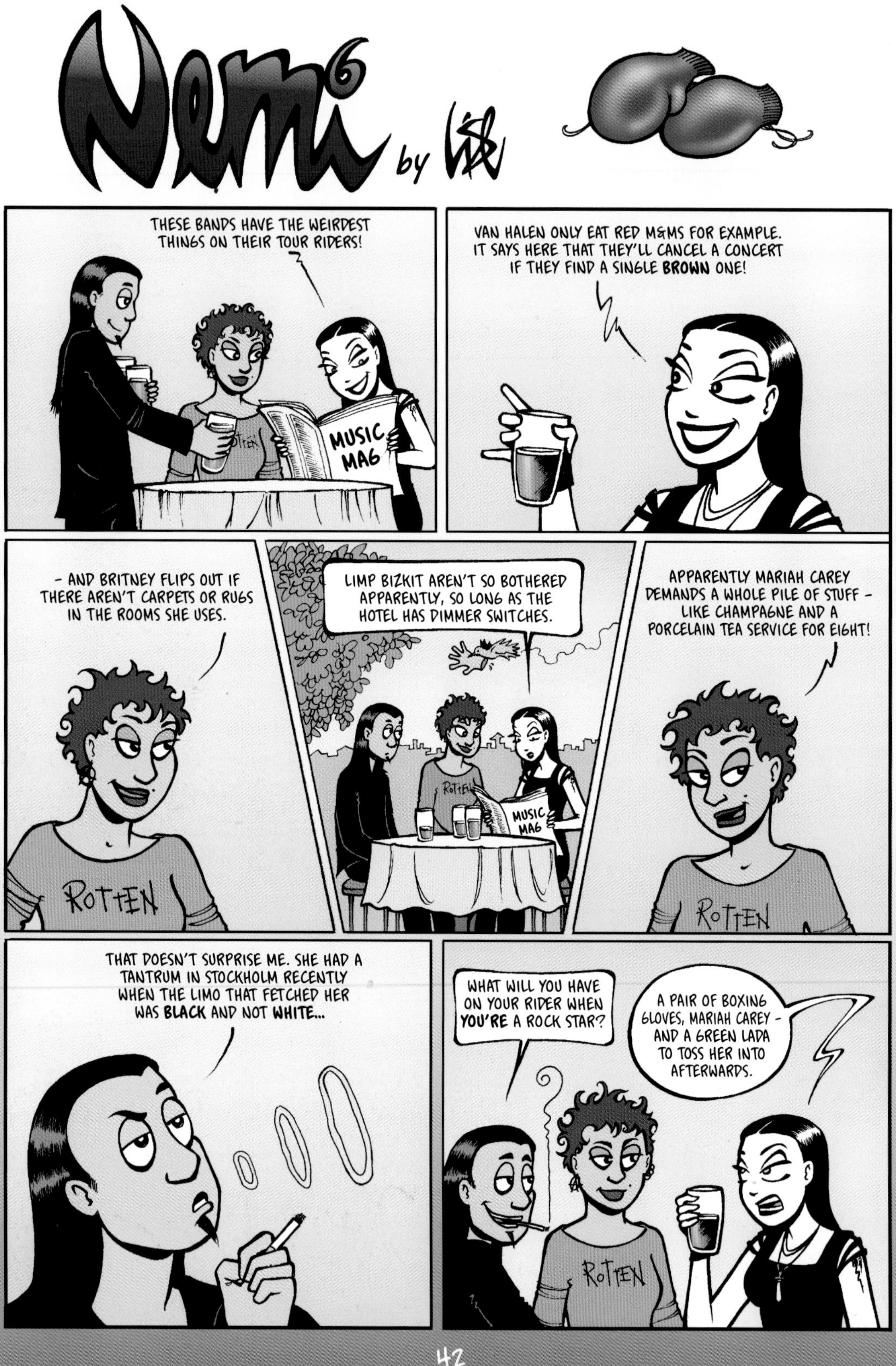
Nemi by Lise
THESE BANDS HAVE THE WEIRDEST THINGS ON THEIR TOUR RIDERS!
MUSIC MAG
ROTTEN
VAN HALEN ONLY EAT RED M&MS FOR EXAMPLE. IT SAYS HERE THAT THEY'LL CANCEL A CONCERT IF THEY FIND A SINGLE **BROWN** ONE!
- AND BRITNEY FLIPS OUT IF THERE AREN'T CARPETS OR RUGS IN THE ROOMS SHE USES.
LIMP BIZKIT AREN'T SO BOTHERED APPARENTLY, SO LONG AS THE HOTEL HAS DIMMER SWITCHES.
APPARENTLY MARIAH CAREY DEMANDS A WHOLE PILE OF STUFF - LIKE CHAMPAGNE AND A PORCELAIN TEA SERVICE FOR EIGHT!
THAT DOESN'T SURPRISE ME. SHE HAD A TANTRUM IN STOCKHOLM RECENTLY WHEN THE LIMO THAT FETCHED HER WAS **BLACK** AND NOT **WHITE...**
WHAT WILL YOU HAVE ON YOUR RIDER WHEN **YOU'RE** A ROCK STAR?
A PAIR OF BOXING GLOVES, MARIAH CAREY - AND A GREEN LADA TO TOSS HER INTO AFTERWARDS.

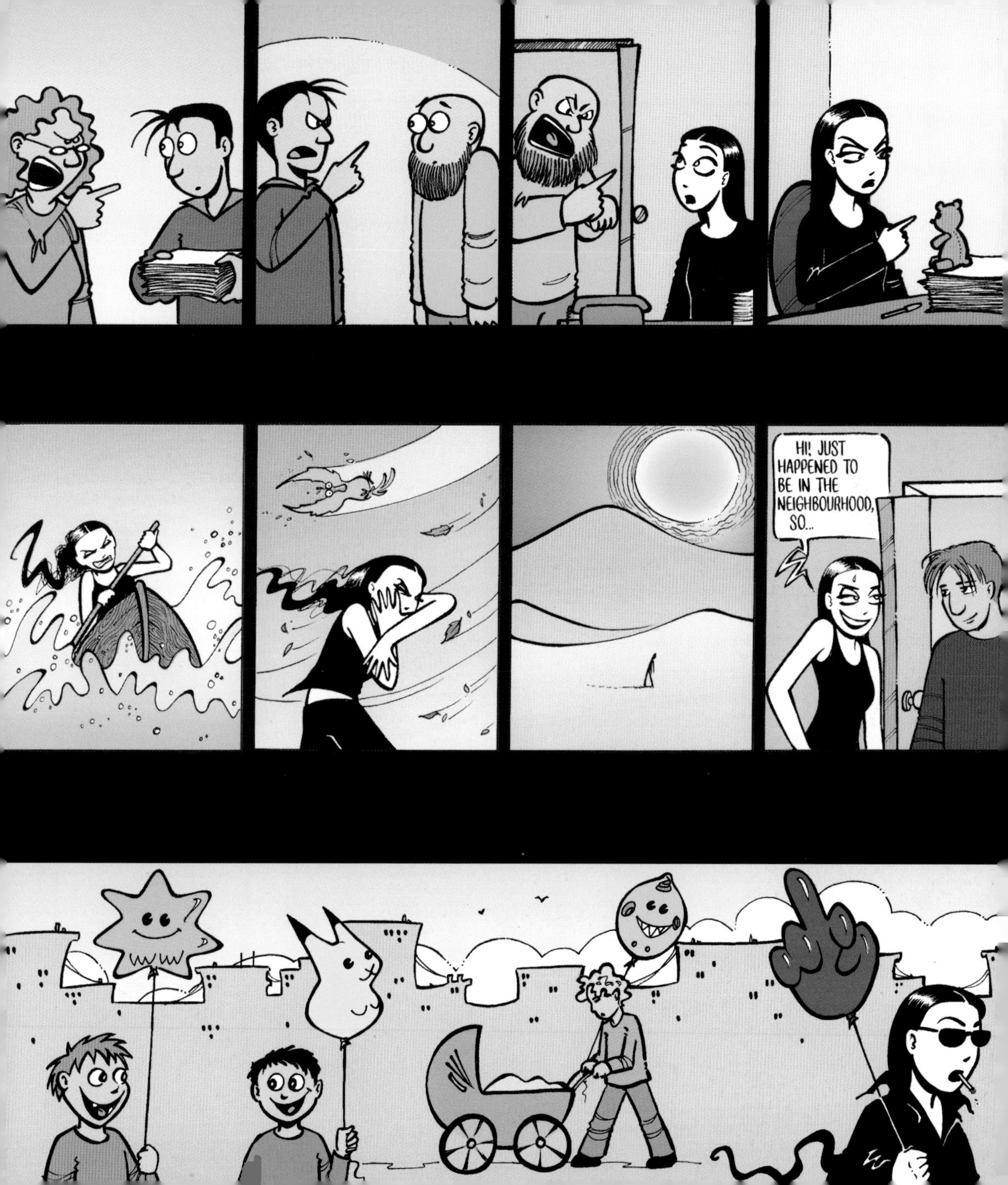
HI! JUST HAPPENED TO BE IN THE NEIGHBOURHOOD, SO...

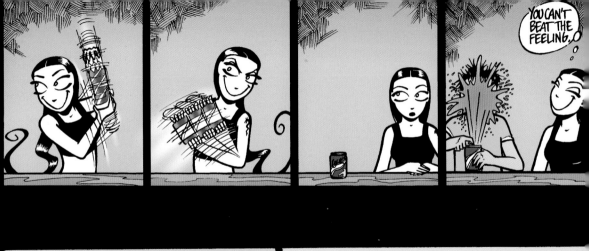

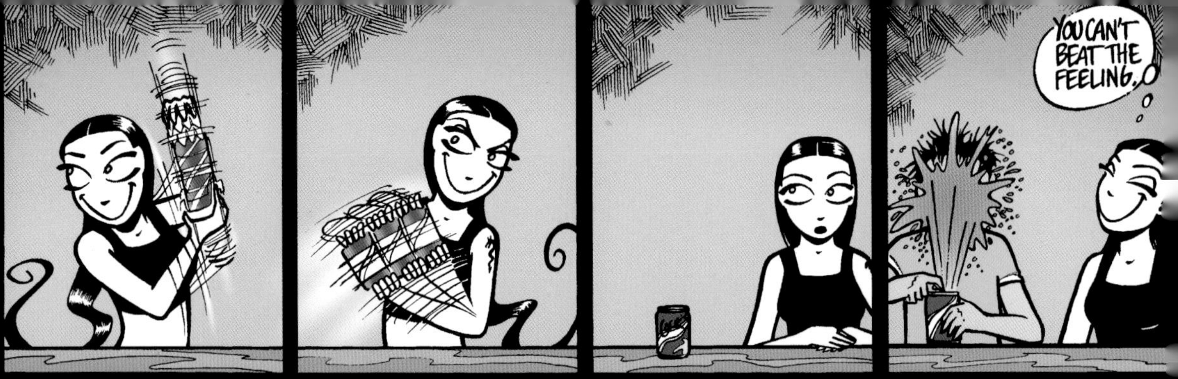
YOU CAN'T BEAT THE FEELING.

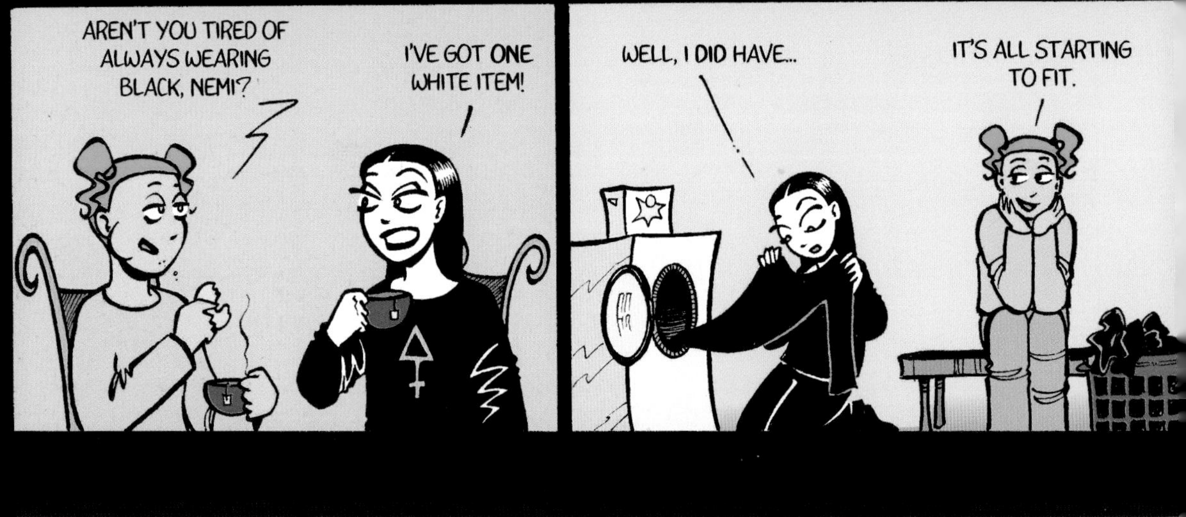
AREN'T YOU TIRED OF ALWAYS WEARING BLACK, NEMI?
I'VE GOT ONE WHITE ITEM!
WELL, I DID HAVE...
IT'S ALL STARTING TO FIT.

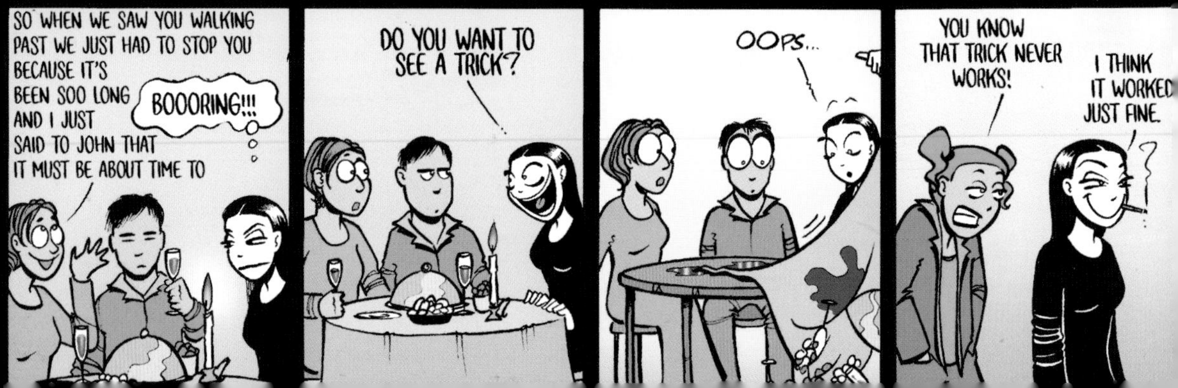
SO WHEN WE SAW YOU WALKING PAST WE JUST HAD TO STOP YOU BECAUSE IT'S BEEN SOO LONG AND I JUST SAID TO JOHN THAT IT MUST BE ABOUT TIME TO
BOOORING!!!
DO YOU WANT TO SEE A TRICK?
OOPS...
YOU KNOW THAT TRICK NEVER WORKS!
I THINK IT WORKED JUST FINE.

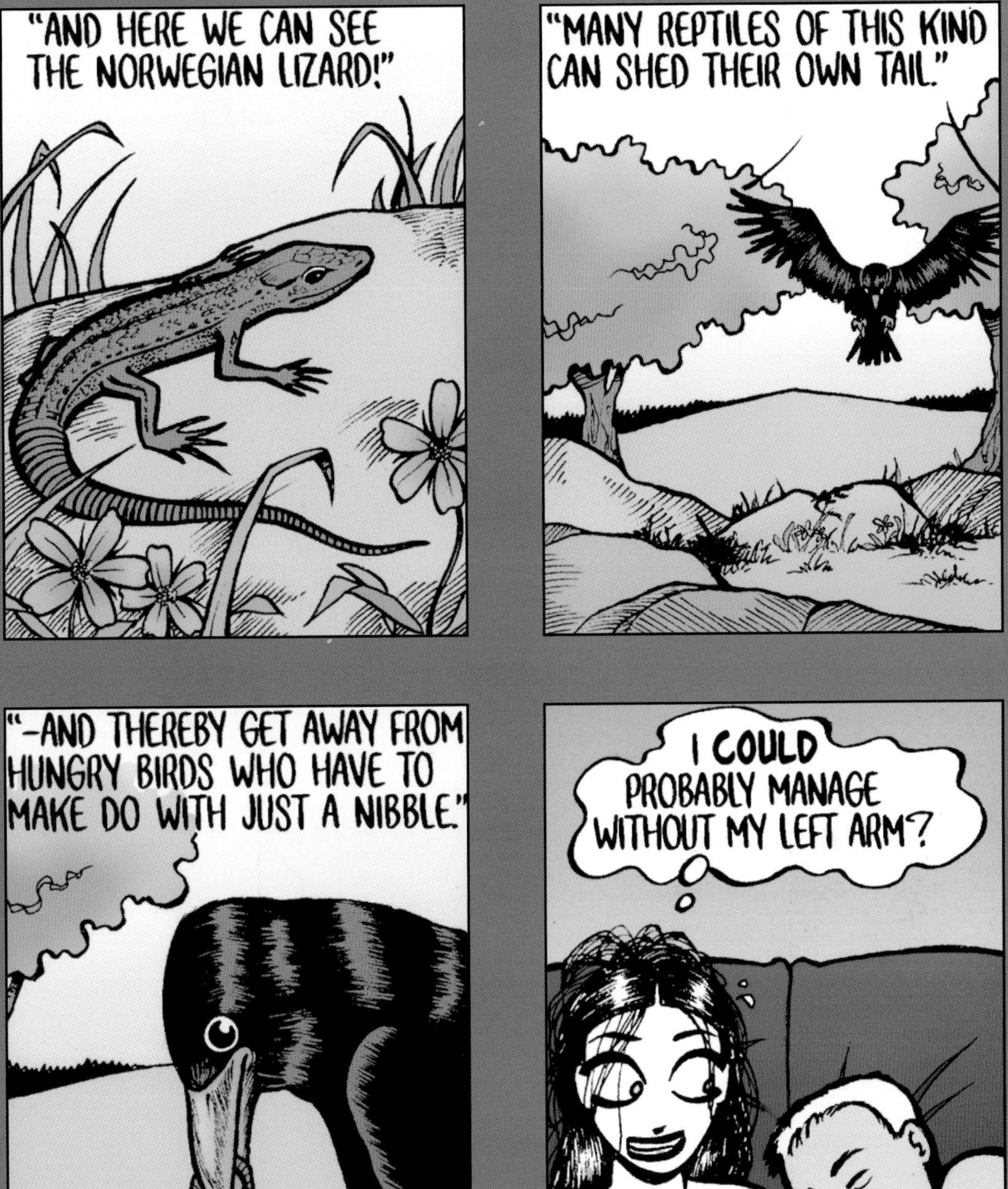
"AND HERE WE CAN SEE THE NORWEGIAN LIZARD!"
"MANY REPTILES OF THIS KIND CAN SHED THEIR OWN TAIL."
"-AND THEREBY GET AWAY FROM HUNGRY BIRDS WHO HAVE TO MAKE DO WITH JUST A NIBBLE."
I COULD PROBABLY MANAGE WITHOUT MY LEFT ARM?

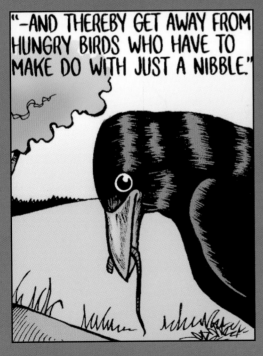

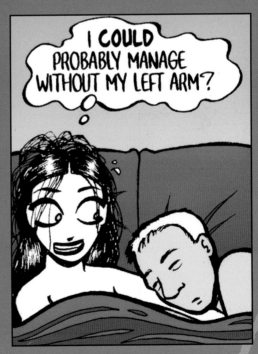

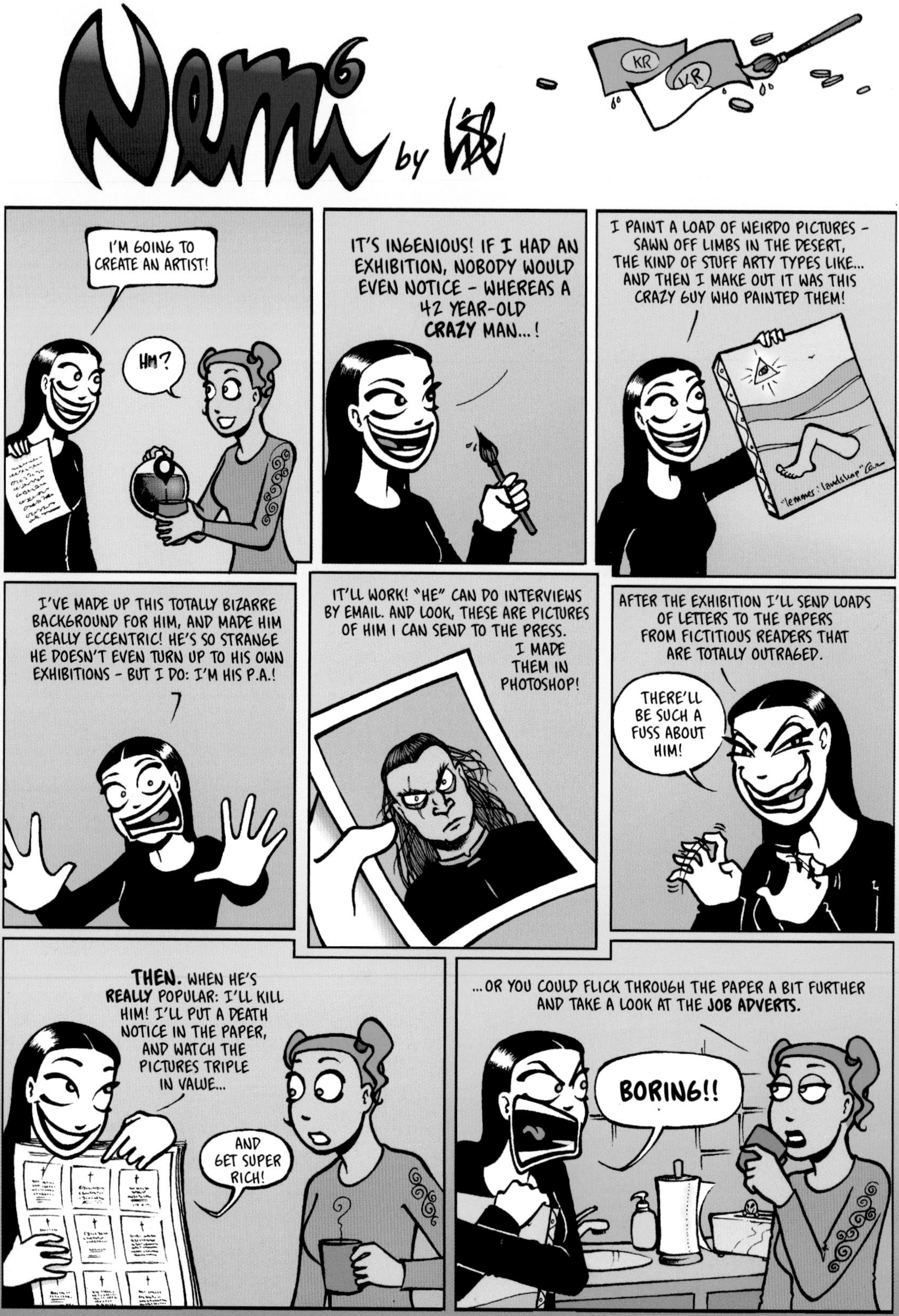
Nemi by Lise
I'M GOING TO CREATE AN ARTIST!
HM?
IT'S INGENIOUS! IF I HAD AN EXHIBITION, NOBODY WOULD EVEN NOTICE – WHEREAS A 42 YEAR-OLD CRAZY MAN...!
I PAINT A LOAD OF WEIRDO PICTURES – SAWN OFF LIMBS IN THE DESERT, THE KIND OF STUFF ARTY TYPES LIKE... AND THEN I MAKE OUT IT WAS THIS CRAZY GUY WHO PAINTED THEM!
I'VE MADE UP THIS TOTALLY BIZARRE BACKGROUND FOR HIM, AND MADE HIM REALLY ECCENTRIC! HE'S SO STRANGE HE DOESN'T EVEN TURN UP TO HIS OWN EXHIBITIONS – BUT I DO: I'M HIS P.A.!
IT'LL WORK! "HE" CAN DO INTERVIEWS BY EMAIL. AND LOOK, THESE ARE PICTURES OF HIM I CAN SEND TO THE PRESS.
I MADE THEM IN PHOTOSHOP!
AFTER THE EXHIBITION I'LL SEND LOADS OF LETTERS TO THE PAPERS FROM FICTITIOUS READERS THAT ARE TOTALLY OUTRAGED.
THERE'LL BE SUCH A FUSS ABOUT HIM!
THEN. WHEN HE'S REALLY POPULAR: I'LL KILL HIM! I'LL PUT A DEATH NOTICE IN THE PAPER, AND WATCH THE PICTURES TRIPLE IN VALUE...
AND GET SUPER RICH!
...OR YOU COULD FLICK THROUGH THE PAPER A BIT FURTHER AND TAKE A LOOK AT THE JOB ADVERTS.
BORING!!

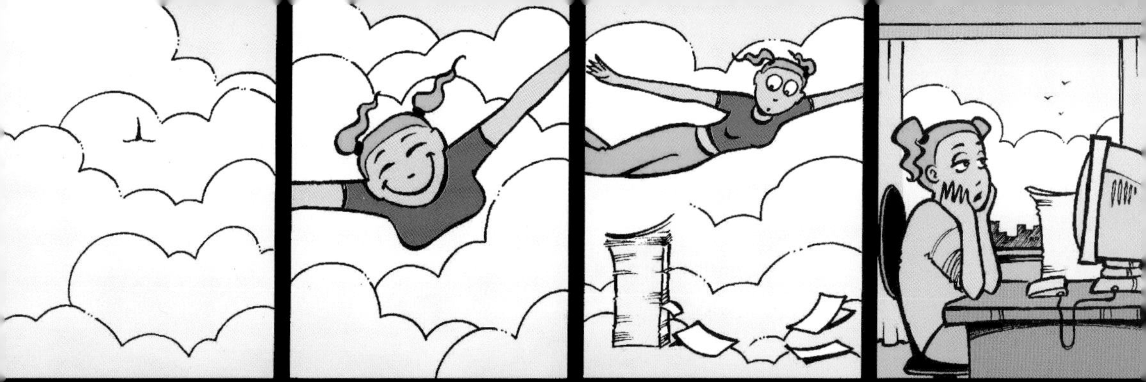

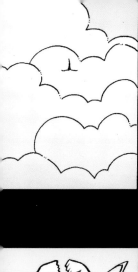

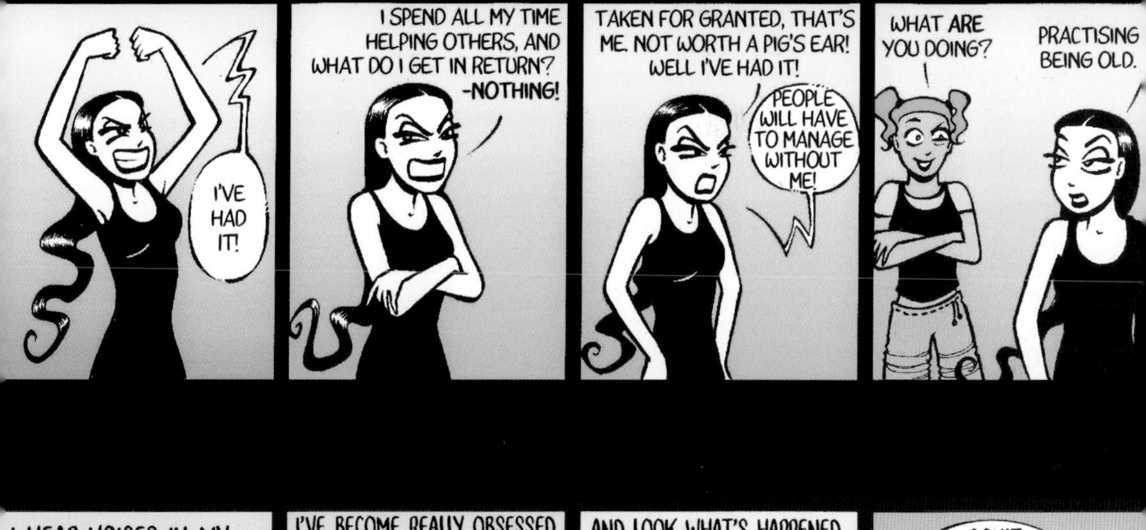
I'VE HAD IT!
I SPEND ALL MY TIME HELPING OTHERS, AND WHAT DO I GET IN RETURN? -NOTHING!
TAKEN FOR GRANTED, THAT'S ME. NOT WORTH A PIG'S EAR! WELL I'VE HAD IT!
PEOPLE WILL HAVE TO MANAGE WITHOUT ME!
WHAT ARE YOU DOING?
PRACTISING BEING OLD.

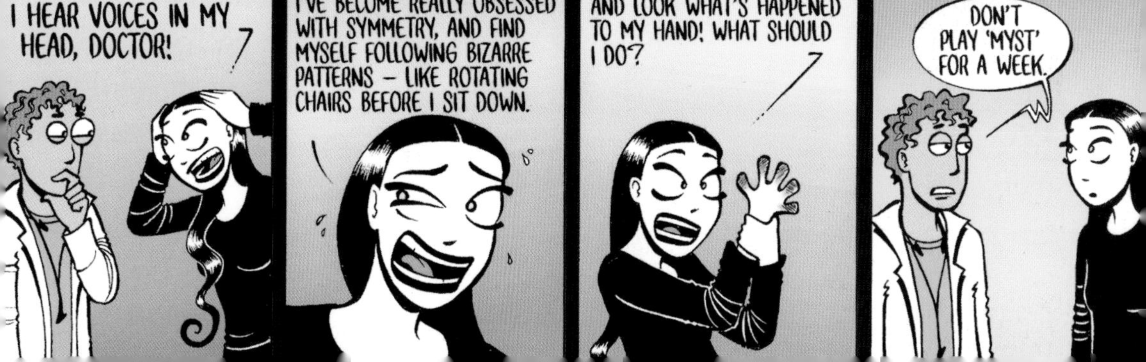
I HEAR VOICES IN MY HEAD, DOCTOR!
I'VE BECOME REALLY OBSESSED WITH SYMMETRY, AND FIND MYSELF FOLLOWING BIZARRE PATTERNS – LIKE ROTATING CHAIRS BEFORE I SIT DOWN.
AND LOOK WHAT'S HAPPENED TO MY HAND! WHAT SHOULD I DO?
DON'T PLAY 'MYST' FOR A WEEK.

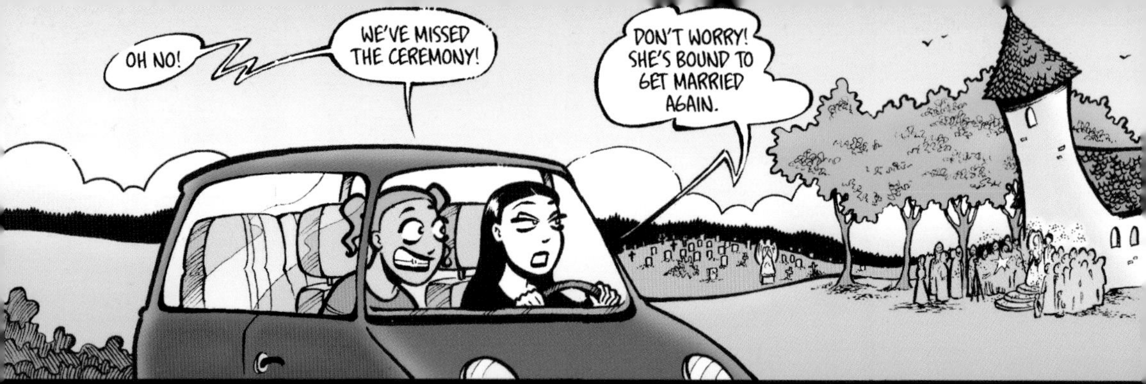
OH NO!
WE'VE MISSED THE CEREMONY!
DON'T WORRY! SHE'S BOUND TO GET MARRIED AGAIN.

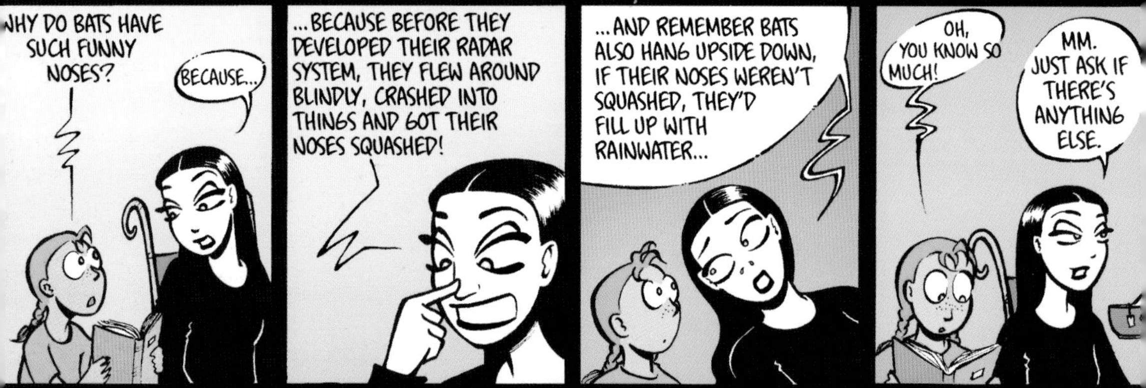
WHY DO BATS HAVE SUCH FUNNY NOSES?
BECAUSE...
...BECAUSE BEFORE THEY DEVELOPED THEIR RADAR SYSTEM, THEY FLEW AROUND BLINDLY, CRASHED INTO THINGS AND GOT THEIR NOSES SQUASHED!
...AND REMEMBER BATS ALSO HANG UPSIDE DOWN, IF THEIR NOSES WEREN'T SQUASHED, THEY'D FILL UP WITH RAINWATER...
OH, YOU KNOW SO MUCH!
MM. JUST ASK IF THERE'S ANYTHING ELSE.

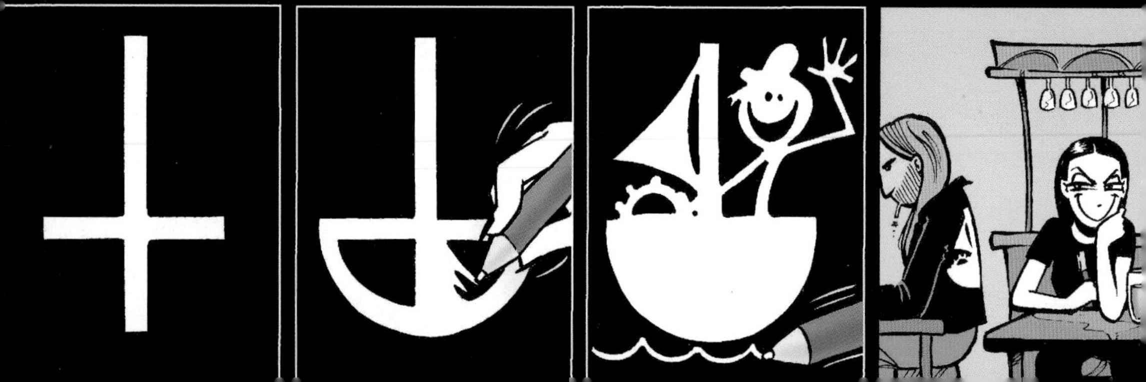

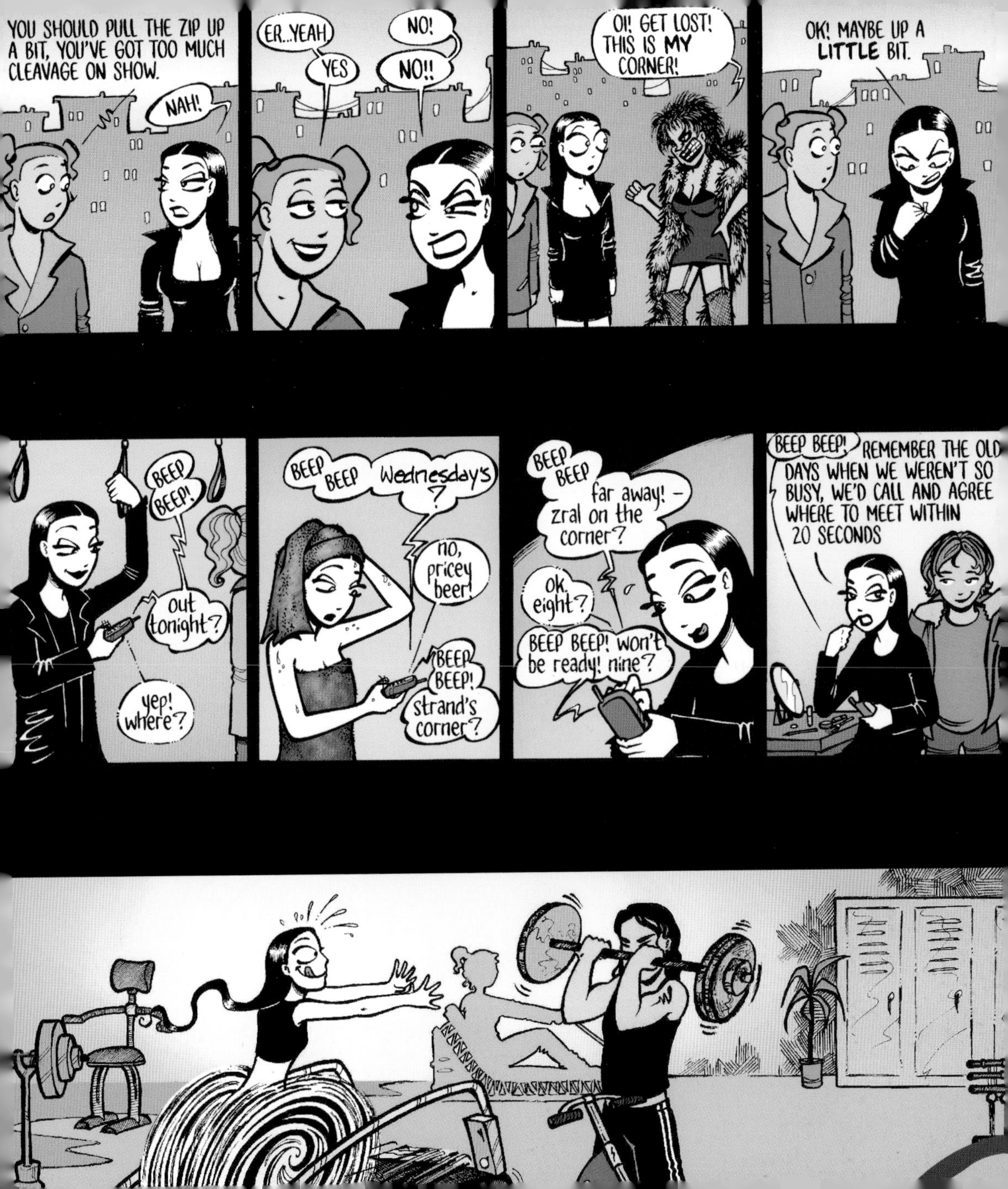

YOU SHOULD PULL THE ZIP UP A BIT, YOU'VE GOT TOO MUCH CLEAVAGE ON SHOW.
NAH!
ER...YEAH
YES
NO!
NO!!
OI! GET LOST! THIS IS MY CORNER!
OK! MAYBE UP A LITTLE BIT.
BEEP BEEP!
out tonight?
yep! where?
BEEP BEEP
Wednesday's?
no, pricey beer!
BEEP BEEP! strand's corner?
BEEP BEEP
far away! - zral on the corner?
ok, eight?
BEEP BEEP! won't be ready! nine?
BEEP BEEP!
REMEMBER THE OLD DAYS WHEN WE WEREN'T SO BUSY, WE'D CALL AND AGREE WHERE TO MEET WITHIN 20 SECONDS

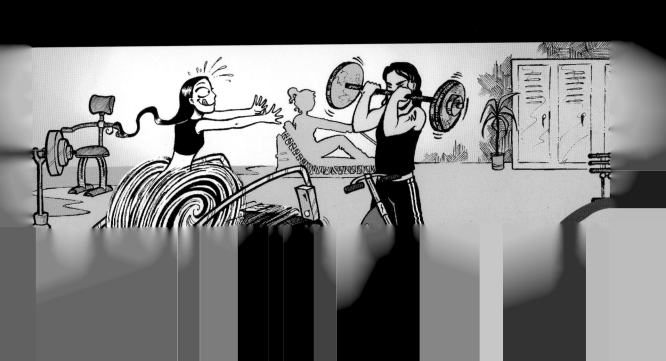

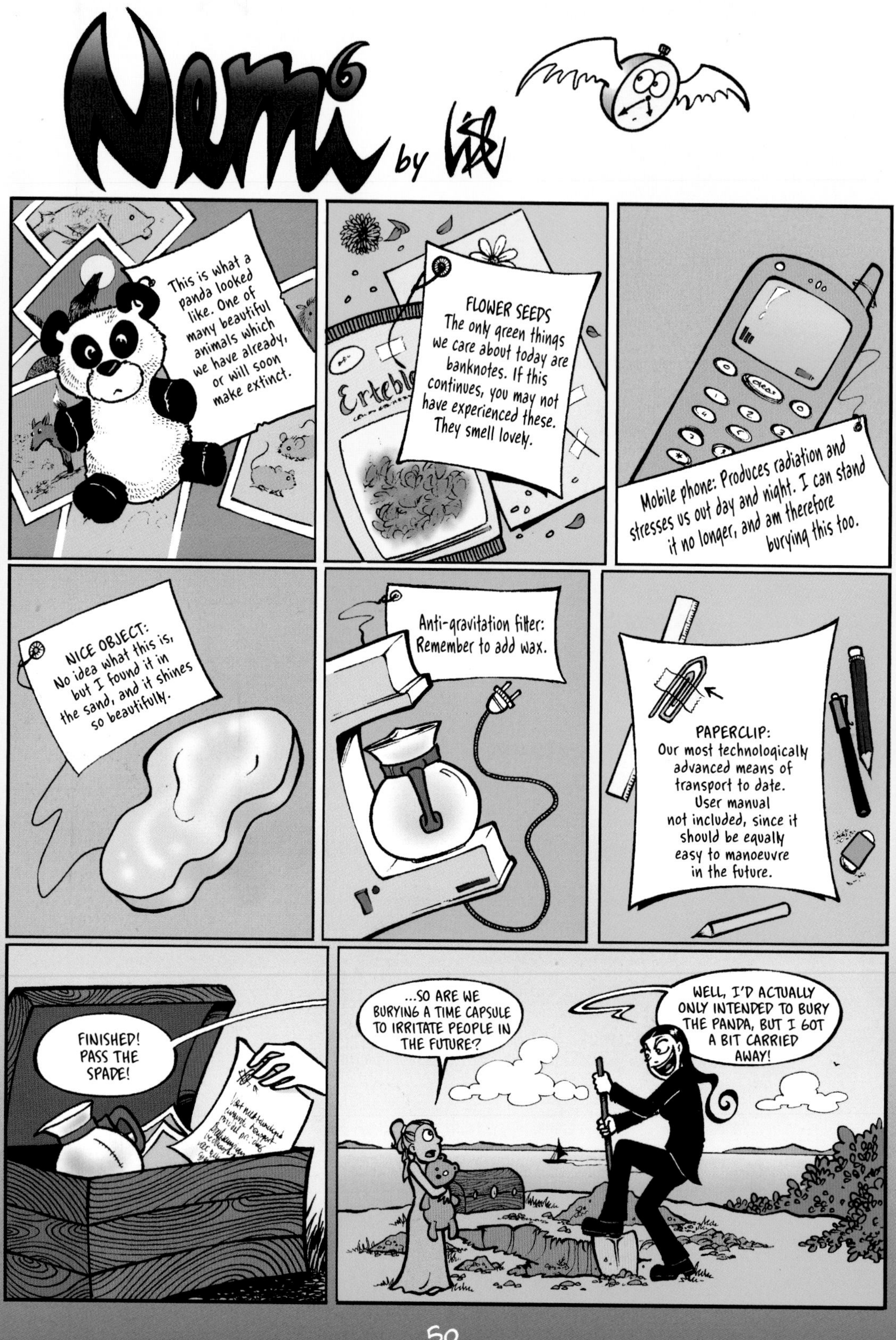
Nemi by Lise
This is what a panda looked like. One of many beautiful animals which we have already, or will soon make extinct.
FLOWER SEEDS
The only green things we care about today are banknotes. If this continues, you may not have experienced these. They smell lovely.
Mobile phone: Produces radiation and stresses us out day and night. I can stand it no longer, and am therefore burying this too.
NICE OBJECT:
No idea what this is, but I found it in the sand, and it shines so beautifully.
Anti-gravitation filter:
Remember to add wax.
PAPERCLIP:
Our most technologically advanced means of transport to date. User manual not included, since it should be equally easy to manoeuvre in the future.
FINISHED! PASS THE SPADE!
...SO ARE WE BURYING A TIME CAPSULE TO IRRITATE PEOPLE IN THE FUTURE?
WELL, I'D ACTUALLY ONLY INTENDED TO BURY THE PANDA, BUT I GOT A BIT CARRIED AWAY!

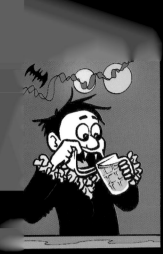

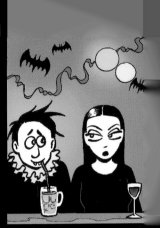

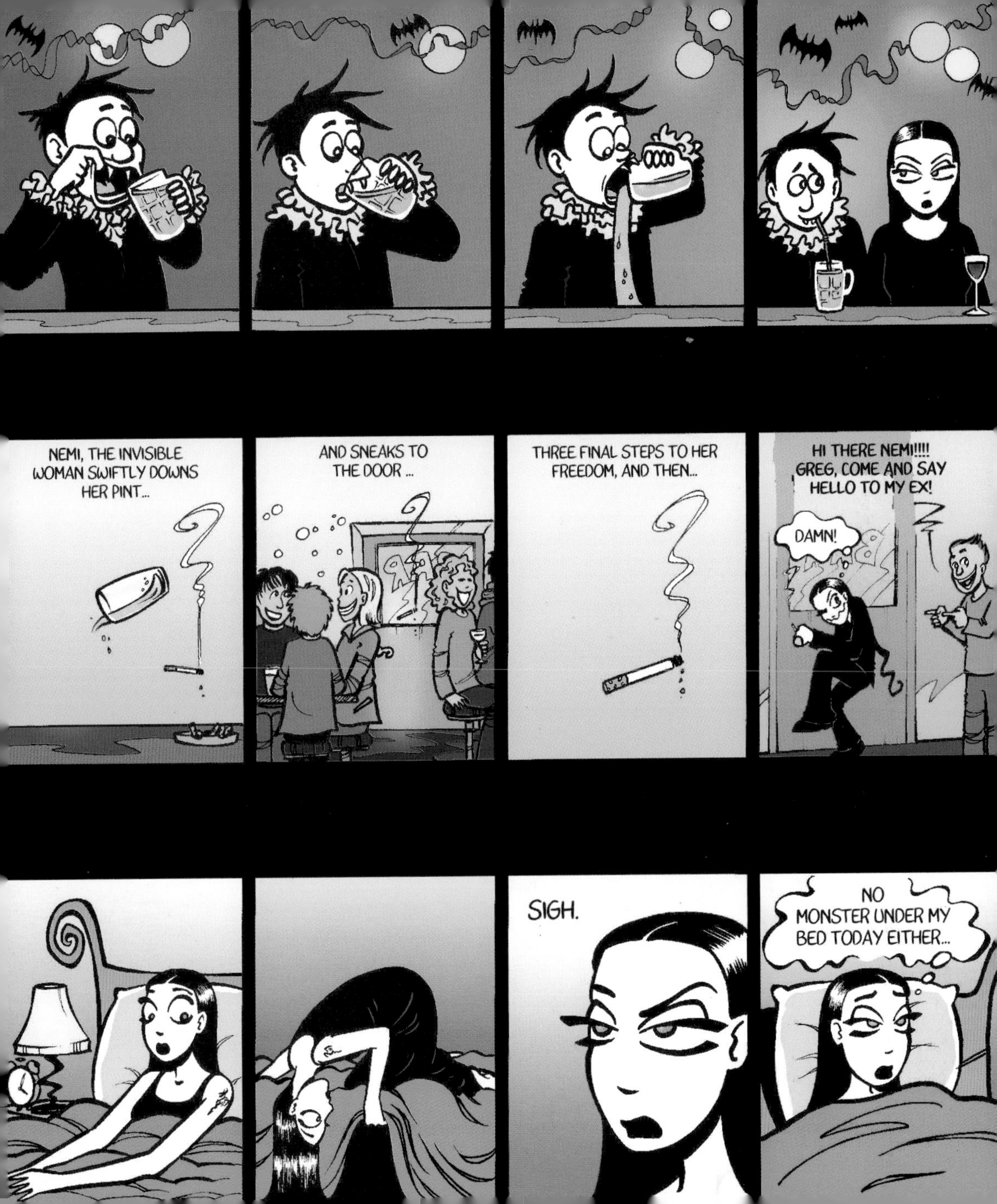
NEMI, THE INVISIBLE WOMAN SWIFTLY DOWNS HER PINT...
AND SNEAKS TO THE DOOR ...
THREE FINAL STEPS TO HER FREEDOM, AND THEN...
HI THERE NEMI!!!! GREG, COME AND SAY HELLO TO MY EX!
DAMN!
SIGH.
NO MONSTER UNDER MY BED TODAY EITHER...

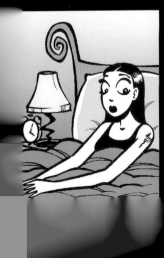

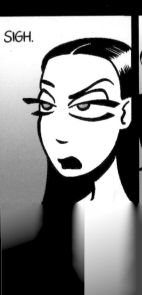

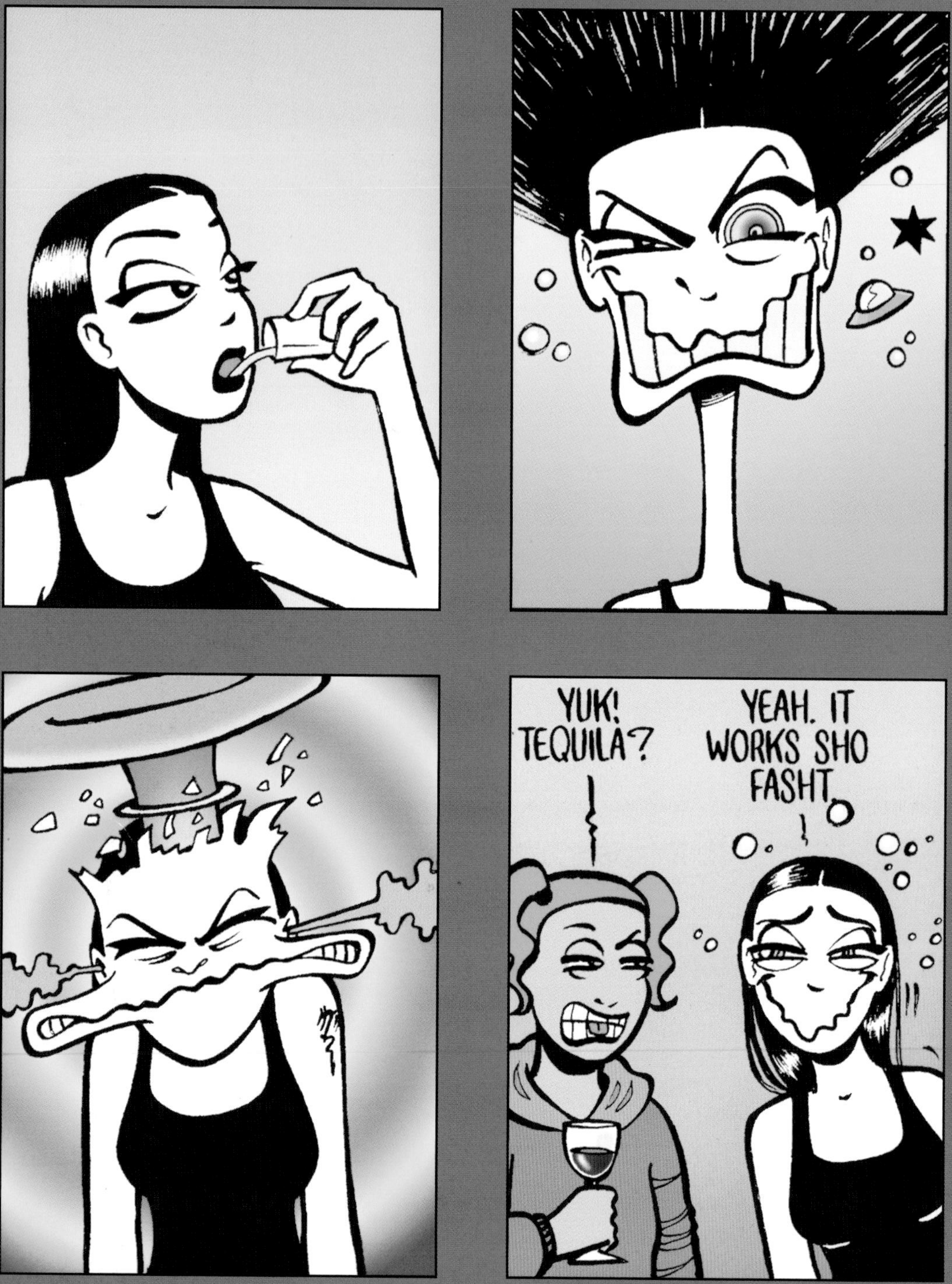
YUK! TEQUILA?
YEAH. IT WORKS SHO FASHT.

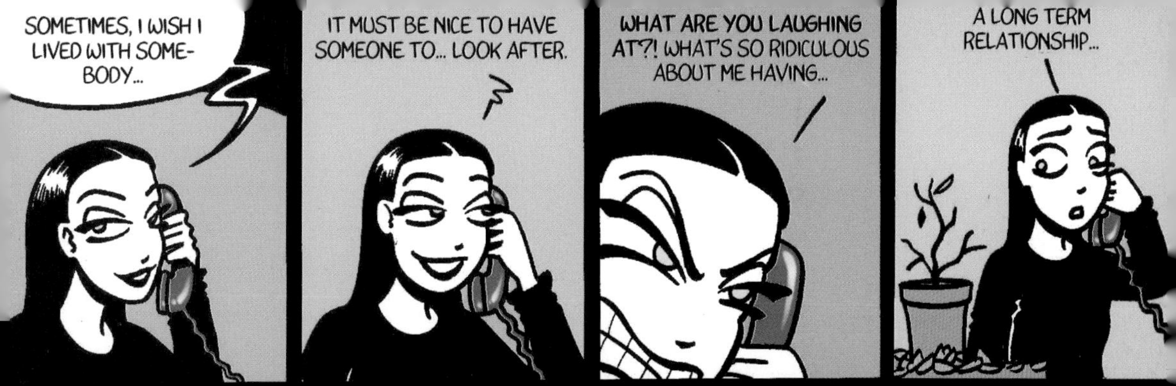
SOMETIMES, I WISH I LIVED WITH SOME-BODY...
IT MUST BE NICE TO HAVE SOMEONE TO... LOOK AFTER.
WHAT ARE YOU LAUGHING AT?! WHAT'S SO RIDICULOUS ABOUT ME HAVING...
A LONG TERM RELATIONSHIP...

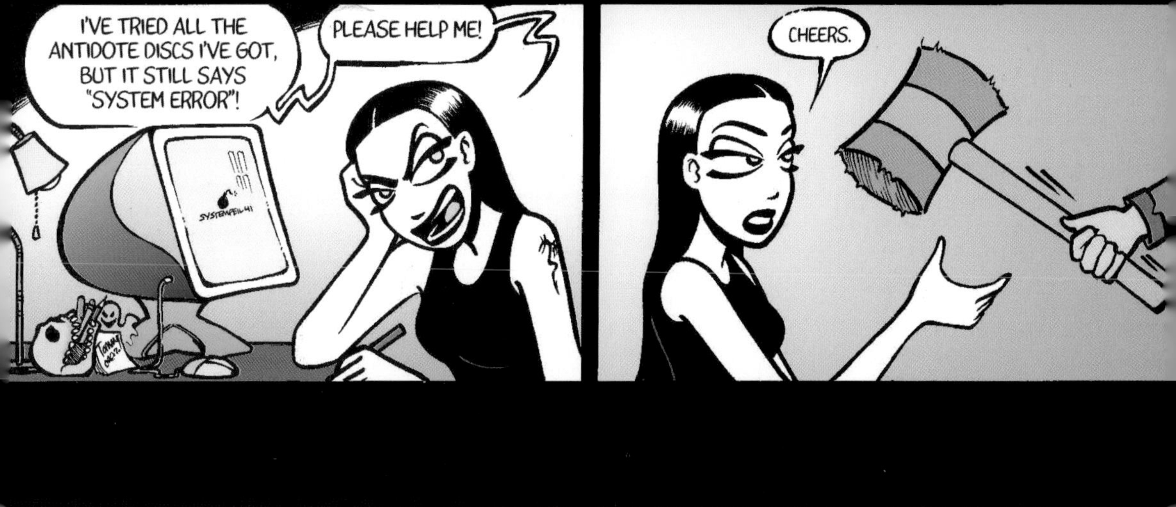
I'VE TRIED ALL THE ANTIDOTE DISCS I'VE GOT, BUT IT STILL SAYS "SYSTEM ERROR"!
PLEASE HELP ME!
CHEERS.

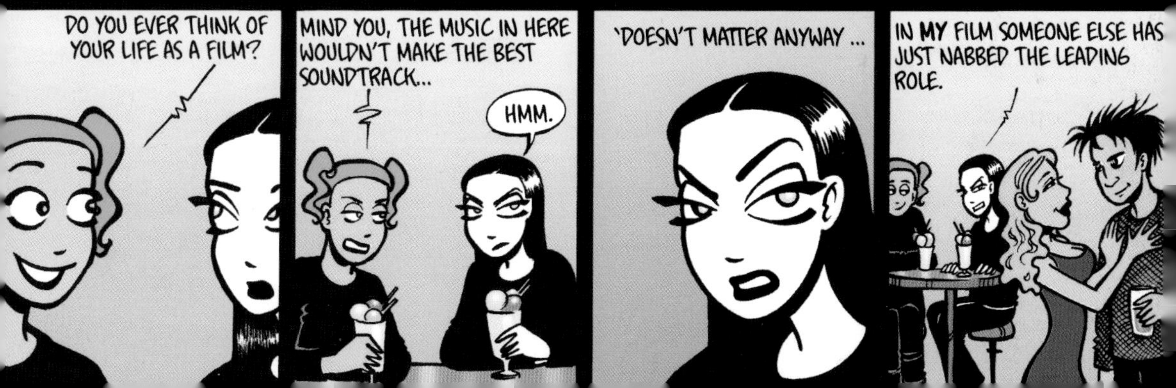
DO YOU EVER THINK OF YOUR LIFE AS A FILM?
MIND YOU, THE MUSIC IN HERE WOULDN'T MAKE THE BEST SOUNDTRACK...
HMM.
'DOESN'T MATTER ANYWAY ...
IN MY FILM SOMEONE ELSE HAS JUST NABBED THE LEADING ROLE.

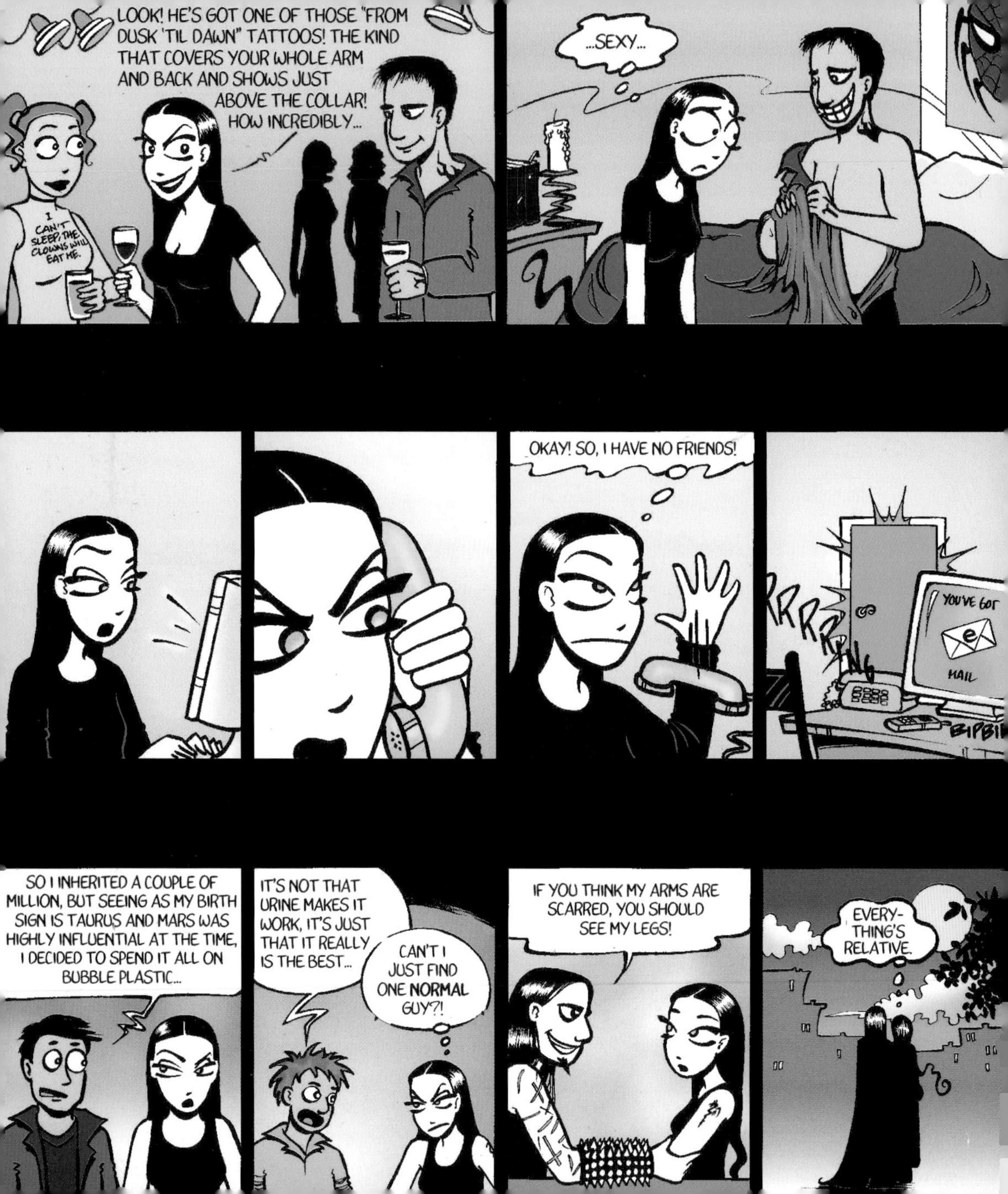

LOOK! HE'S GOT ONE OF THOSE "FROM DUSK 'TIL DAWN" TATTOOS! THE KIND THAT COVERS YOUR WHOLE ARM AND BACK AND SHOWS JUST ABOVE THE COLLAR! HOW INCREDIBLY...
I CAN'T SLEEP, THE CLOWNS WILL EAT ME.
...SEXY...
OKAY! SO, I HAVE NO FRIENDS!
RRRRRING
YOU'VE GOT e MAIL
BIPBI
SO I INHERITED A COUPLE OF MILLION, BUT SEEING AS MY BIRTH SIGN IS TAURUS AND MARS WAS HIGHLY INFLUENTIAL AT THE TIME, I DECIDED TO SPEND IT ALL ON BUBBLE PLASTIC...
IT'S NOT THAT URINE MAKES IT WORK, IT'S JUST THAT IT REALLY IS THE BEST...
CAN'T I JUST FIND ONE **NORMAL** GUY?!
IF YOU THINK MY ARMS ARE SCARRED, YOU SHOULD SEE MY LEGS!
EVERY-THING'S RELATIVE.

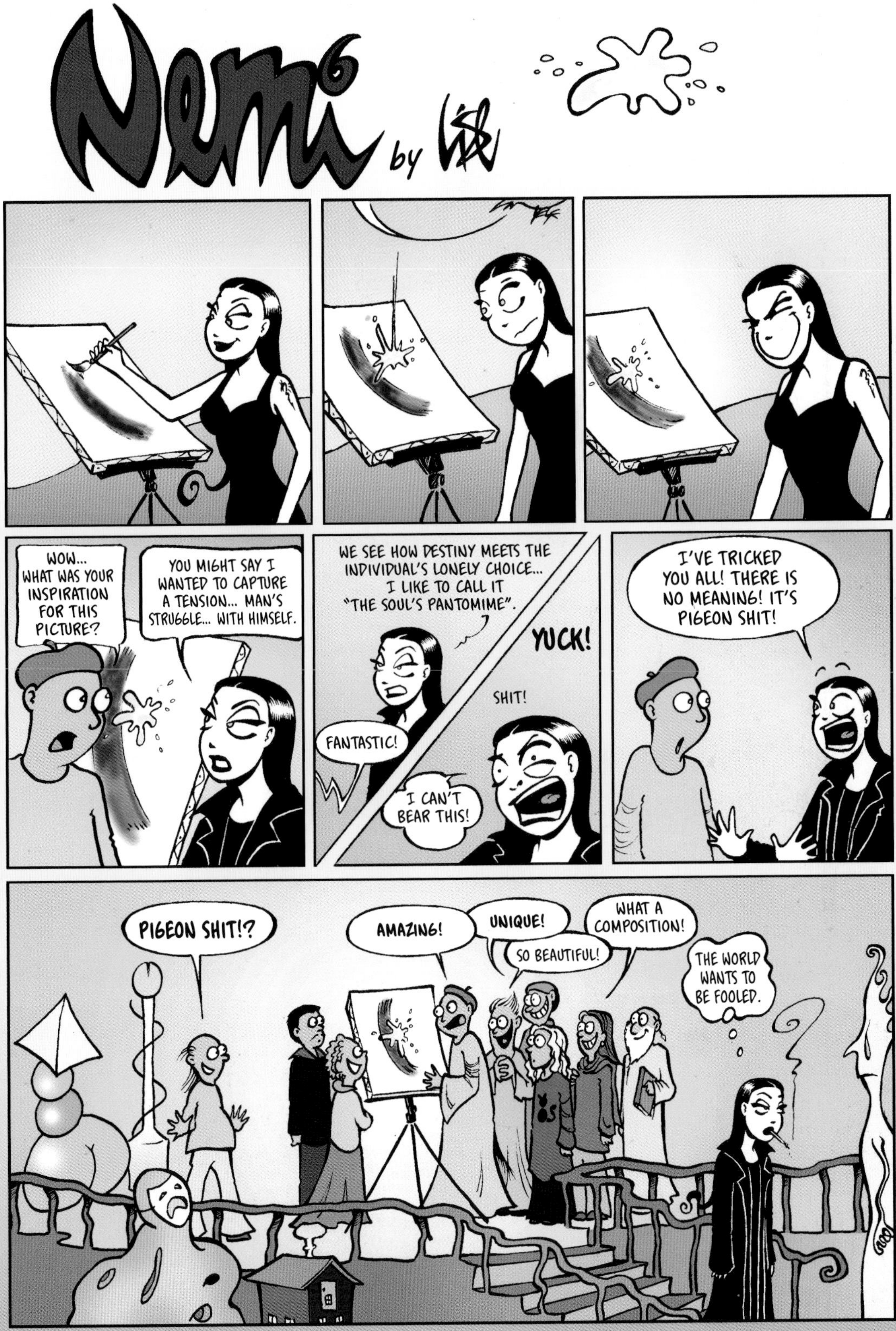
Nemi by Lise
WOW... WHAT WAS YOUR INSPIRATION FOR THIS PICTURE?
YOU MIGHT SAY I WANTED TO CAPTURE A TENSION... MAN'S STRUGGLE... WITH HIMSELF.
WE SEE HOW DESTINY MEETS THE INDIVIDUAL'S LONELY CHOICE... I LIKE TO CALL IT "THE SOUL'S PANTOMIME".
FANTASTIC!
YUCK!
SHIT!
I CAN'T BEAR THIS!
I'VE TRICKED YOU ALL! THERE IS NO MEANING! IT'S PIGEON SHIT!
PIGEON SHIT!?
AMAZING!
UNIQUE!
SO BEAUTIFUL!
WHAT A COMPOSITION!
THE WORLD WANTS TO BE FOOLED.

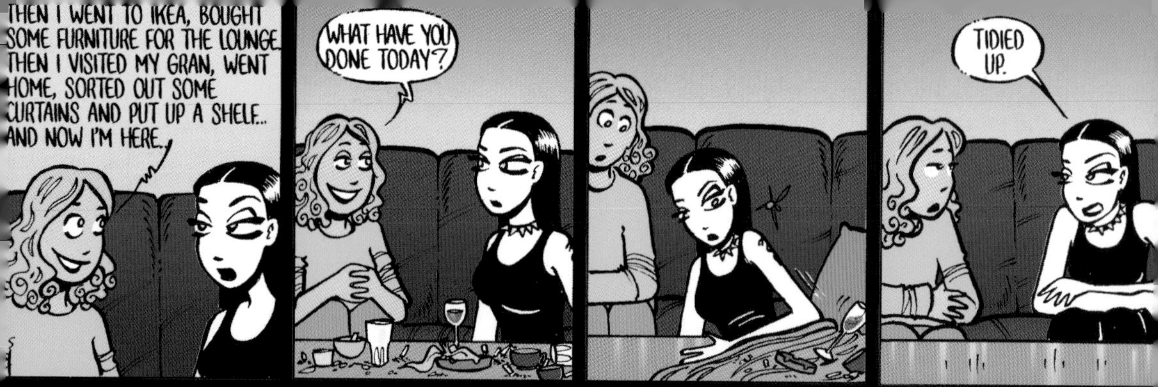
THEN I WENT TO IKEA, BOUGHT SOME FURNITURE FOR THE LOUNGE. THEN I VISITED MY GRAN, WENT HOME, SORTED OUT SOME CURTAINS AND PUT UP A SHELF... AND NOW I'M HERE.
WHAT HAVE YOU DONE TODAY?
TIDIED UP.

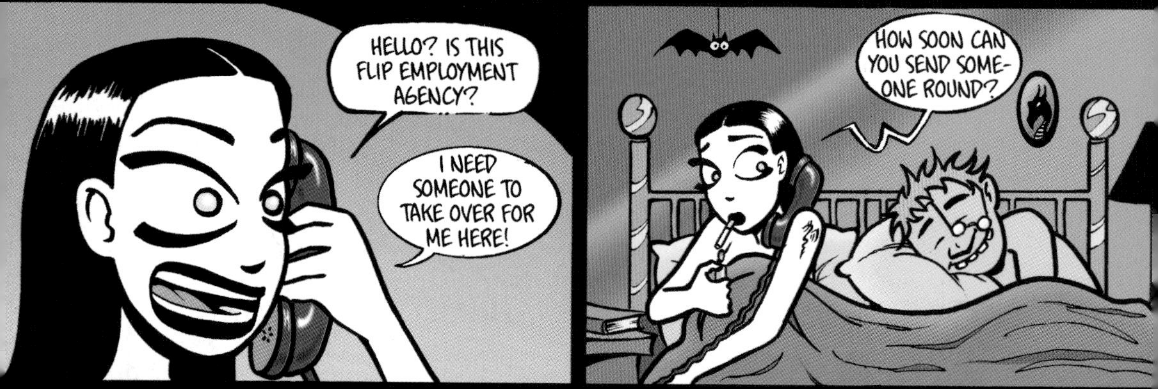
HELLO? IS THIS FLIP EMPLOYMENT AGENCY?
I NEED SOMEONE TO TAKE OVER FOR ME HERE!
HOW SOON CAN YOU SEND SOME-ONE ROUND?

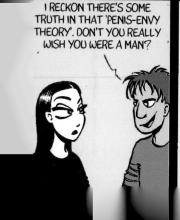

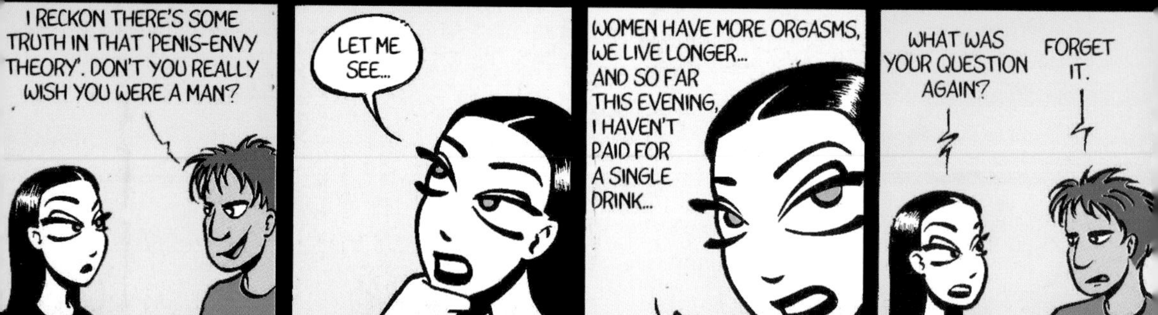
I RECKON THERE'S SOME TRUTH IN THAT 'PENIS-ENVY THEORY'. DON'T YOU REALLY WISH YOU WERE A MAN?
LET ME SEE...
WOMEN HAVE MORE ORGASMS, WE LIVE LONGER... AND SO FAR THIS EVENING, I HAVEN'T PAID FOR A SINGLE DRINK...
WHAT WAS YOUR QUESTION AGAIN?
FORGET IT.

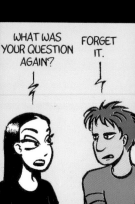

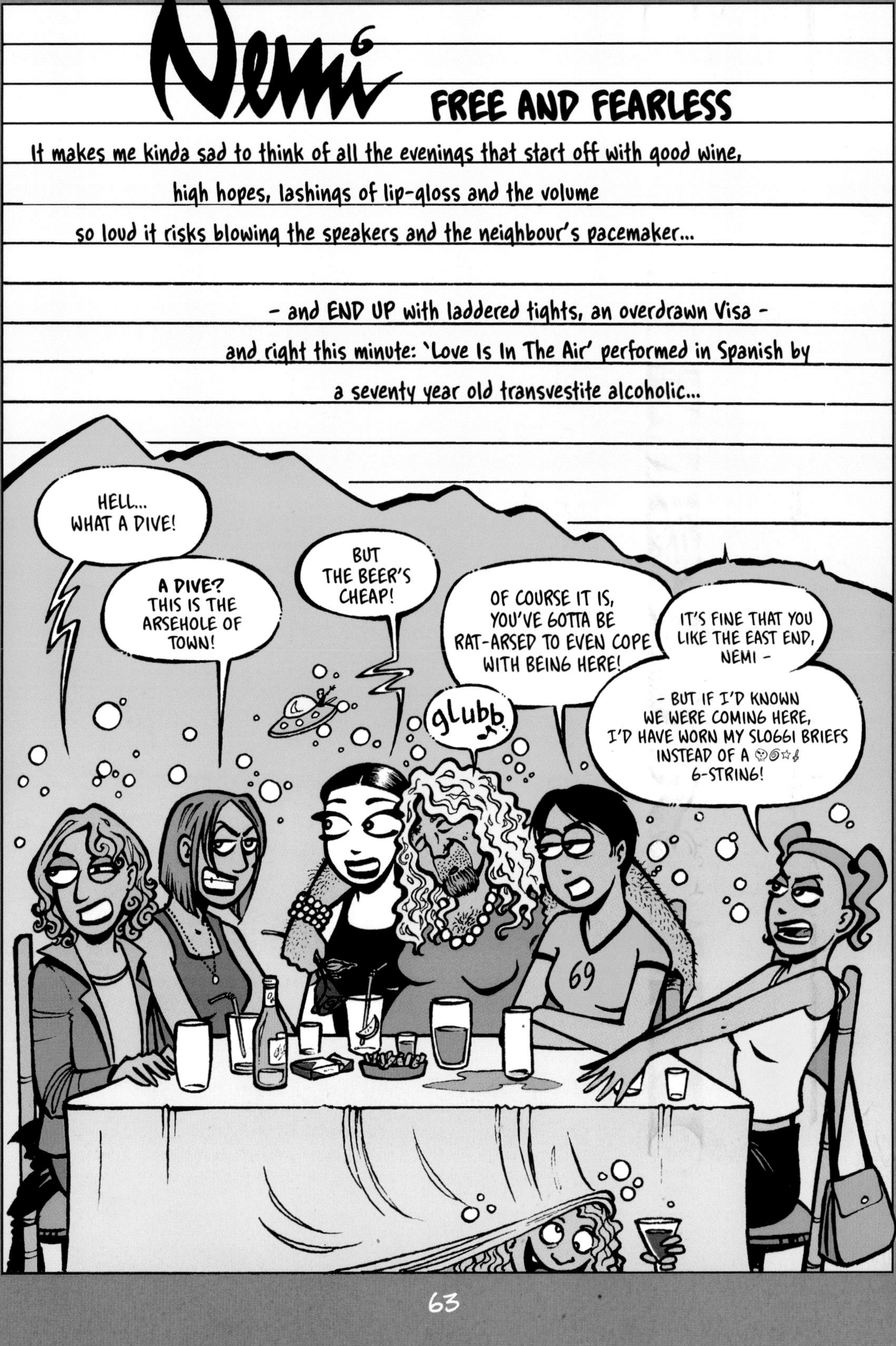
Nemi 6
FREE AND FEARLESS
It makes me kinda sad to think of all the evenings that start off with good wine, high hopes, lashings of lip-gloss and the volume so loud it risks blowing the speakers and the neighbour's pacemaker...
- and END UP with laddered tights, an overdrawn Visa -
and right this minute: 'Love Is In The Air' performed in Spanish by a seventy year old transvestite alcoholic...
HELL... WHAT A DIVE!
A DIVE? THIS IS THE ARSEHOLE OF TOWN!
BUT THE BEER'S CHEAP!
glubb
OF COURSE IT IS, YOU'VE GOTTA BE RAT-ARSED TO EVEN COPE WITH BEING HERE!
IT'S FINE THAT YOU LIKE THE EAST END, NEMI -
- BUT IF I'D KNOWN WE WERE COMING HERE, I'D HAVE WORN MY SLOGGI BRIEFS INSTEAD OF A
6-STRING!

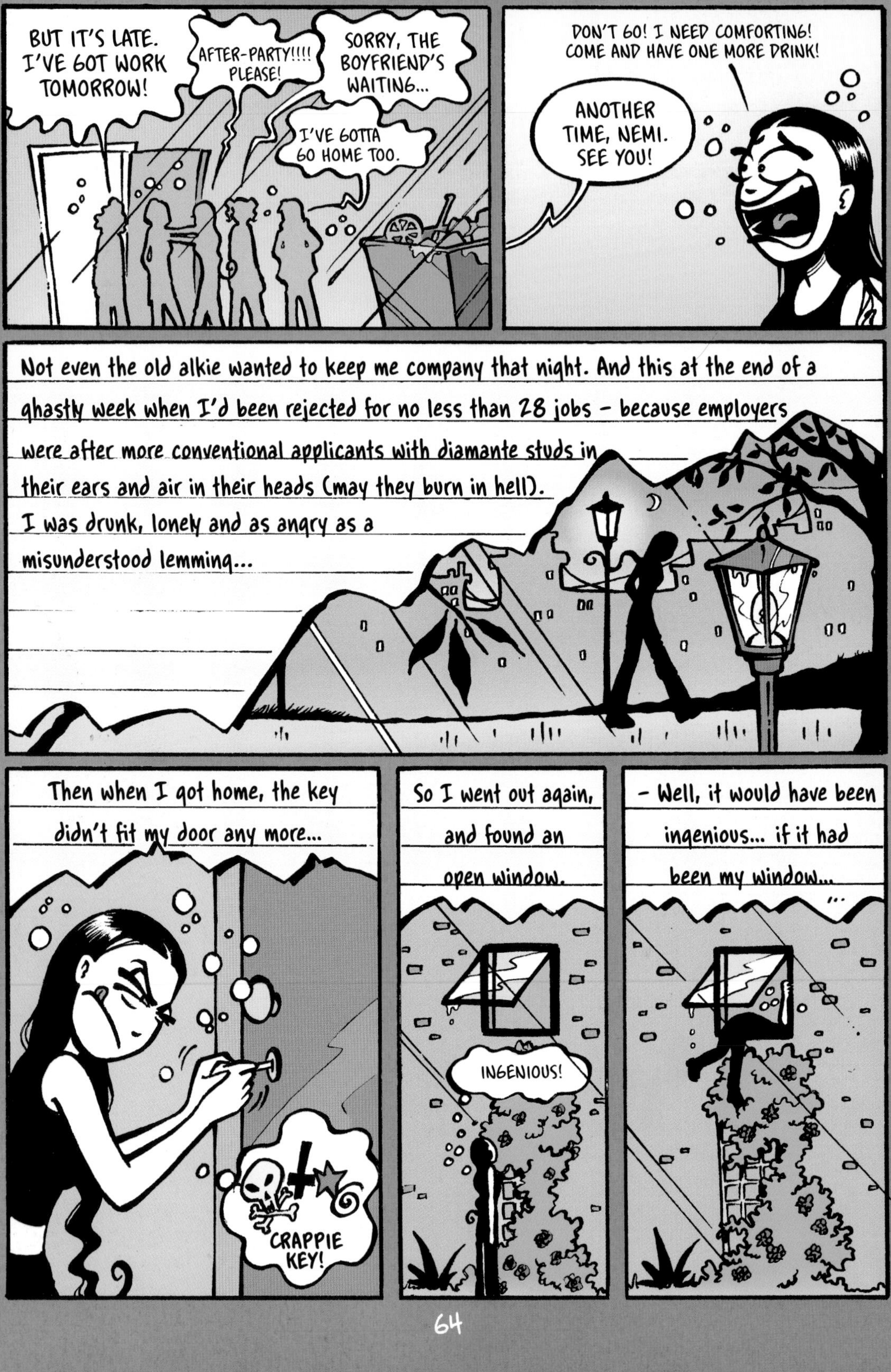
BUT IT'S LATE. I'VE GOT WORK TOMORROW!
AFTER-PARTY!!!! PLEASE!
SORRY, THE BOYFRIEND'S WAITING...
I'VE GOTTA GO HOME TOO.
DON'T GO! I NEED COMFORTING! COME AND HAVE ONE MORE DRINK!
ANOTHER TIME, NEMI. SEE YOU!
Not even the old alkie wanted to keep me company that night. And this at the end of a ghastly week when I'd been rejected for no less than 28 jobs – because employers were after more conventional applicants with diamante studs in their ears and air in their heads (may they burn in hell).
I was drunk, lonely and as angry as a misunderstood lemming...
Then when I got home, the key didn't fit my door any more...
CRAPPIE KEY!
So I went out again, and found an open window.
INGENIOUS!
– Well, it would have been ingenious... if it had been my window...

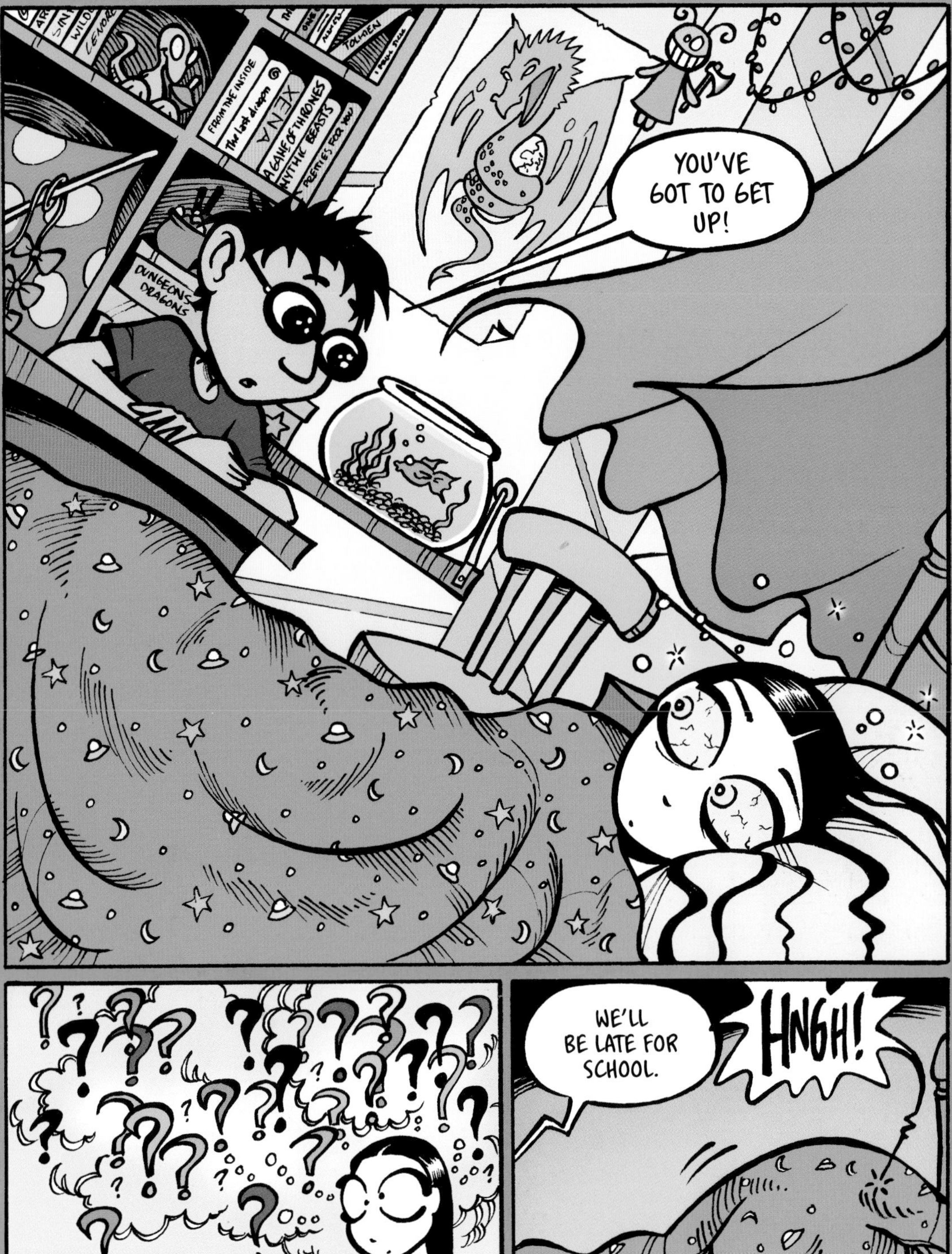
FROM THE INSIDE
The last dragon
XENA
A GAME OF THRONES
MYTHIC BEASTS
PRETTIES FOR YOU
DUNGEONS DRAGONS
YOU'VE GOT TO GET UP!
WE'LL BE LATE FOR SCHOOL.
HNGH!

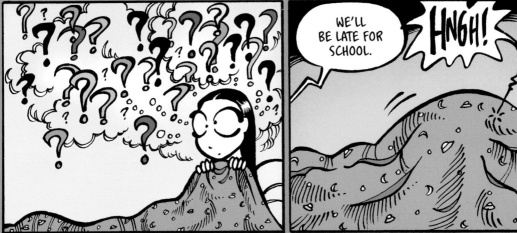

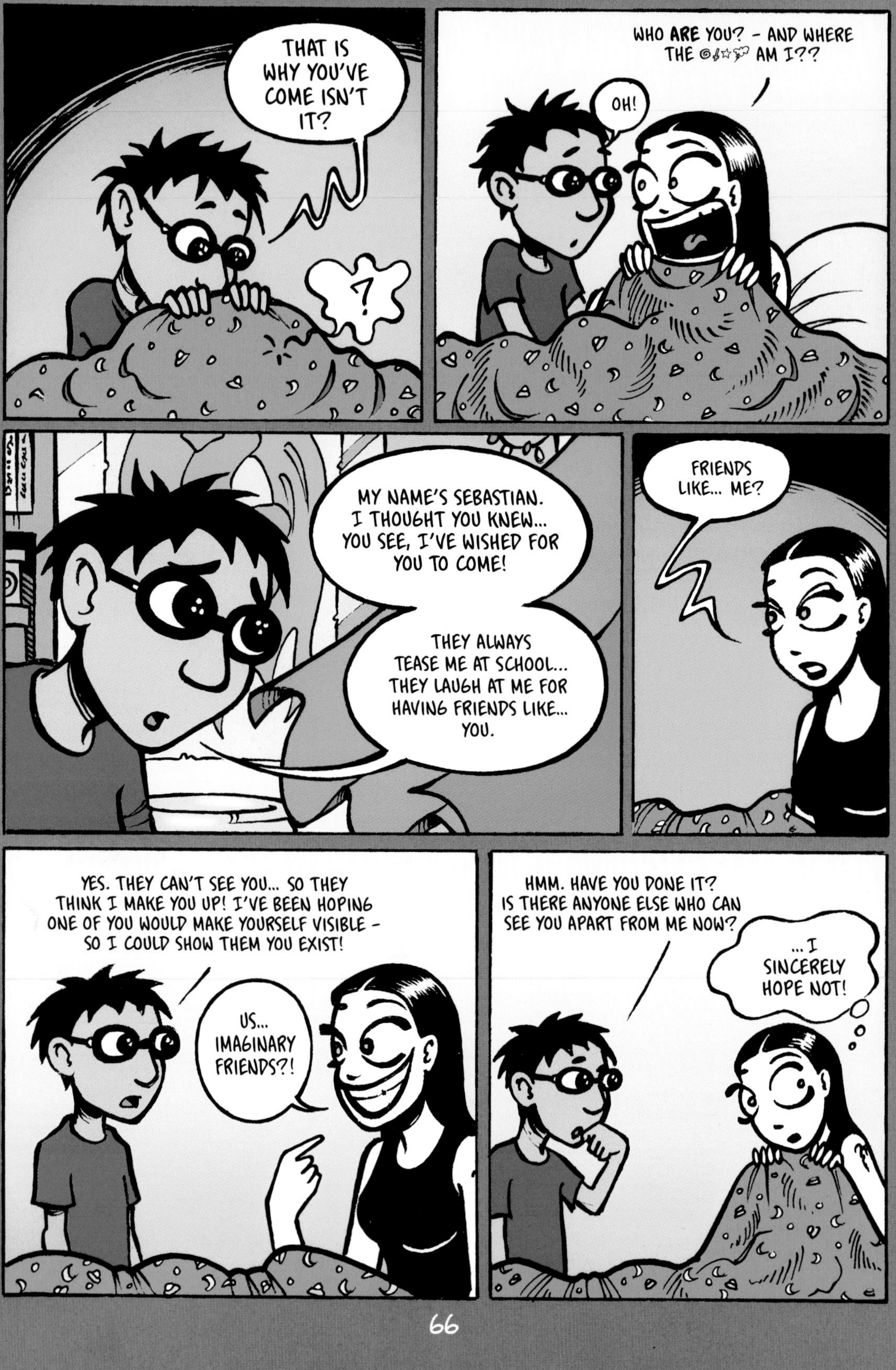
THAT IS WHY YOU'VE COME ISN'T IT?
?
WHO ARE YOU? - AND WHERE THE @#☆% AM I??
OH!
MY NAME'S SEBASTIAN. I THOUGHT YOU KNEW... YOU SEE, I'VE WISHED FOR YOU TO COME!
THEY ALWAYS TEASE ME AT SCHOOL... THEY LAUGH AT ME FOR HAVING FRIENDS LIKE... YOU.
FRIENDS LIKE... ME?
YES. THEY CAN'T SEE YOU... SO THEY THINK I MAKE YOU UP! I'VE BEEN HOPING ONE OF YOU WOULD MAKE YOURSELF VISIBLE - SO I COULD SHOW THEM YOU EXIST!
US... IMAGINARY FRIENDS?!
HMM. HAVE YOU DONE IT? IS THERE ANYONE ELSE WHO CAN SEE YOU APART FROM ME NOW?
... I SINCERELY HOPE NOT!

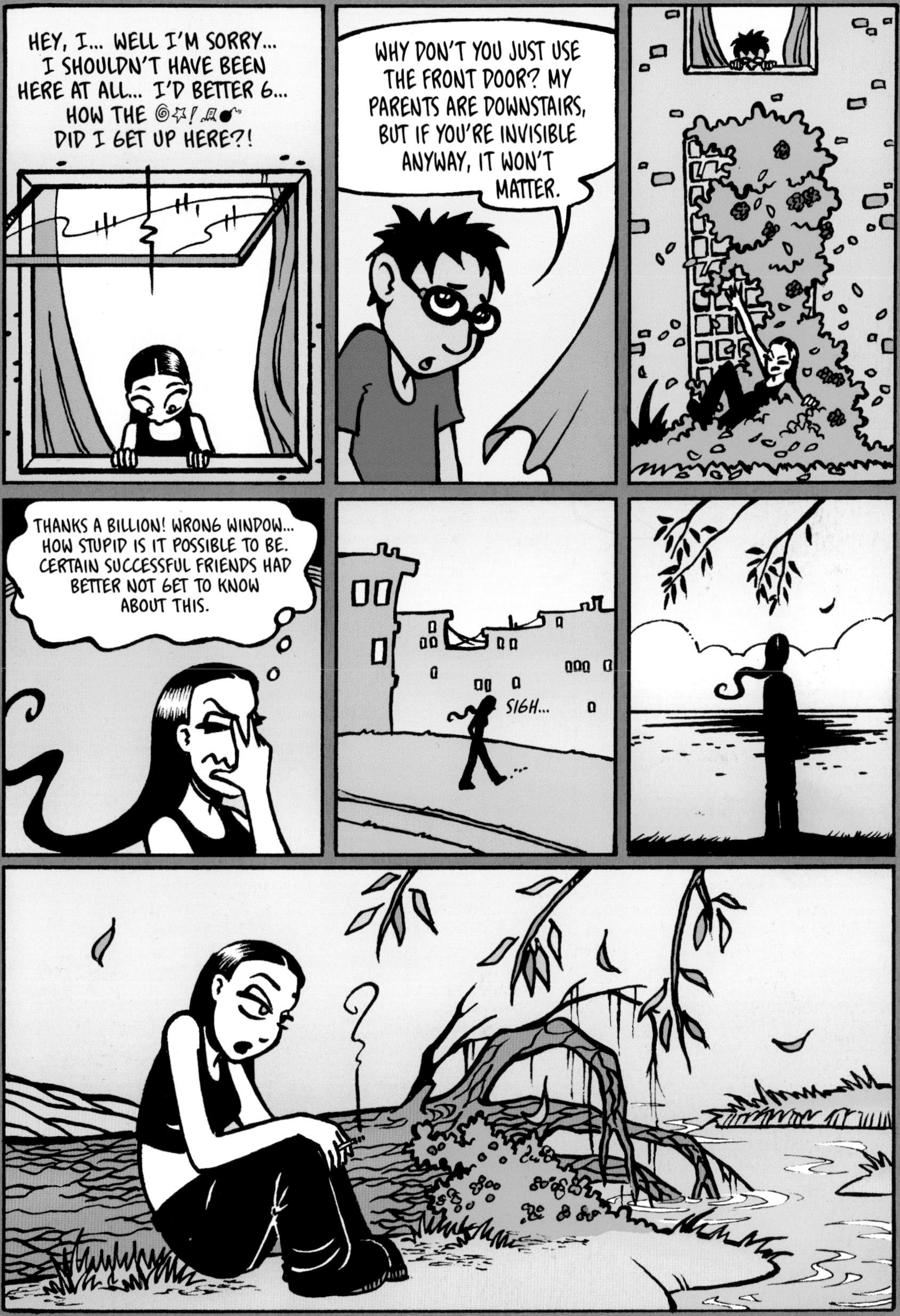
HEY, I... WELL I'M SORRY... I SHOULDN'T HAVE BEEN HERE AT ALL... I'D BETTER G... HOW THE
DID I GET UP HERE?!
WHY DON'T YOU JUST USE THE FRONT DOOR? MY PARENTS ARE DOWNSTAIRS, BUT IF YOU'RE INVISIBLE ANYWAY, IT WON'T MATTER.
THANKS A BILLION! WRONG WINDOW... HOW STUPID IS IT POSSIBLE TO BE. CERTAIN SUCCESSFUL FRIENDS HAD BETTER NOT GET TO KNOW ABOUT THIS.
SIGH...

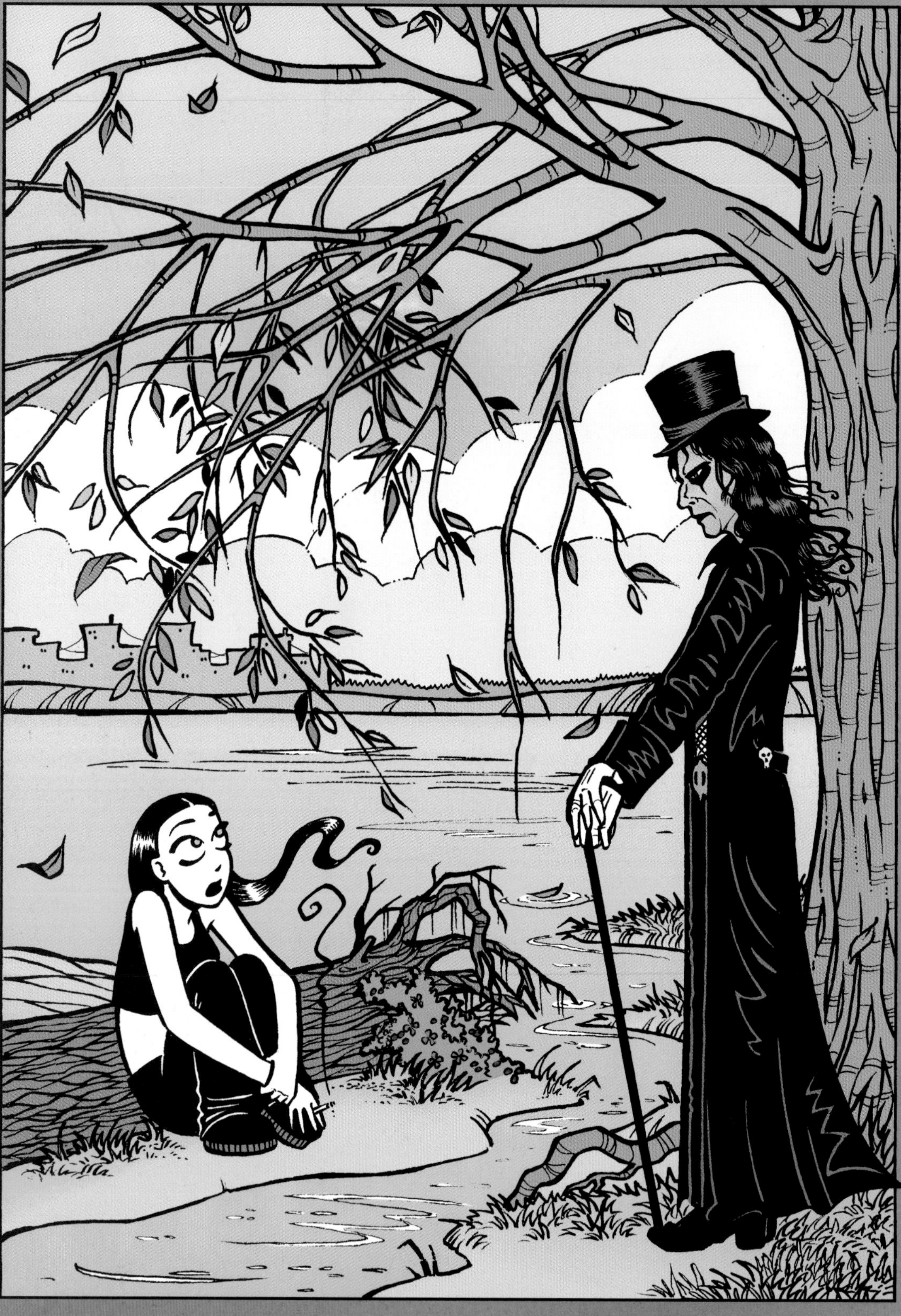

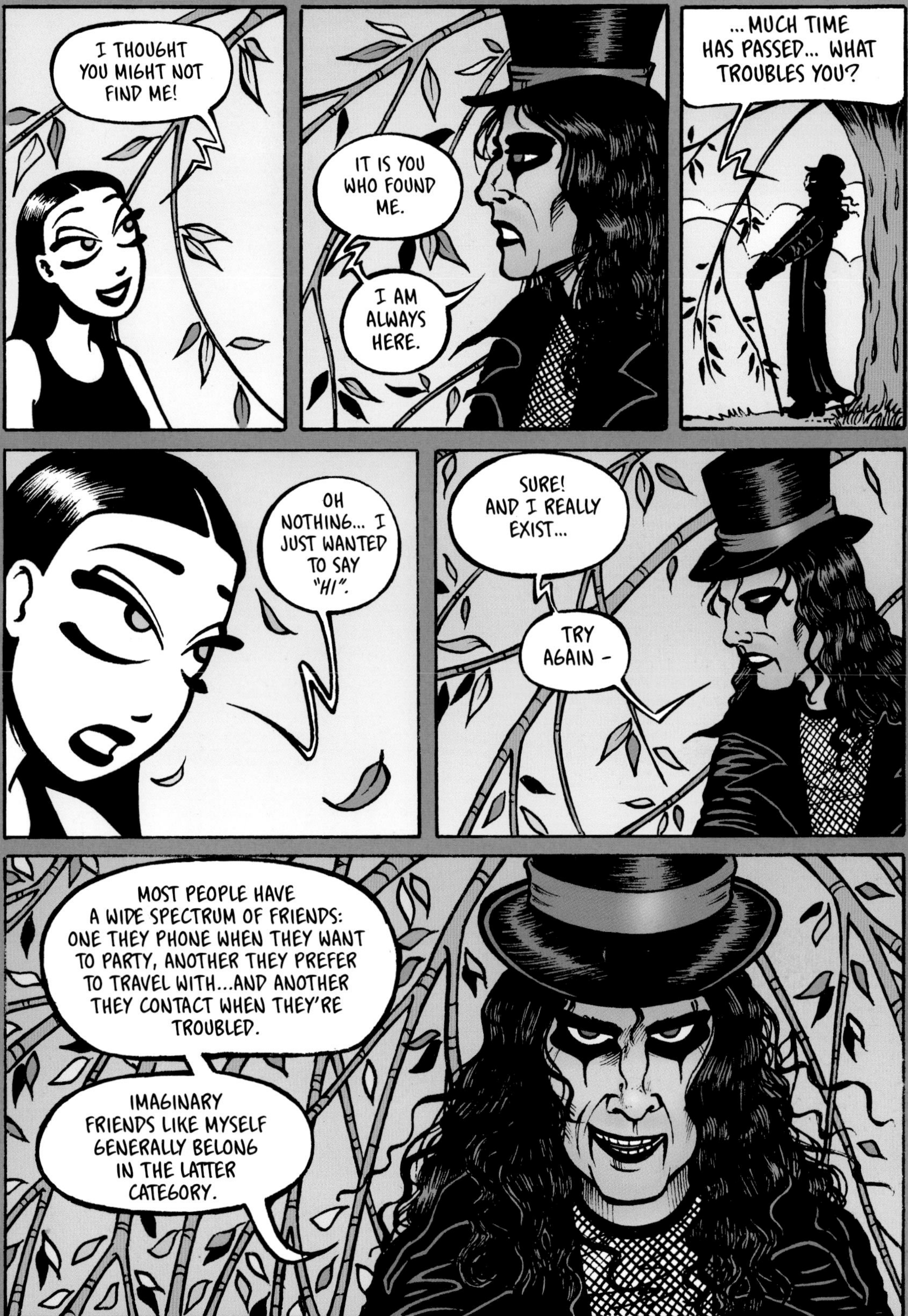
I THOUGHT YOU MIGHT NOT FIND ME!
IT IS YOU WHO FOUND ME.
I AM ALWAYS HERE.
...MUCH TIME HAS PASSED... WHAT TROUBLES YOU?
OH NOTHING... I JUST WANTED TO SAY "HI".
SURE! AND I REALLY EXIST...
TRY AGAIN -
MOST PEOPLE HAVE A WIDE SPECTRUM OF FRIENDS: ONE THEY PHONE WHEN THEY WANT TO PARTY, ANOTHER THEY PREFER TO TRAVEL WITH...AND ANOTHER THEY CONTACT WHEN THEY'RE TROUBLED.
IMAGINARY FRIENDS LIKE MYSELF GENERALLY BELONG IN THE LATTER CATEGORY.

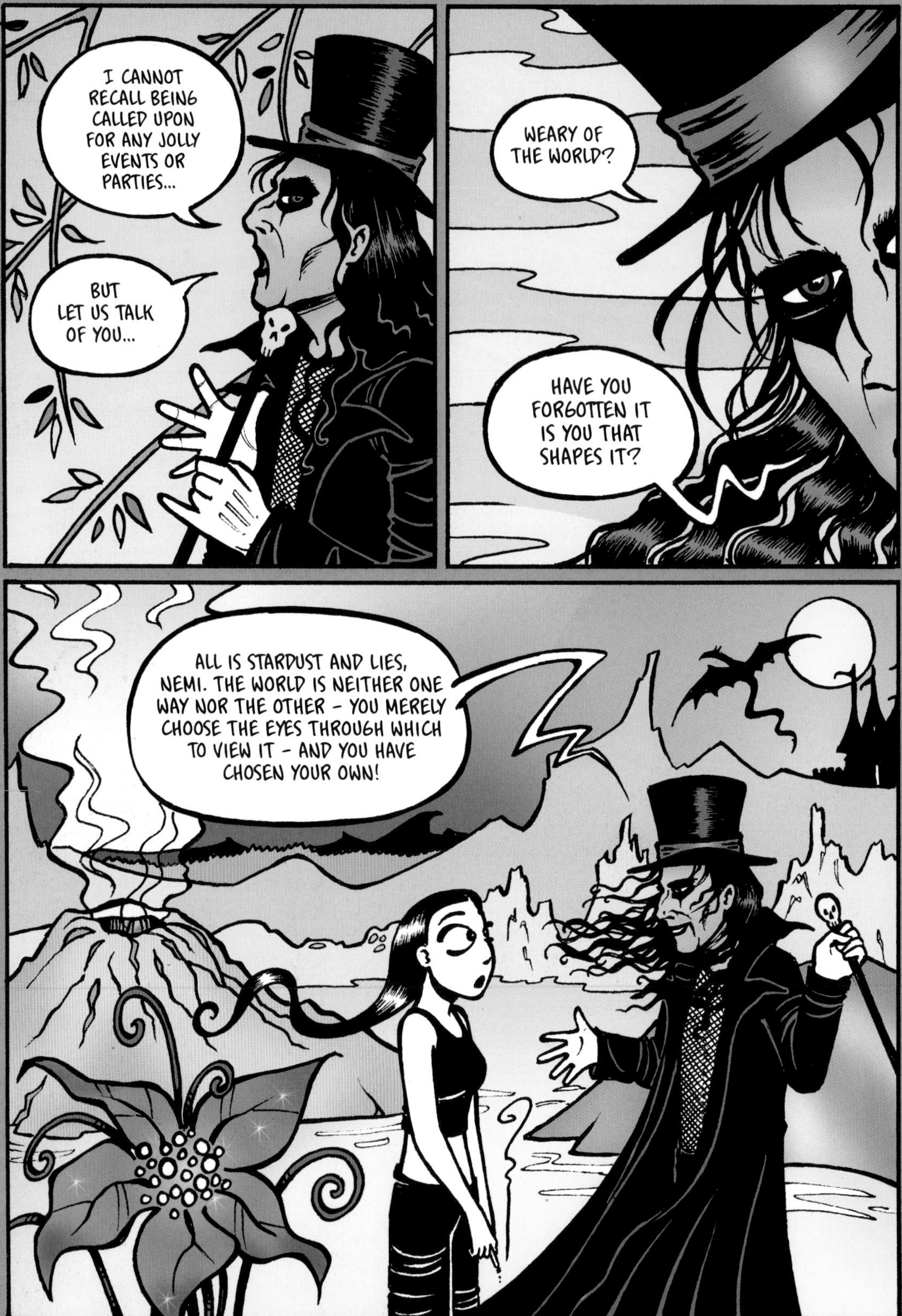
I CANNOT RECALL BEING CALLED UPON FOR ANY JOLLY EVENTS OR PARTIES...
BUT LET US TALK OF YOU...
WEARY OF THE WORLD?
HAVE YOU FORGOTTEN IT IS YOU THAT SHAPES IT?
ALL IS STARDUST AND LIES, NEMI. THE WORLD IS NEITHER ONE WAY NOR THE OTHER - YOU MERELY CHOOSE THE EYES THROUGH WHICH TO VIEW IT - AND YOU HAVE CHOSEN YOUR OWN!

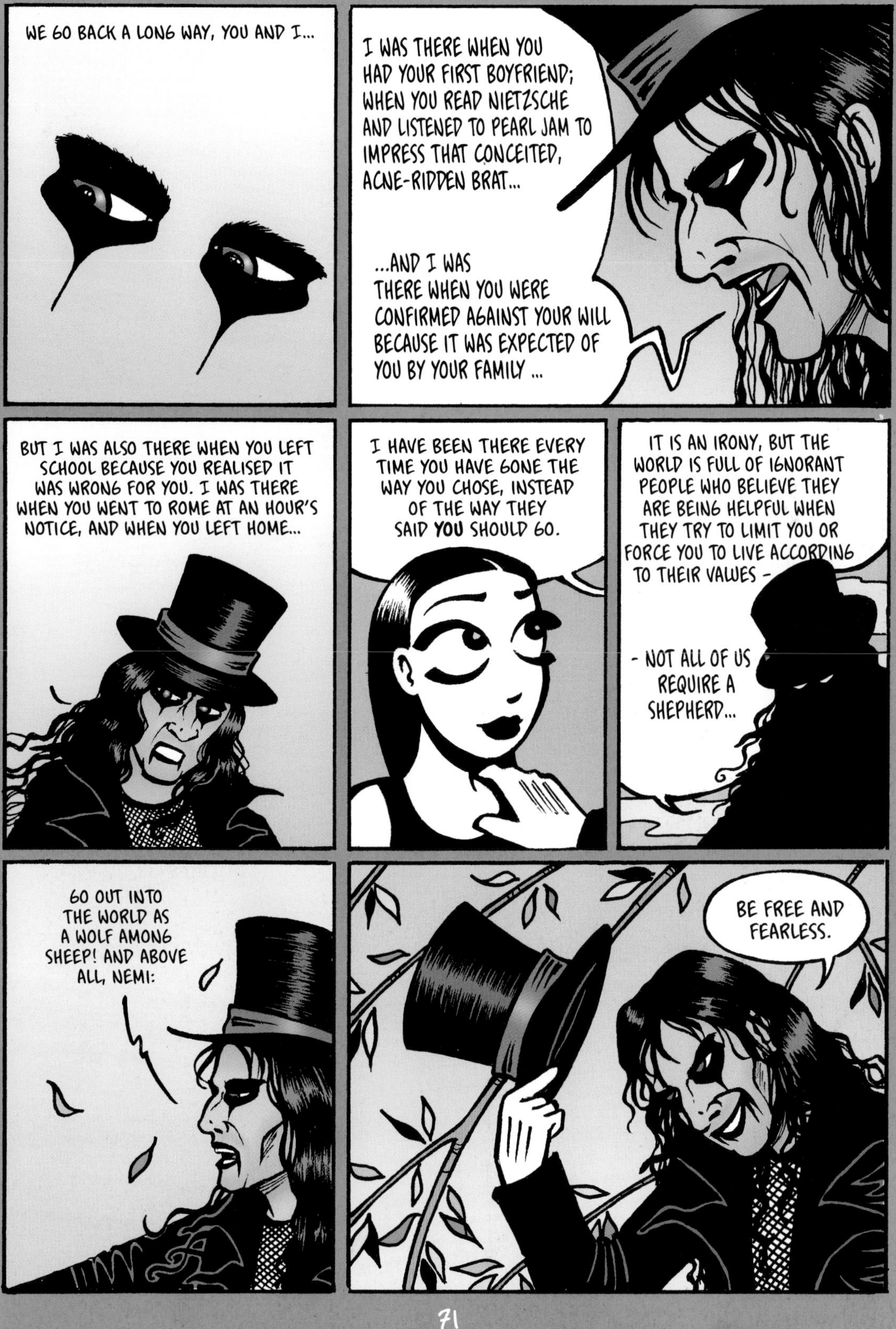
WE GO BACK A LONG WAY, YOU AND I...
I WAS THERE WHEN YOU HAD YOUR FIRST BOYFRIEND; WHEN YOU READ NIETZSCHE AND LISTENED TO PEARL JAM TO IMPRESS THAT CONCEITED, ACNE-RIDDEN BRAT...
...AND I WAS THERE WHEN YOU WERE CONFIRMED AGAINST YOUR WILL BECAUSE IT WAS EXPECTED OF YOU BY YOUR FAMILY ...
BUT I WAS ALSO THERE WHEN YOU LEFT SCHOOL BECAUSE YOU REALISED IT WAS WRONG FOR YOU. I WAS THERE WHEN YOU WENT TO ROME AT AN HOUR'S NOTICE, AND WHEN YOU LEFT HOME...
I HAVE BEEN THERE EVERY TIME YOU HAVE GONE THE WAY YOU CHOSE, INSTEAD OF THE WAY THEY SAID **YOU** SHOULD GO.
IT IS AN IRONY, BUT THE WORLD IS FULL OF IGNORANT PEOPLE WHO BELIEVE THEY ARE BEING HELPFUL WHEN THEY TRY TO LIMIT YOU OR FORCE YOU TO LIVE ACCORDING TO THEIR VALUES –
– NOT ALL OF US REQUIRE A SHEPHERD...
GO OUT INTO THE WORLD AS A WOLF AMONG SHEEP! AND ABOVE ALL, NEMI:
BE FREE AND FEARLESS.

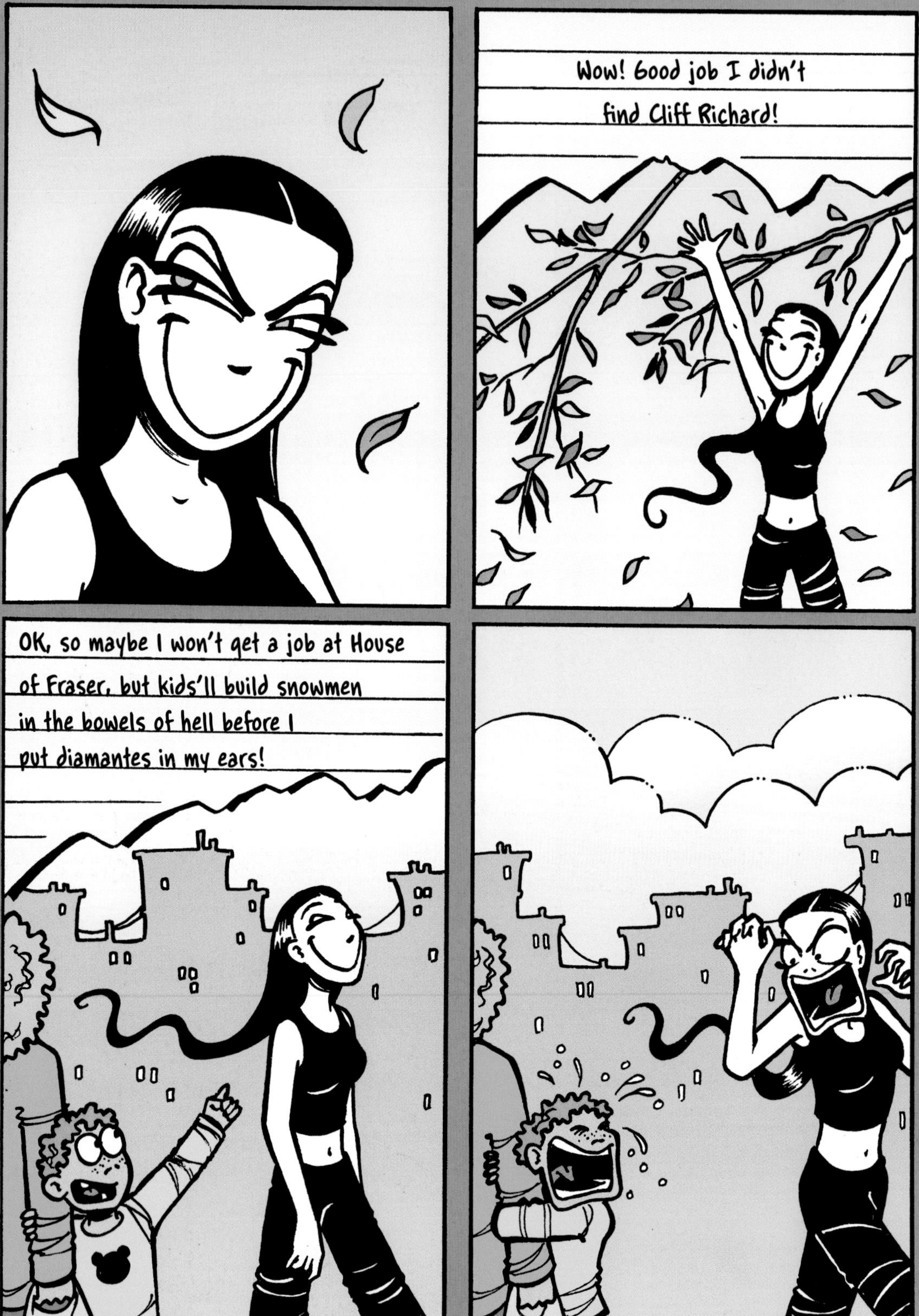
Wow! Good job I didn't find Cliff Richard!
OK, so maybe I won't get a job at House of Fraser, but kid's'll build snowmen in the bowels of hell before I put diamantes in my ears!

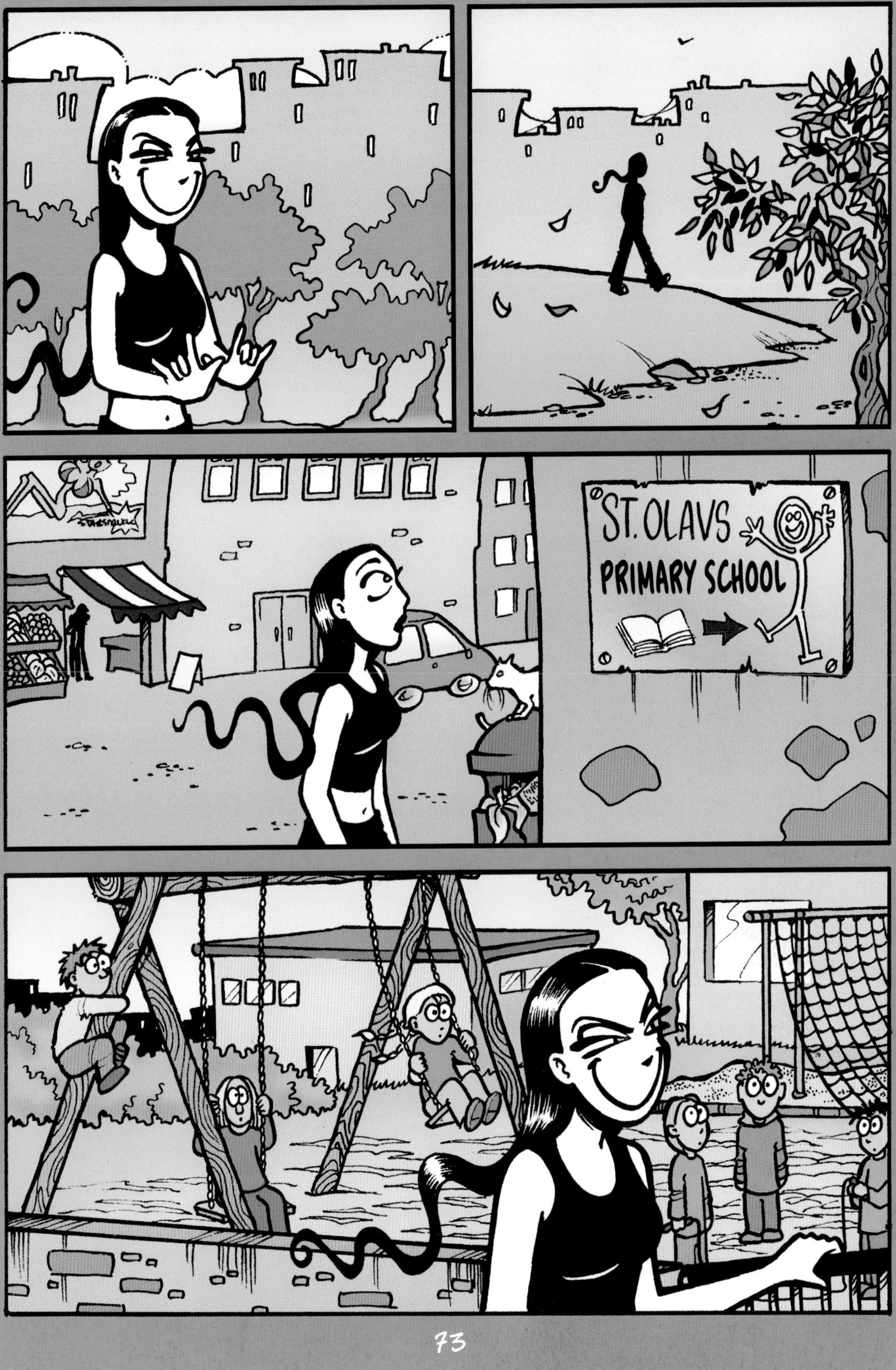
ST. OLAVS
PRIMARY SCHOOL

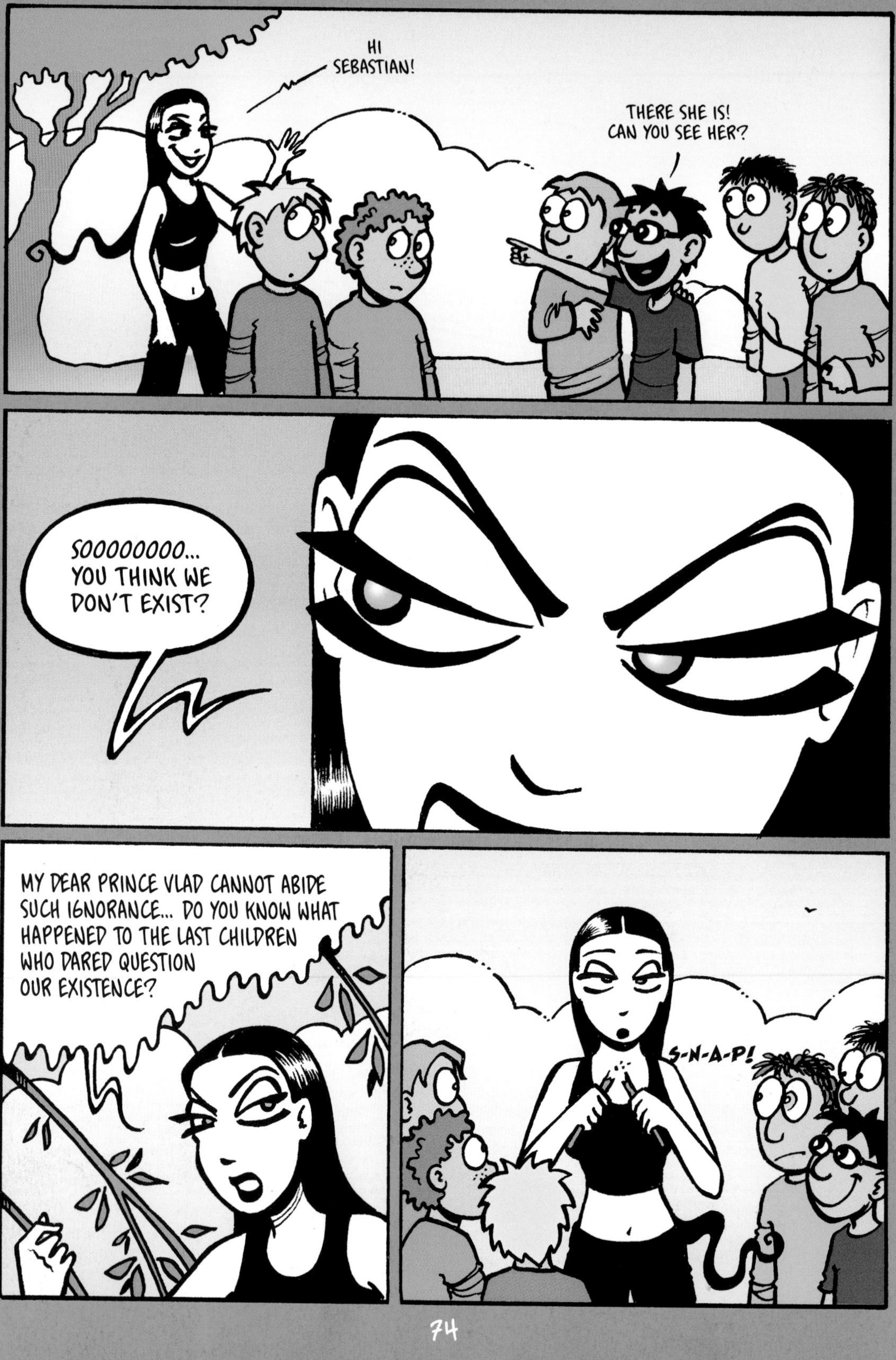
HI SEBASTIAN!
THERE SHE IS! CAN YOU SEE HER?
SOOOOOOOO... YOU THINK WE DON'T EXIST?
MY DEAR PRINCE VLAD CANNOT ABIDE SUCH IGNORANCE... DO YOU KNOW WHAT HAPPENED TO THE LAST CHILDREN WHO DARED QUESTION OUR EXISTENCE?
S-N-A-P!

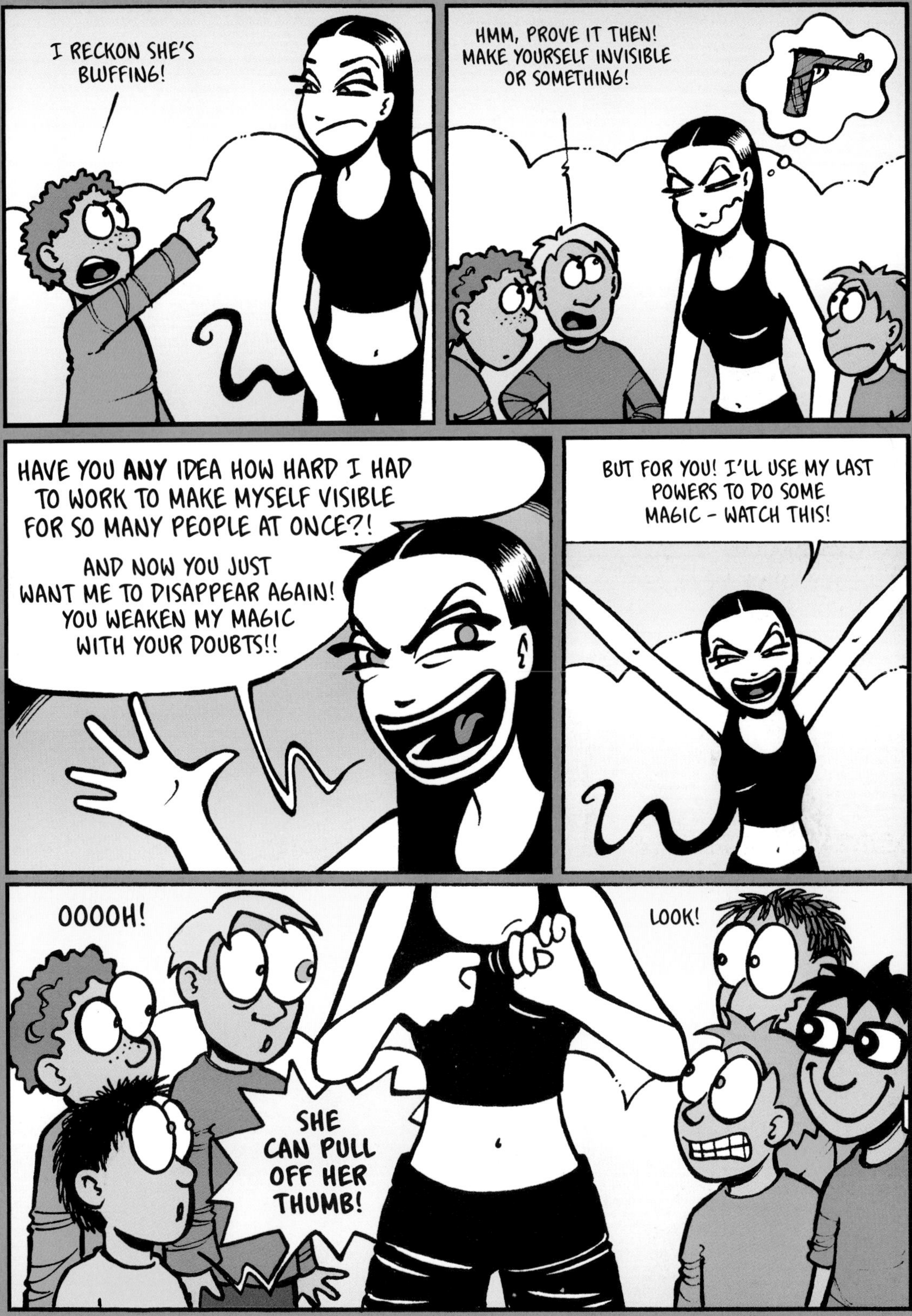
I RECKON SHE'S BLUFFING!
HMM, PROVE IT THEN! MAKE YOURSELF INVISIBLE OR SOMETHING!
HAVE YOU **ANY** IDEA HOW HARD I HAD TO WORK TO MAKE MYSELF VISIBLE FOR SO MANY PEOPLE AT ONCE?!
AND NOW YOU JUST WANT ME TO DISAPPEAR AGAIN! YOU WEAKEN MY MAGIC WITH YOUR DOUBTS!!
BUT FOR YOU! I'LL USE MY LAST POWERS TO DO SOME MAGIC – WATCH THIS!
OOOOH!
LOOK!
SHE CAN PULL OFF HER THUMB!

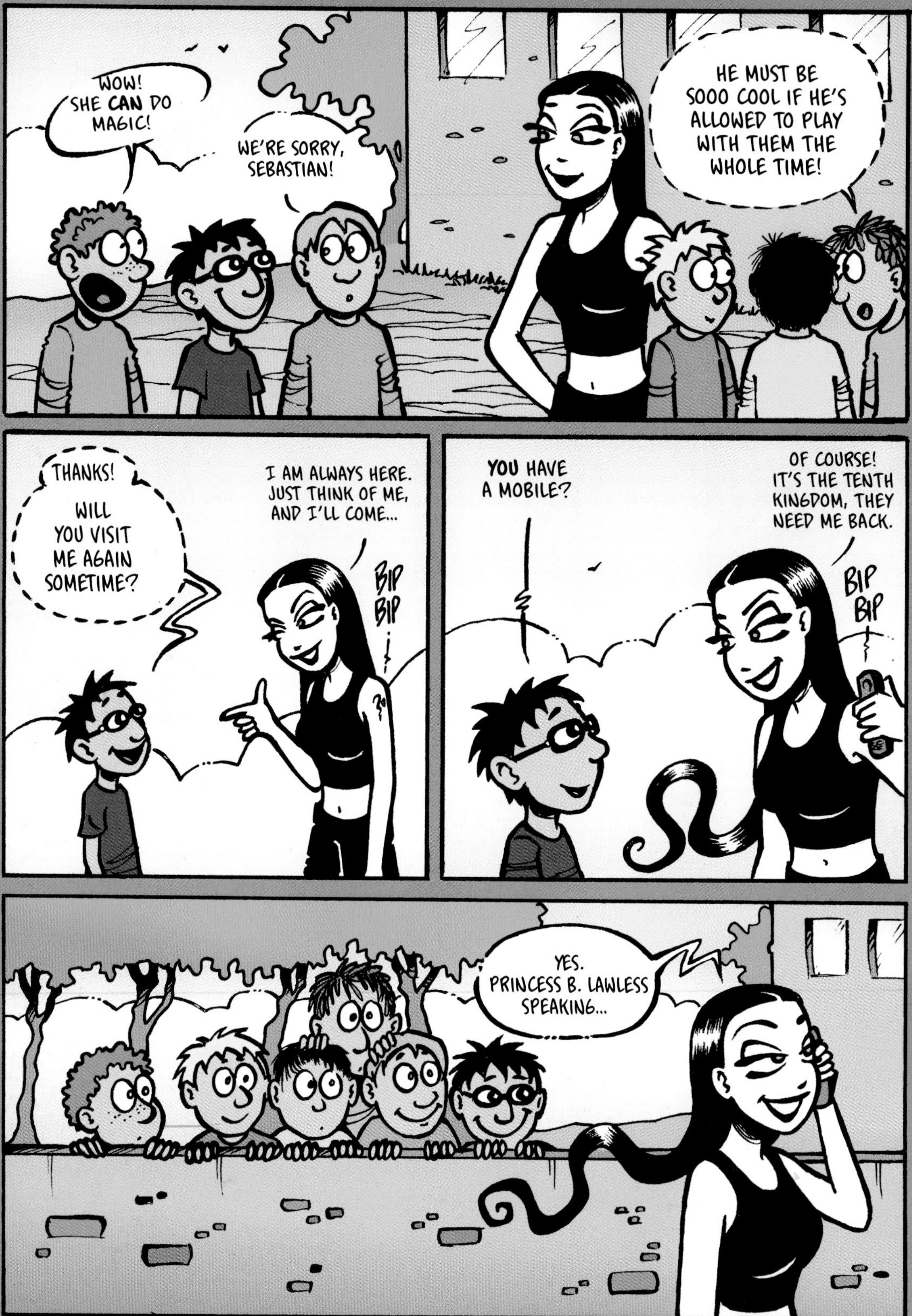
WOW! SHE CAN DO MAGIC!
WE'RE SORRY, SEBASTIAN!
HE MUST BE SOOO COOL IF HE'S ALLOWED TO PLAY WITH THEM THE WHOLE TIME!
THANKS!
WILL YOU VISIT ME AGAIN SOMETIME?
I AM ALWAYS HERE. JUST THINK OF ME, AND I'LL COME...
BIP BIP
YOU HAVE A MOBILE?
OF COURSE! IT'S THE TENTH KINGDOM, THEY NEED ME BACK.
BIP BIP
YES. PRINCESS B. LAWLESS SPEAKING...

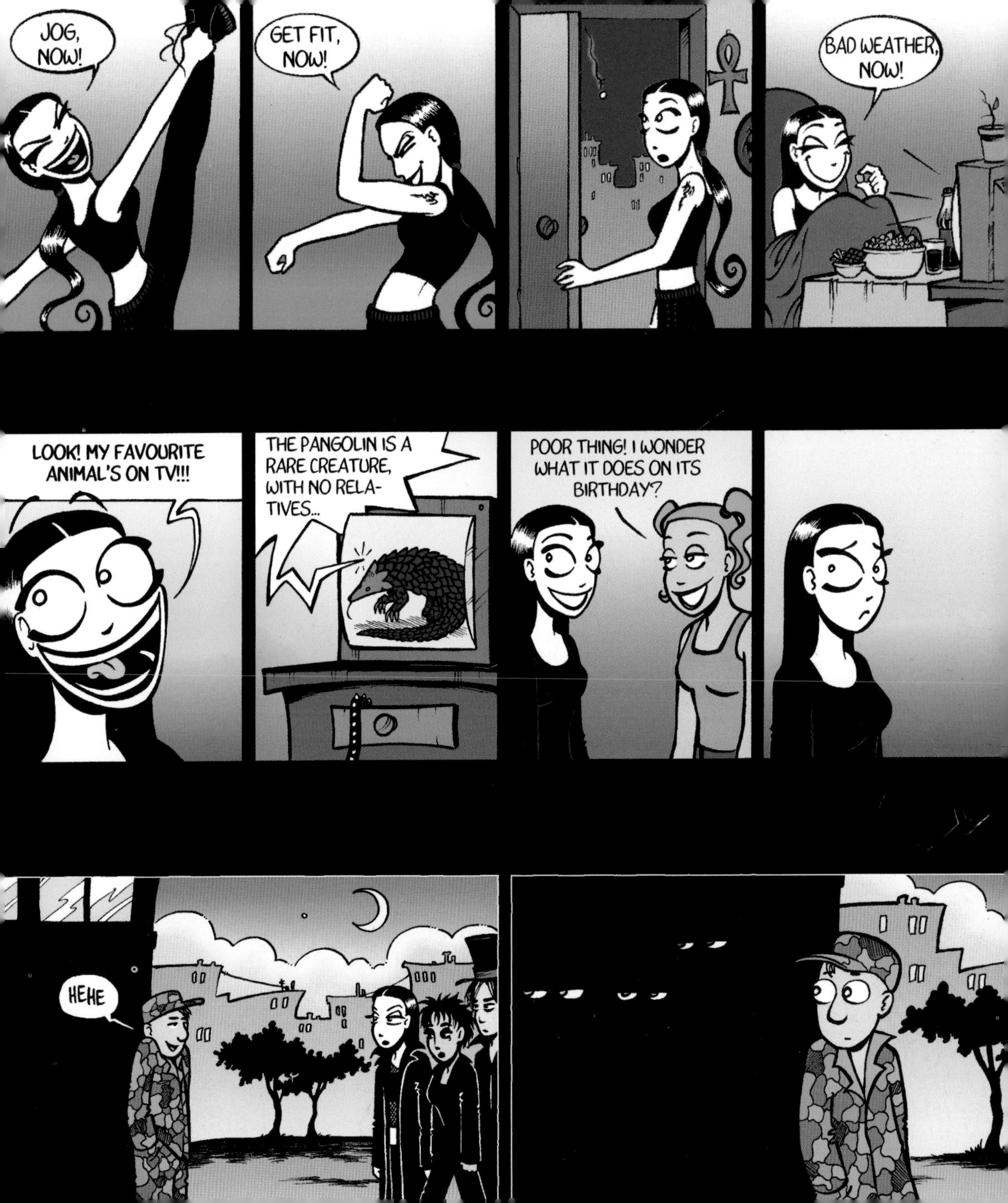
JOG, NOW!
GET FIT, NOW!
BAD WEATHER, NOW!
LOOK! MY FAVOURITE ANIMAL'S ON TV!!!
THE PANGOLIN IS A RARE CREATURE, WITH NO RELA-TIVES...
POOR THING! I WONDER WHAT IT DOES ON ITS BIRTHDAY?
HEHE

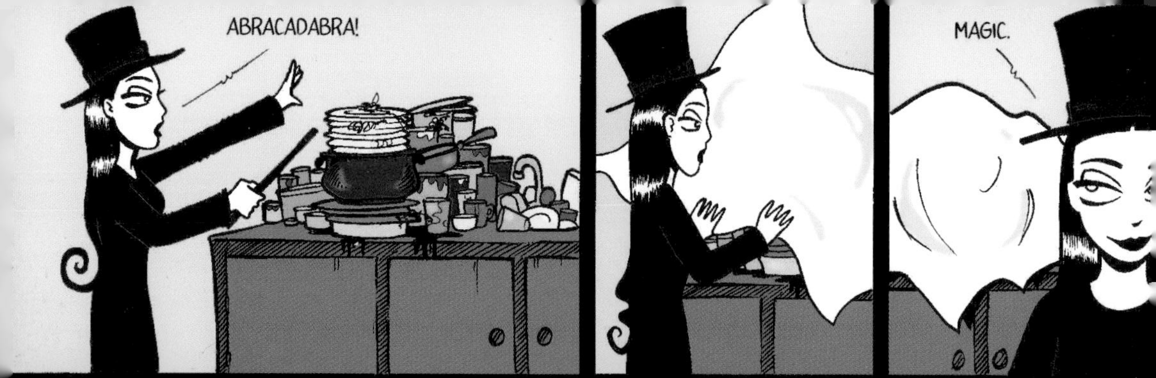
ABRACADABRA!
MAGIC.

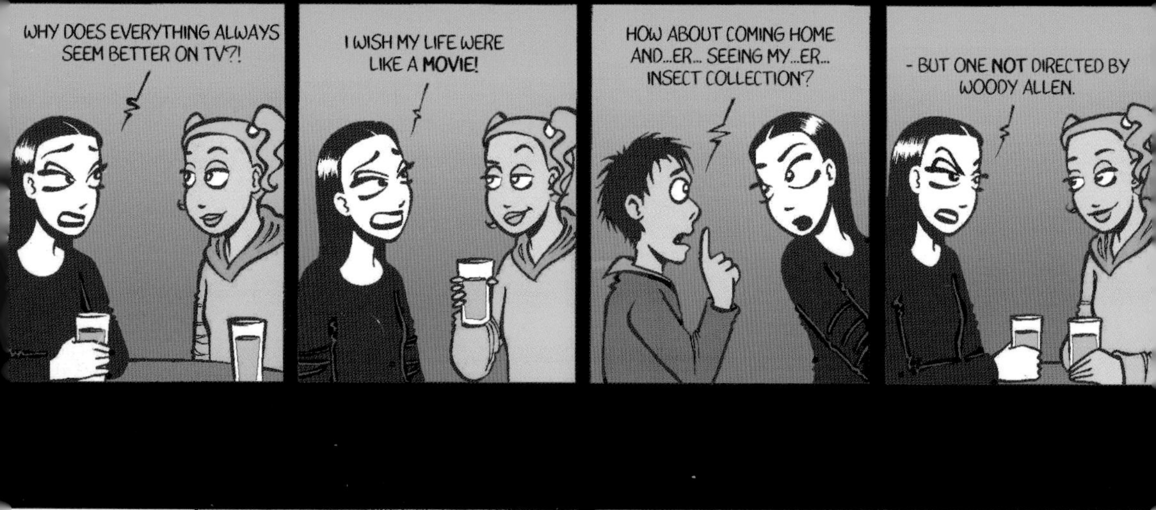
WHY DOES EVERYTHING ALWAYS SEEM BETTER ON TV?!
I WISH MY LIFE WERE LIKE A **MOVIE**!
HOW ABOUT COMING HOME AND...ER... SEEING MY...ER... INSECT COLLECTION?
- BUT ONE **NOT** DIRECTED BY WOODY ALLEN.

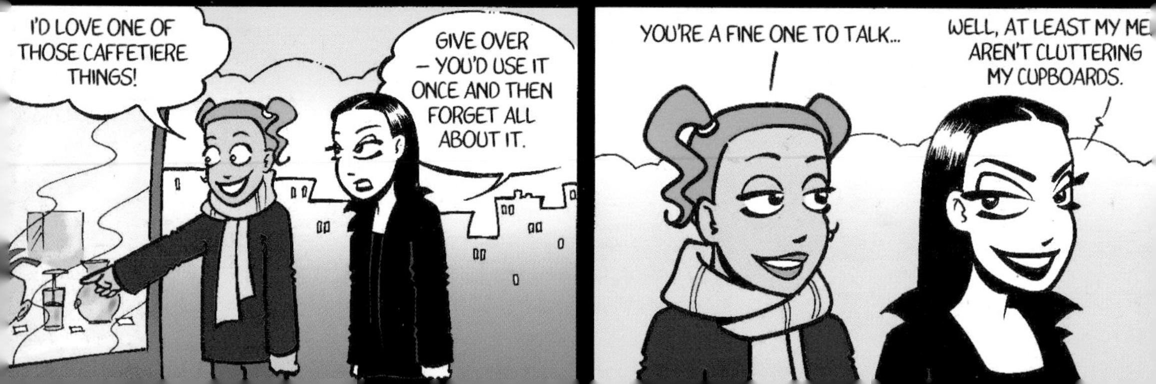
I'D LOVE ONE OF THOSE CAFFETIERE THINGS!
GIVE OVER – YOU'D USE IT ONCE AND THEN FORGET ALL ABOUT IT.
YOU'RE A FINE ONE TO TALK...
WELL, AT LEAST MY ME
AREN'T CLUTTERING MY CUPBOARDS.

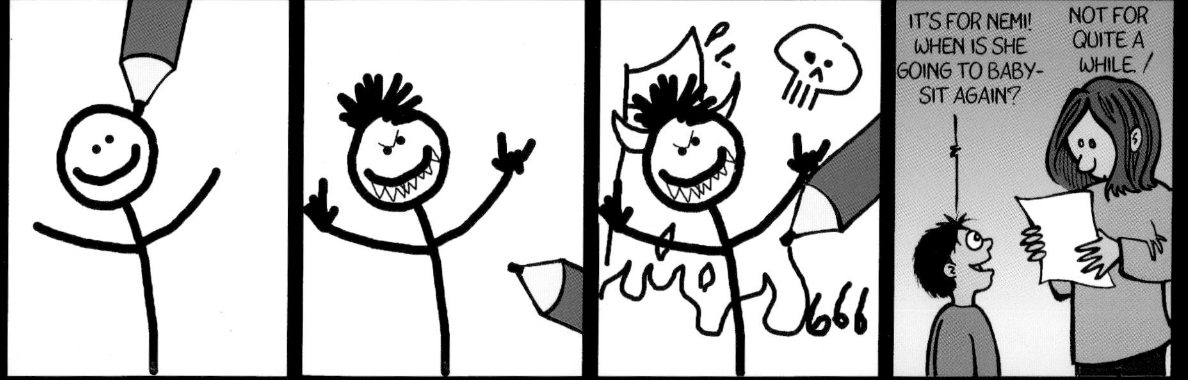
IT'S FOR NEMI! WHEN IS SHE GOING TO BABY-SIT AGAIN?
NOT FOR QUITE A WHILE.

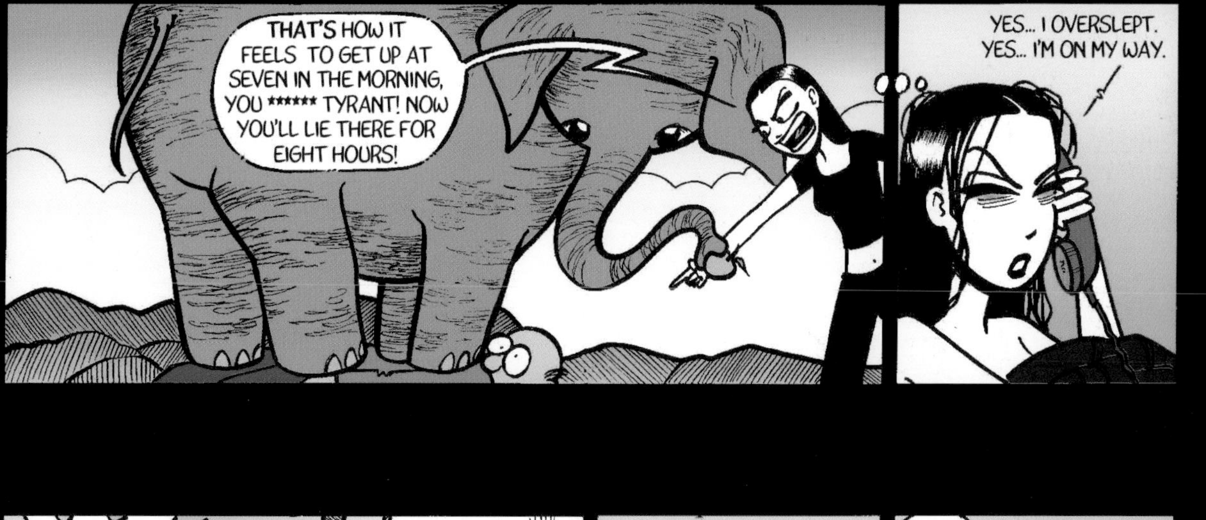
THAT'S HOW IT FEELS TO GET UP AT SEVEN IN THE MORNING, YOU ****** TYRANT! NOW YOU'LL LIE THERE FOR EIGHT HOURS!
YES... I OVERSLEPT. YES... I'M ON MY WAY.

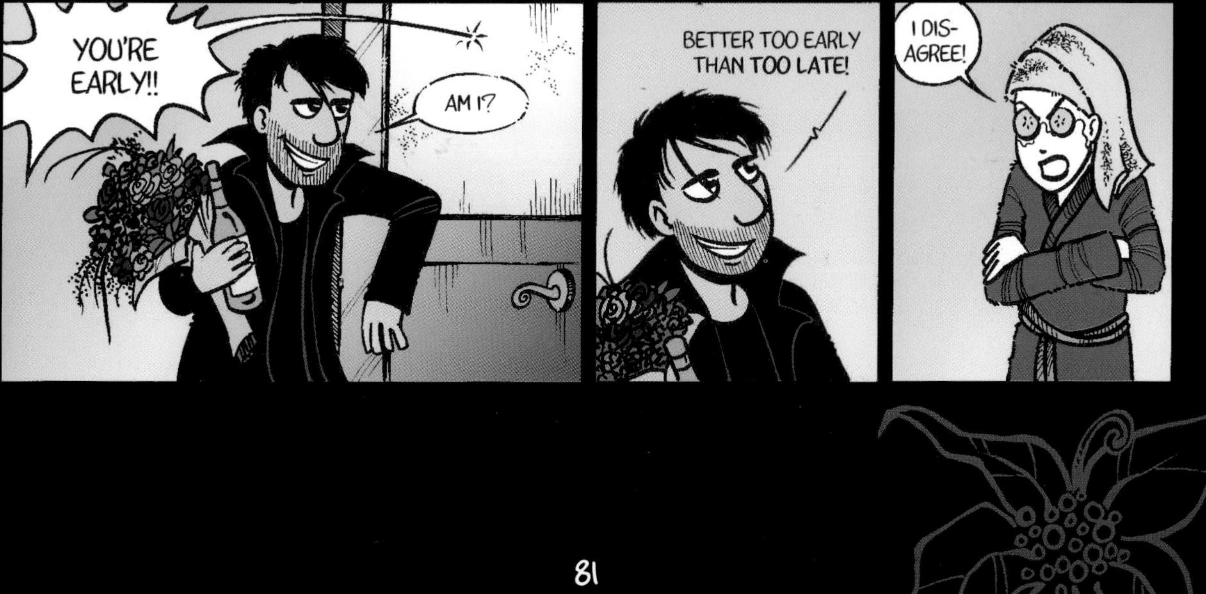
YOU'RE EARLY!!
AM I?
BETTER TOO EARLY THAN TOO LATE!
I DIS-AGREE!

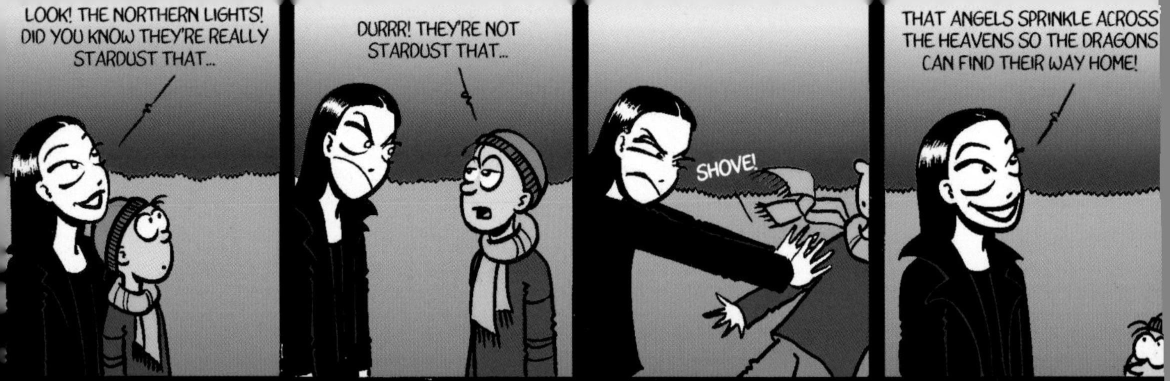
LOOK! THE NORTHERN LIGHTS! DID YOU KNOW THEY'RE REALLY STARDUST THAT...
DURRR! THEY'RE NOT STARDUST THAT...
SHOVE!
THAT ANGELS SPRINKLE ACROSS THE HEAVENS SO THE DRAGONS CAN FIND THEIR WAY HOME!

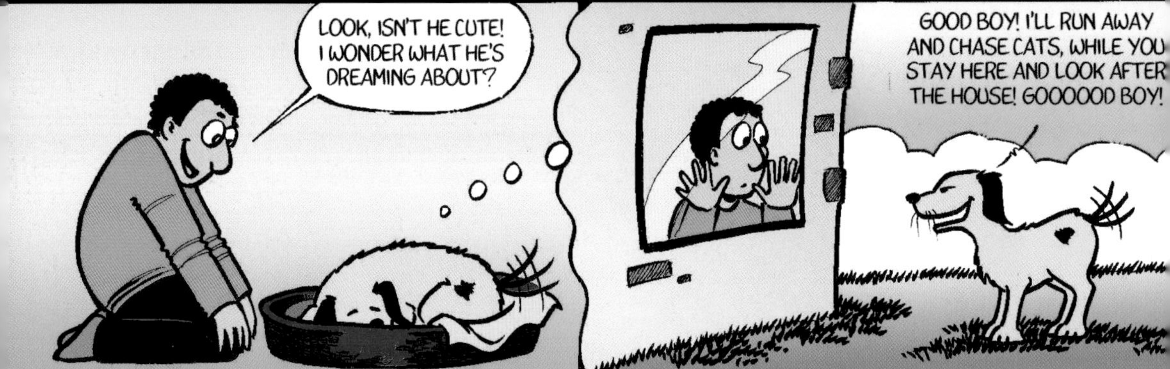
LOOK, ISN'T HE CUTE! I WONDER WHAT HE'S DREAMING ABOUT?
GOOD BOY! I'LL RUN AWAY AND CHASE CATS, WHILE YOU STAY HERE AND LOOK AFTER THE HOUSE! GOOOOOD BOY!

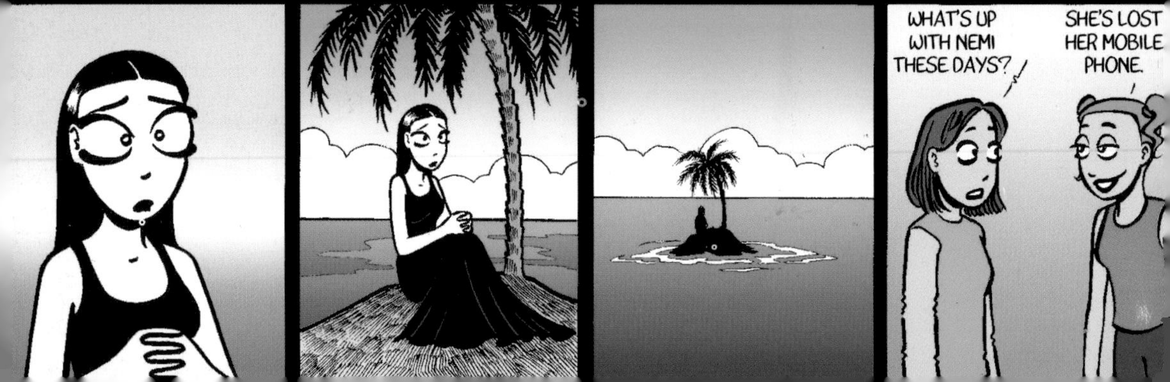
WHAT'S UP WITH NEMI THESE DAYS?
SHE'S LOST HER MOBILE PHONE.

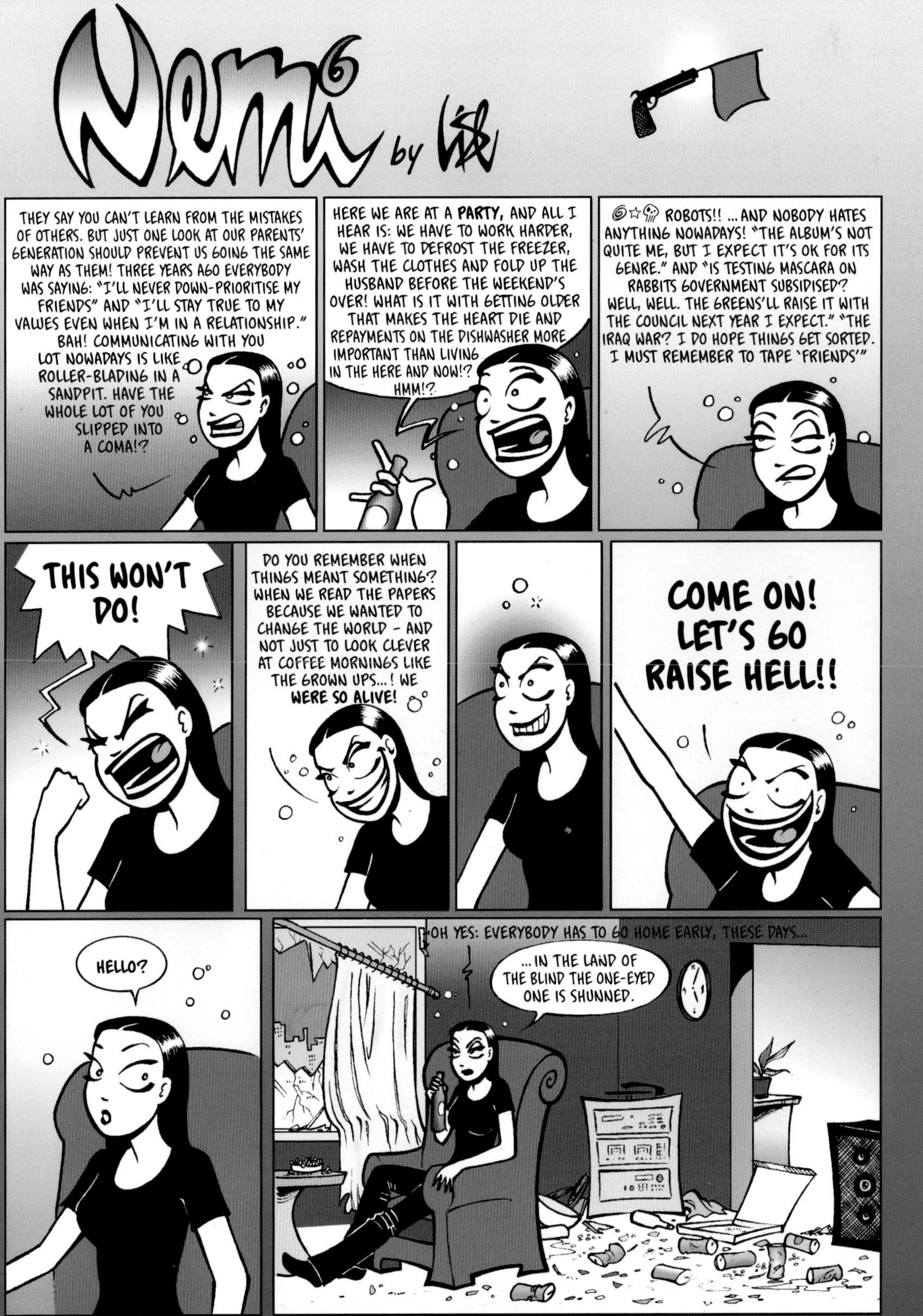
Nemi by Lise
THEY SAY YOU CAN'T LEARN FROM THE MISTAKES OF OTHERS. BUT JUST ONE LOOK AT OUR PARENTS' GENERATION SHOULD PREVENT US GOING THE SAME WAY AS THEM! THREE YEARS AGO EVERYBODY WAS SAYING: "I'LL NEVER DOWN-PRIORITISE MY FRIENDS" AND "I'LL STAY TRUE TO MY VALUES EVEN WHEN I'M IN A RELATIONSHIP." BAH! COMMUNICATING WITH YOU LOT NOWADAYS IS LIKE ROLLER-BLADING IN A SANDPIT. HAVE THE WHOLE LOT OF YOU SLIPPED INTO A COMA!?
HERE WE ARE AT A PARTY, AND ALL I HEAR IS: WE HAVE TO WORK HARDER, WE HAVE TO DEFROST THE FREEZER, WASH THE CLOTHES AND FOLD UP THE HUSBAND BEFORE THE WEEKEND'S OVER! WHAT IS IT WITH GETTING OLDER THAT MAKES THE HEART DIE AND REPAYMENTS ON THE DISHWASHER MORE IMPORTANT THAN LIVING IN THE HERE AND NOW!? HMM!?
ROBOTS!! ...AND NOBODY HATES ANYTHING NOWADAYS! "THE ALBUM'S NOT QUITE ME, BUT I EXPECT IT'S OK FOR ITS GENRE." AND "IS TESTING MASCARA ON RABBITS GOVERNMENT SUBSIDISED? WELL, WELL. THE GREENS'LL RAISE IT WITH THE COUNCIL NEXT YEAR I EXPECT." "THE IRAQ WAR? I DO HOPE THINGS GET SORTED. I MUST REMEMBER TO TAPE 'FRIENDS'"
THIS WON'T DO!
DO YOU REMEMBER WHEN THINGS MEANT SOMETHING? WHEN WE READ THE PAPERS BECAUSE WE WANTED TO CHANGE THE WORLD – AND NOT JUST TO LOOK CLEVER AT COFFEE MORNINGS LIKE THE GROWN UPS...! WE WERE SO ALIVE!
COME ON! LET'S GO RAISE HELL!!
HELLO?
OH YES: EVERYBODY HAS TO GO HOME EARLY, THESE DAYS...
...IN THE LAND OF THE BLIND THE ONE-EYED ONE IS SHUNNED.

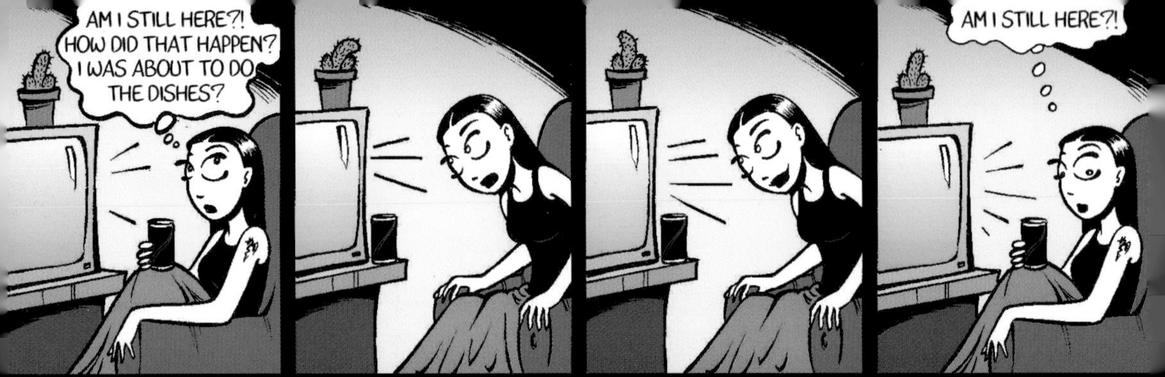
AM I STILL HERE?! HOW DID THAT HAPPEN? I WAS ABOUT TO DO THE DISHES?
AM I STILL HERE?!

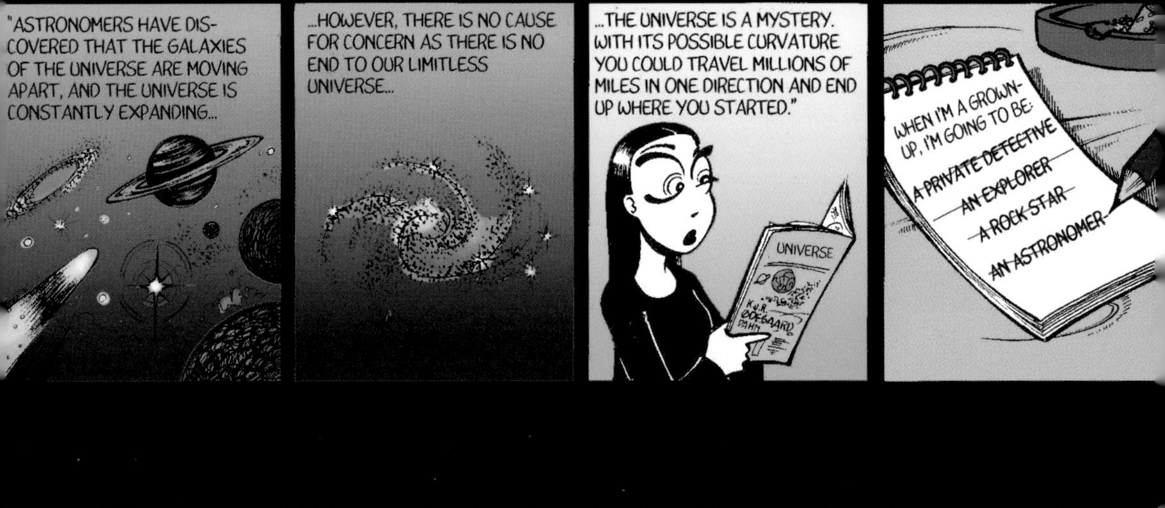
"ASTRONOMERS HAVE DISCOVERED THAT THE GALAXIES OF THE UNIVERSE ARE MOVING APART, AND THE UNIVERSE IS CONSTANTLY EXPANDING...
...HOWEVER, THERE IS NO CAUSE FOR CONCERN AS THERE IS NO END TO OUR LIMITLESS UNIVERSE...
...THE UNIVERSE IS A MYSTERY. WITH ITS POSSIBLE CURVATURE YOU COULD TRAVEL MILLIONS OF MILES IN ONE DIRECTION AND END UP WHERE YOU STARTED."
UNIVERSE
WHEN I'M A GROWN-UP, I'M GOING TO BE:
A PRIVATE DETECTIVE
AN EXPLORER
A ROCK STAR
AN ASTRONOMER

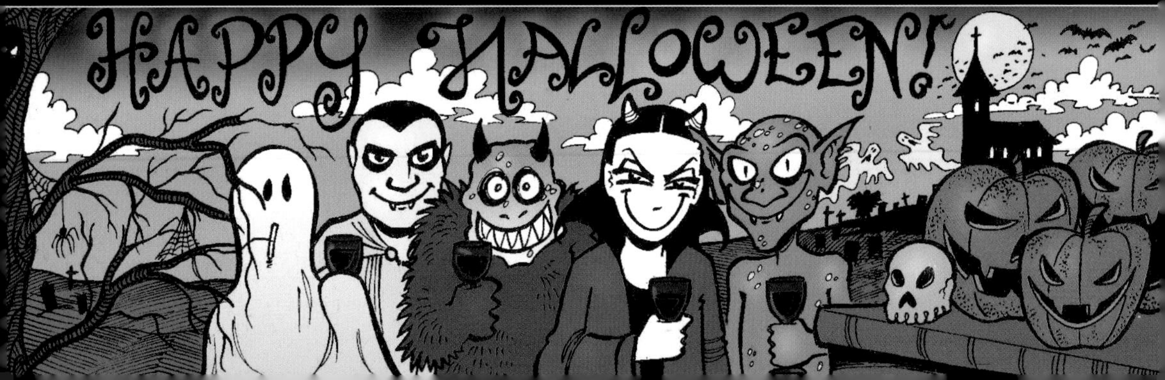
HAPPY HALLOWEEN!

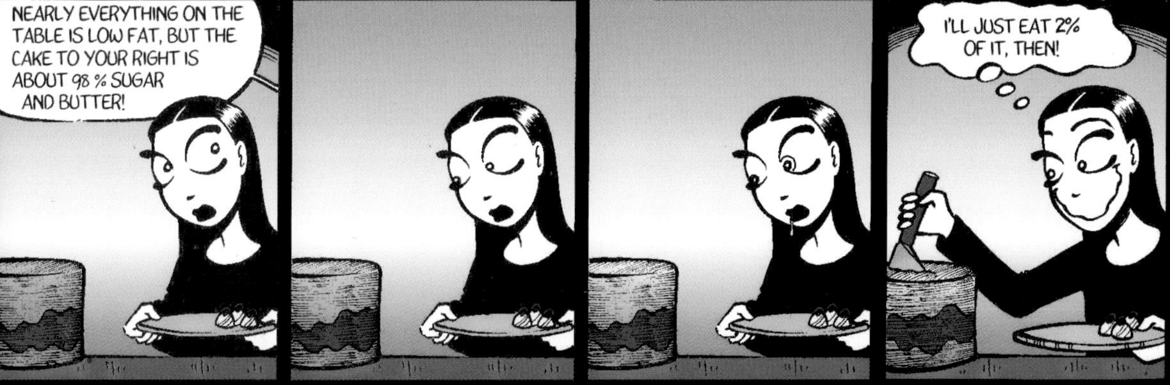
NEARLY EVERYTHING ON THE TABLE IS LOW FAT, BUT THE CAKE TO YOUR RIGHT IS ABOUT 98 % SUGAR AND BUTTER!
I'LL JUST EAT 2% OF IT, THEN!

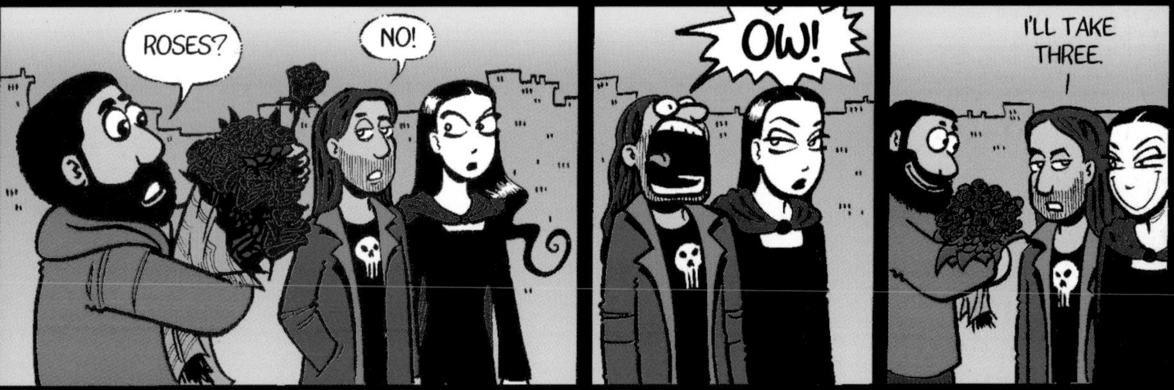
ROSES?
NO!
OW!
I'LL TAKE THREE.

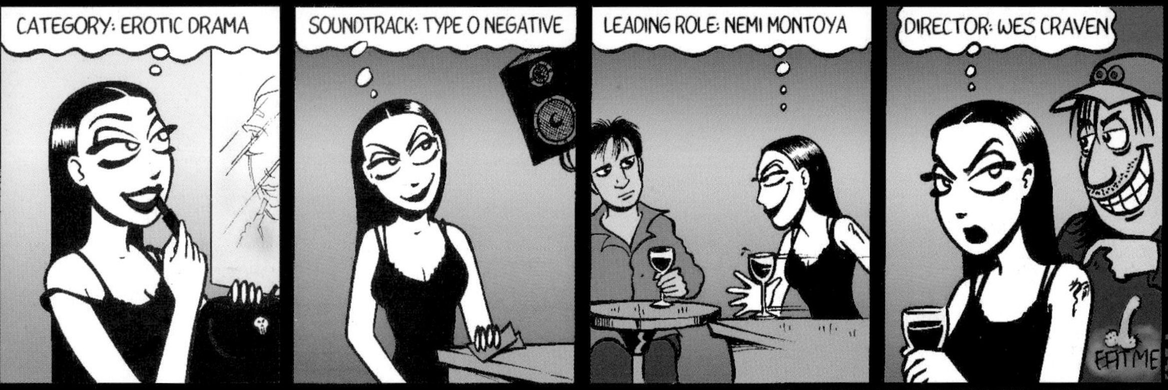
CATEGORY: EROTIC DRAMA
SOUNDTRACK: TYPE O NEGATIVE
LEADING ROLE: NEMI MONTOYA
DIRECTOR: WES CRAVEN
EATME

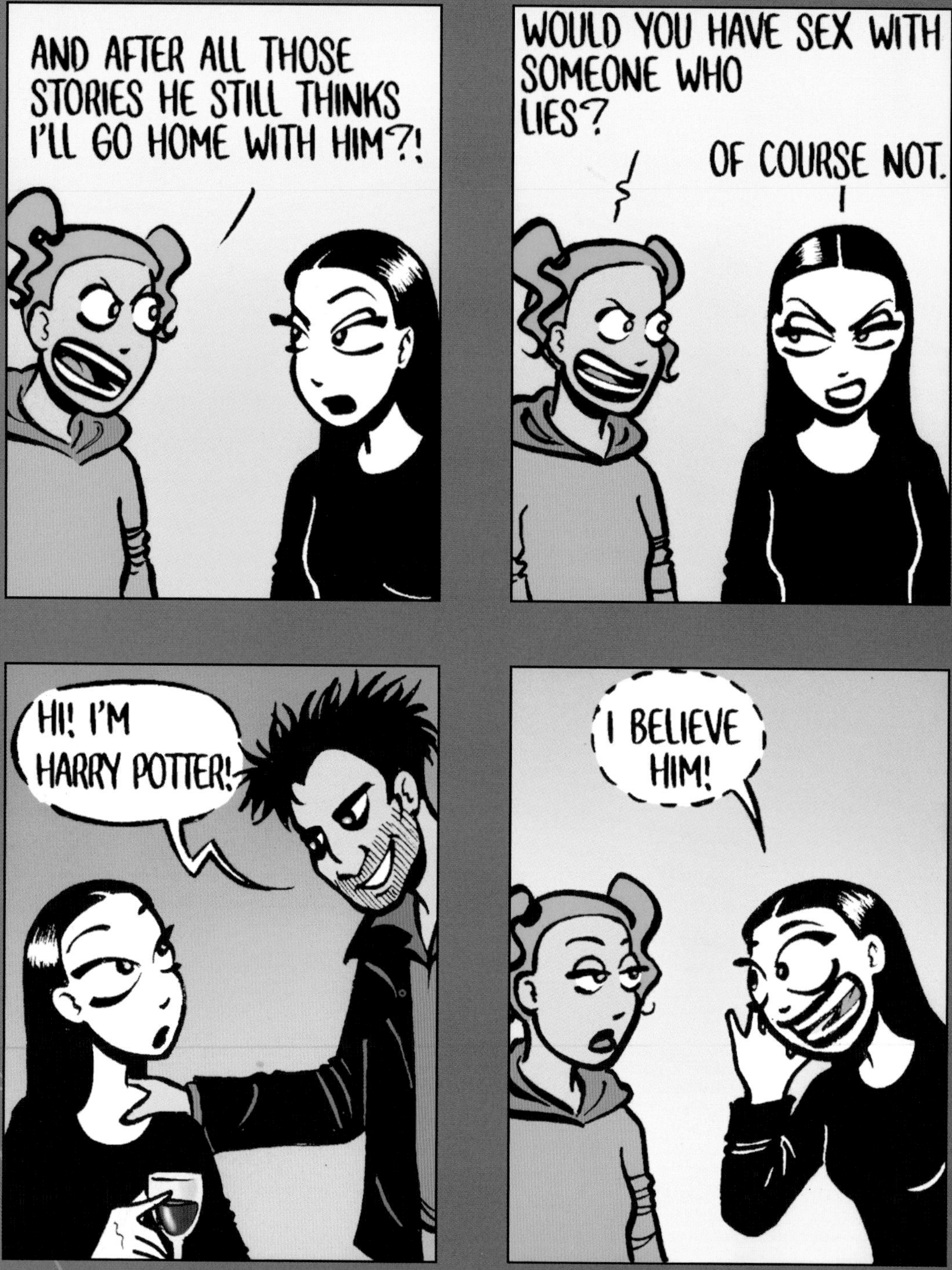

AND AFTER ALL THOSE STORIES HE STILL THINKS I'LL GO HOME WITH HIM?!
WOULD YOU HAVE SEX WITH SOMEONE WHO LIES?
OF COURSE NOT.
HI! I'M HARRY POTTER!
I BELIEVE HIM!

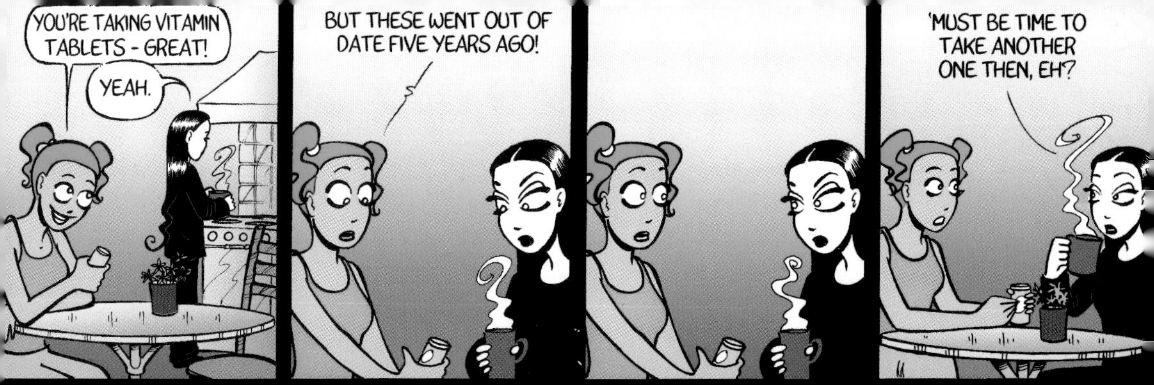
YOU'RE TAKING VITAMIN TABLETS - GREAT!
YEAH.
BUT THESE WENT OUT OF DATE FIVE YEARS AGO!
'MUST BE TIME TO TAKE ANOTHER ONE THEN, EH?

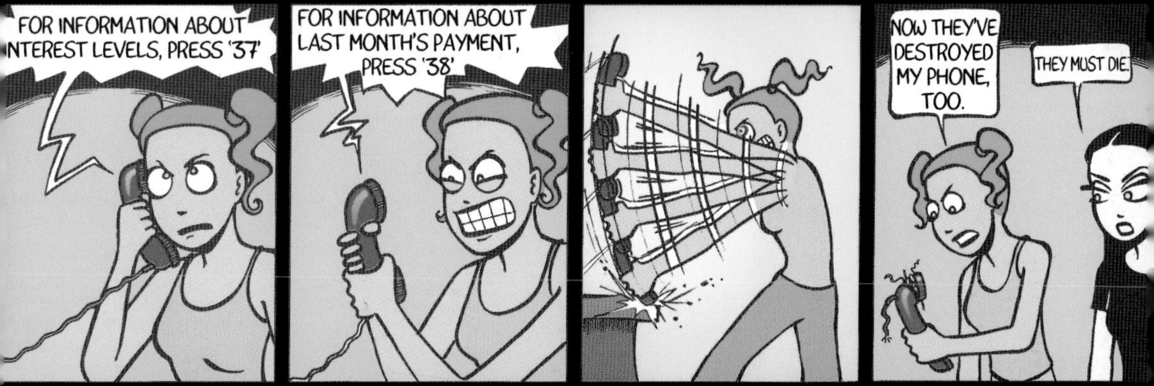
FOR INFORMATION ABOUT INTEREST LEVELS, PRESS '37'
FOR INFORMATION ABOUT LAST MONTH'S PAYMENT, PRESS '38'
NOW THEY'VE DESTROYED MY PHONE, TOO.
THEY MUST DIE.

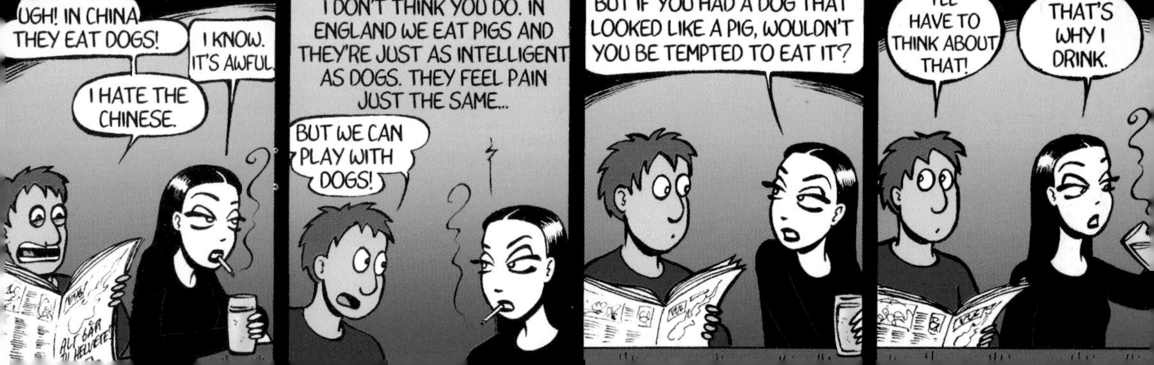
UGH! IN CHINA THEY EAT DOGS!
I KNOW. IT'S AWFUL.
I HATE THE CHINESE.
I DON'T THINK YOU DO. IN ENGLAND WE EAT PIGS AND THEY'RE JUST AS INTELLIGENT AS DOGS. THEY FEEL PAIN JUST THE SAME...
BUT WE CAN PLAY WITH DOGS!
BUT IF YOU HAD A DOG THAT LOOKED LIKE A PIG, WOULDN'T YOU BE TEMPTED TO EAT IT?
I'LL HAVE TO THINK ABOUT THAT!
THAT'S WHY I DRINK.

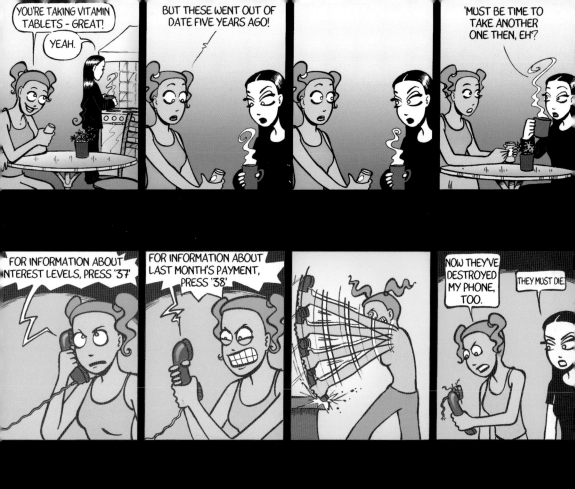

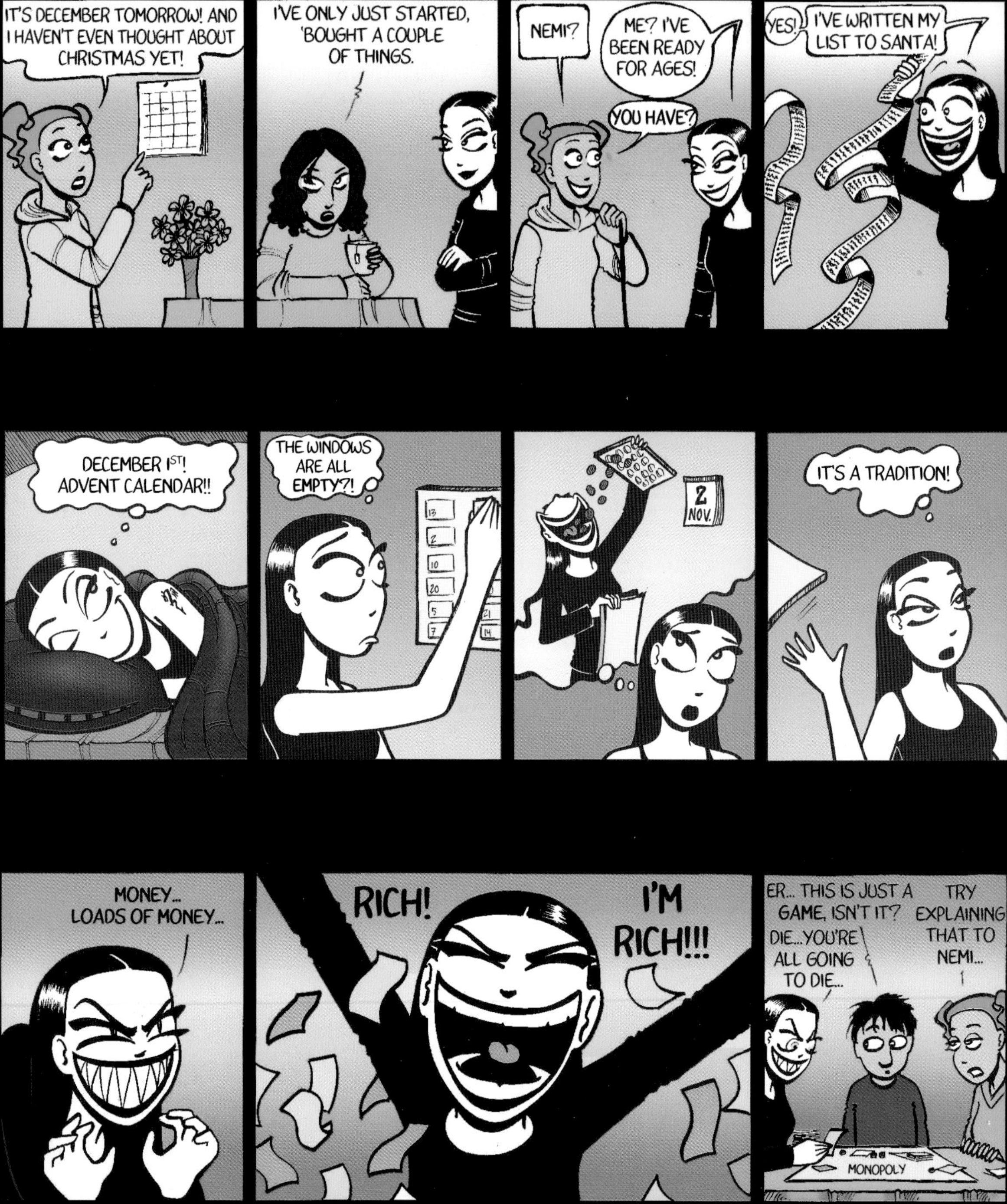
IT'S DECEMBER TOMORROW! AND I HAVEN'T EVEN THOUGHT ABOUT CHRISTMAS YET!
I'VE ONLY JUST STARTED, 'BOUGHT A COUPLE OF THINGS.
NEMI?
ME? I'VE BEEN READY FOR AGES!
YOU HAVE?
YES!
I'VE WRITTEN MY LIST TO SANTA!
DECEMBER 1ST! ADVENT CALENDAR!!
THE WINDOWS ARE ALL EMPTY?!
2 NOV.
IT'S A TRADITION!
MONEY... LOADS OF MONEY...
RICH!
I'M RICH!!!
ER... THIS IS JUST A GAME, ISN'T IT?
DIE... YOU'RE ALL GOING TO DIE...
TRY EXPLAINING THAT TO NEMI...
MONOPOLY

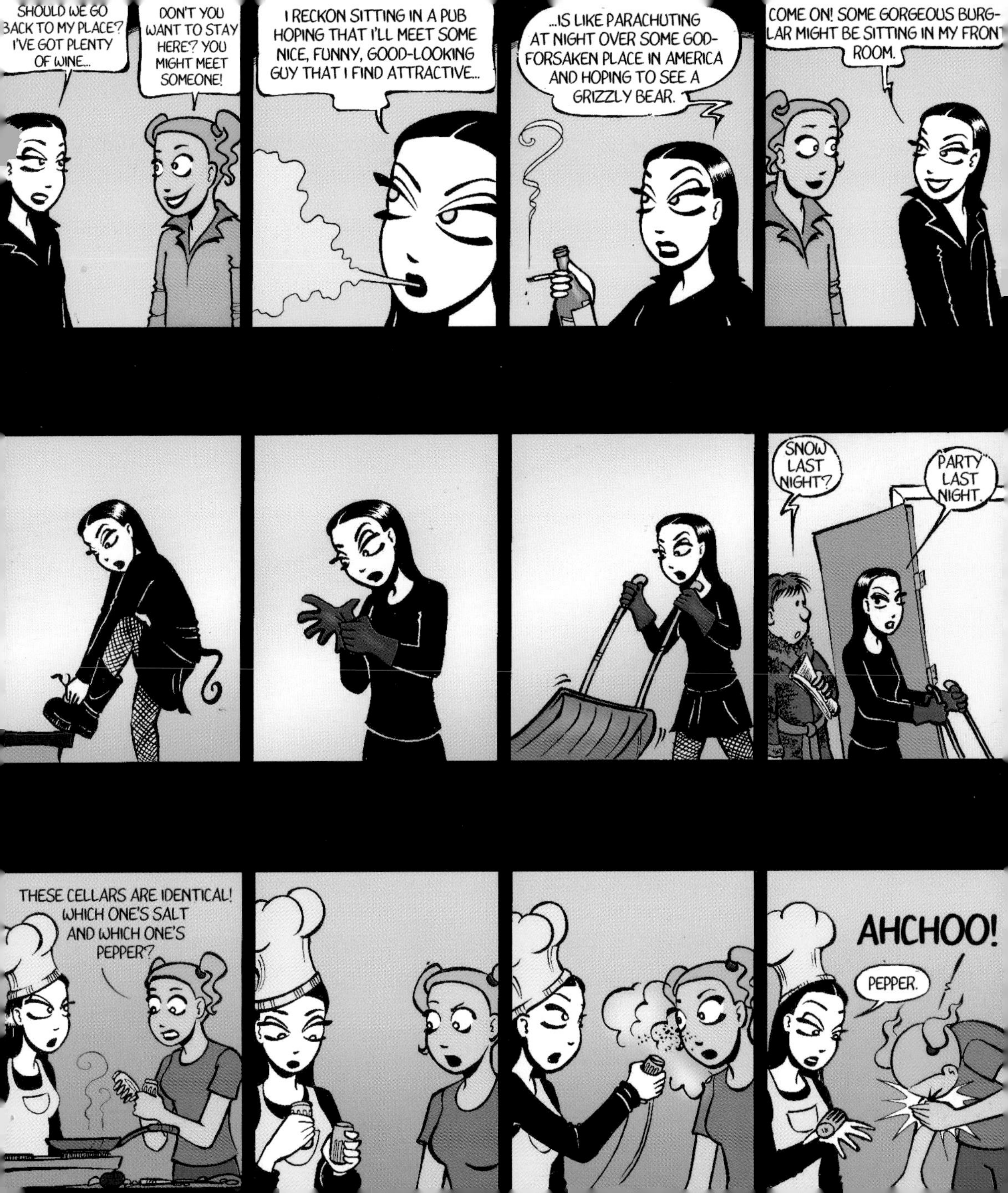

SHOULD WE GO BACK TO MY PLACE? I'VE GOT PLENTY OF WINE...
DON'T YOU WANT TO STAY HERE? YOU MIGHT MEET SOMEONE!
I RECKON SITTING IN A PUB HOPING THAT I'LL MEET SOME NICE, FUNNY, GOOD-LOOKING GUY THAT I FIND ATTRACTIVE...
...IS LIKE PARACHUTING AT NIGHT OVER SOME GOD-FORSAKEN PLACE IN AMERICA AND HOPING TO SEE A GRIZZLY BEAR.
COME ON! SOME GORGEOUS BURG-LAR MIGHT BE SITTING IN MY FRONT ROOM.
SNOW LAST NIGHT?
"PARTY" LAST NIGHT.
THESE CELLARS ARE IDENTICAL! WHICH ONE'S SALT AND WHICH ONE'S PEPPER?
AHCHOO!
PEPPER.

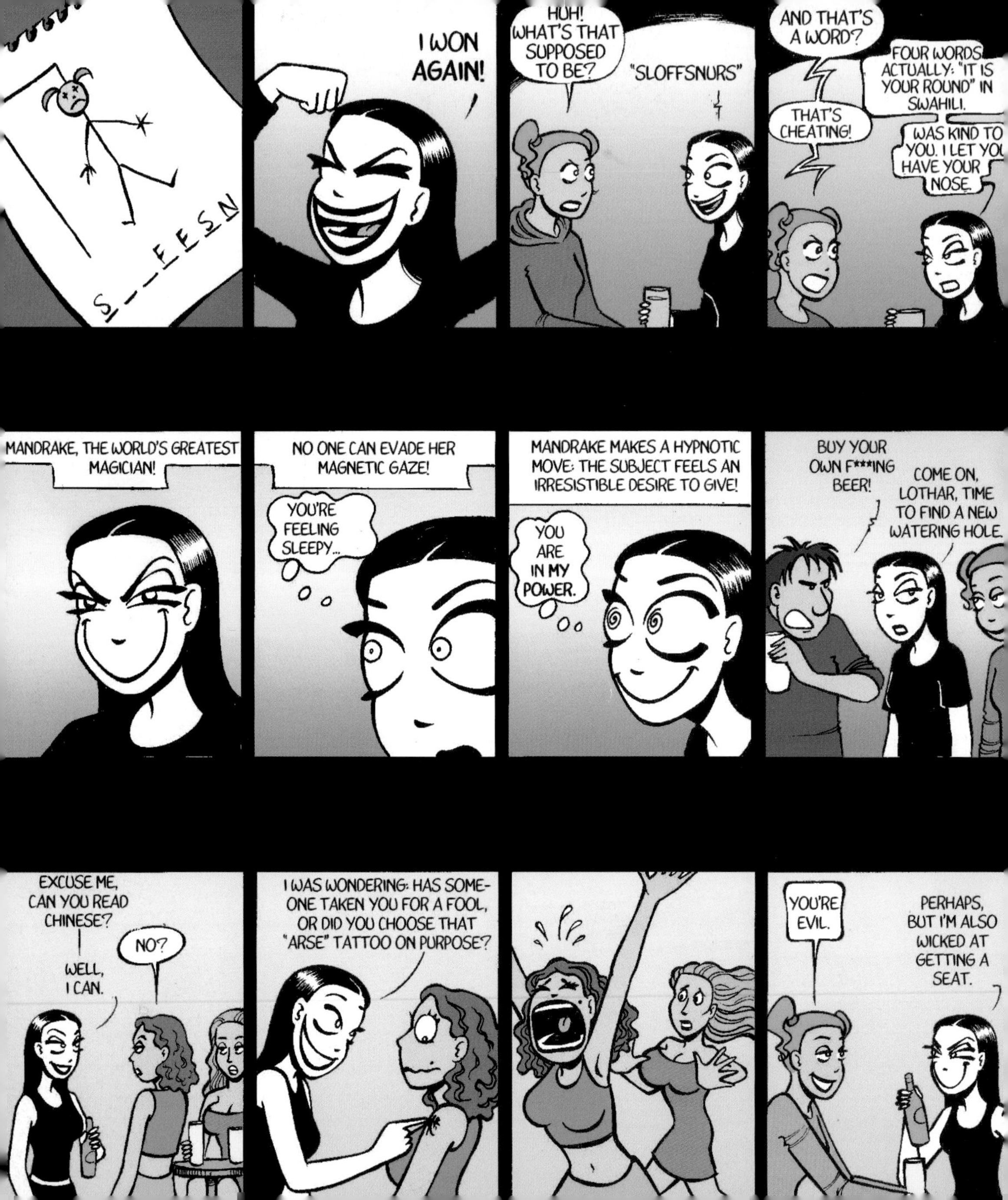
I WON AGAIN!
HUH! WHAT'S THAT SUPPOSED TO BE?
"SLOFFSNURS"
AND THAT'S A WORD?
FOUR WORDS ACTUALLY: "IT IS YOUR ROUND" IN SWAHILI.
THAT'S CHEATING!
WAS KIND TO YOU. I LET YOU HAVE YOUR NOSE.
MANDRAKE, THE WORLD'S GREATEST MAGICIAN!
NO ONE CAN EVADE HER MAGNETIC GAZE!
YOU'RE FEELING SLEEPY...
MANDRAKE MAKES A HYPNOTIC MOVE: THE SUBJECT FEELS AN IRRESISTIBLE DESIRE TO GIVE!
YOU ARE IN MY POWER.
BUY YOUR OWN F***ING BEER!
COME ON, LOTHAR, TIME TO FIND A NEW WATERING HOLE.
EXCUSE ME, CAN YOU READ CHINESE?
NO?
WELL, I CAN.
I WAS WONDERING: HAS SOMEONE TAKEN YOU FOR A FOOL, OR DID YOU CHOOSE THAT "ARSE" TATTOO ON PURPOSE?
YOU'RE EVIL.
PERHAPS, BUT I'M ALSO WICKED AT GETTING A SEAT.

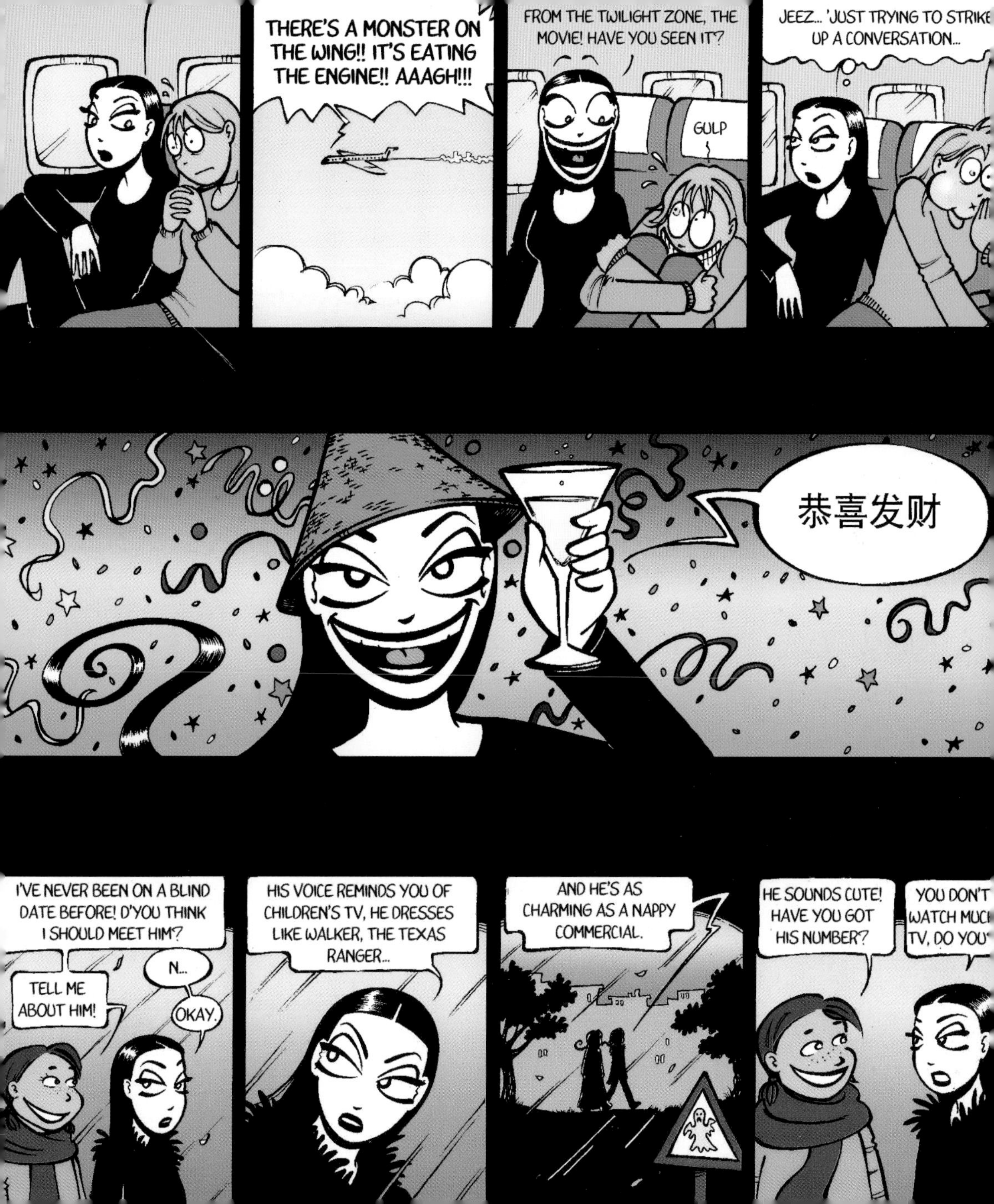
THERE'S A MONSTER ON THE WING!! IT'S EATING THE ENGINE!! AAAGH!!!
FROM THE TWILIGHT ZONE, THE MOVIE! HAVE YOU SEEN IT?
GULP
JEEZ... 'JUST TRYING TO STRIKE UP A CONVERSATION...
恭喜发财
I'VE NEVER BEEN ON A BLIND DATE BEFORE! D'YOU THINK I SHOULD MEET HIM?
N...
TELL ME ABOUT HIM!
OKAY.
HIS VOICE REMINDS YOU OF CHILDREN'S TV, HE DRESSES LIKE WALKER, THE TEXAS RANGER...
AND HE'S AS CHARMING AS A NAPPY COMMERCIAL.
HE SOUNDS CUTE! HAVE YOU GOT HIS NUMBER?
YOU DON'T WATCH MUCH TV, DO YOU

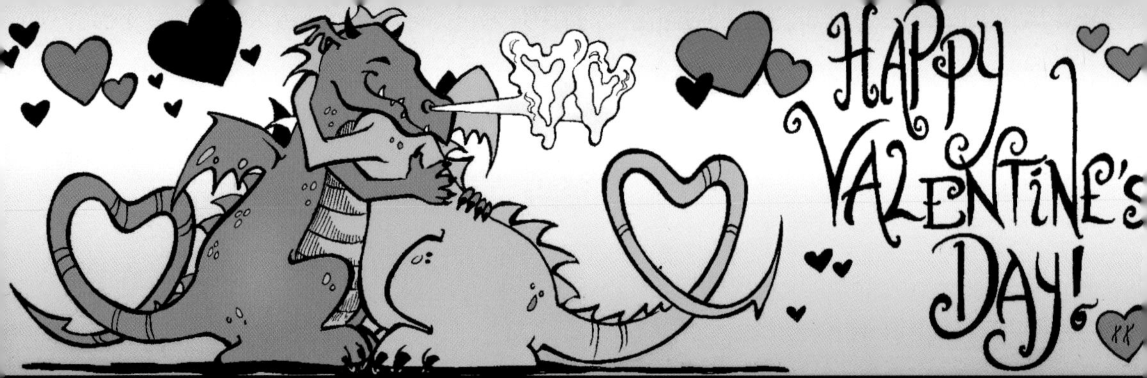
HAPPY VALENTINE'S DAY!
XX

[redacted]

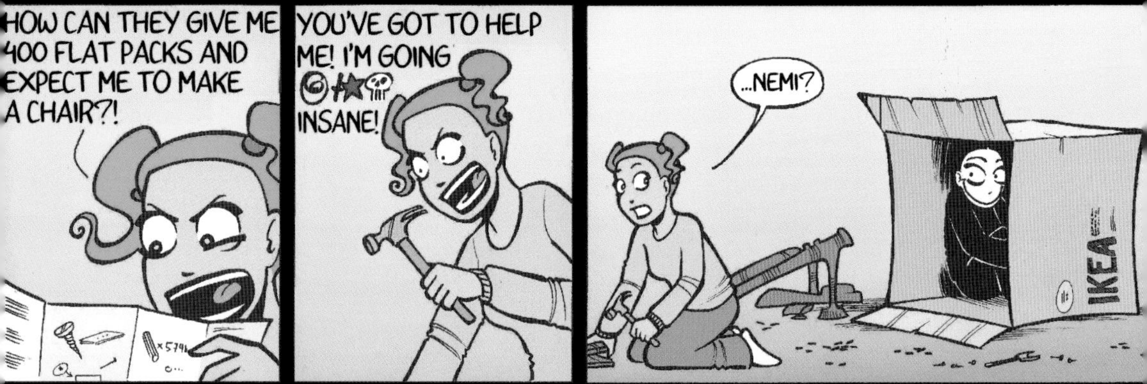
HOW CAN THEY GIVE ME 400 FLAT PACKS AND EXPECT ME TO MAKE A CHAIR?!
YOU'VE GOT TO HELP ME! I'M GOING
INSANE!
...NEMI?
IKEA

[redacted]

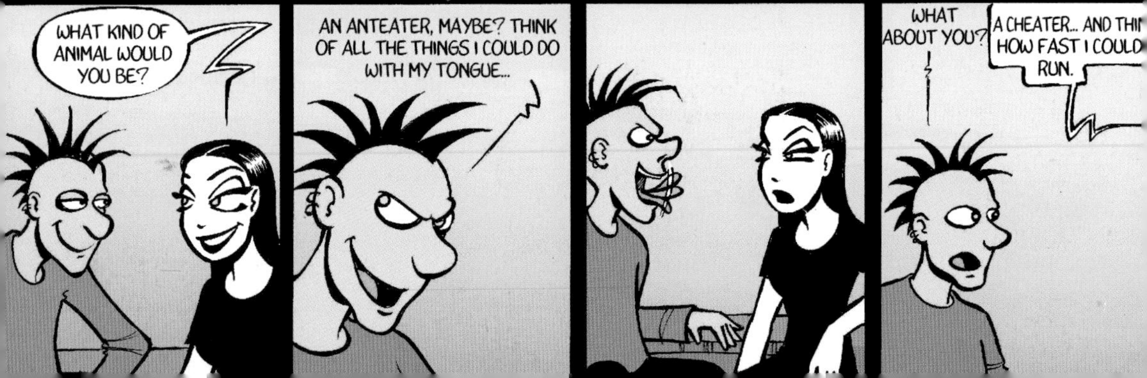
WHAT KIND OF ANIMAL WOULD YOU BE?
AN ANTEATER, MAYBE? THINK OF ALL THE THINGS I COULD DO WITH MY TONGUE...
WHAT ABOUT YOU?
A CHEATER... AND THI
HOW FAST I COULD
RUN.

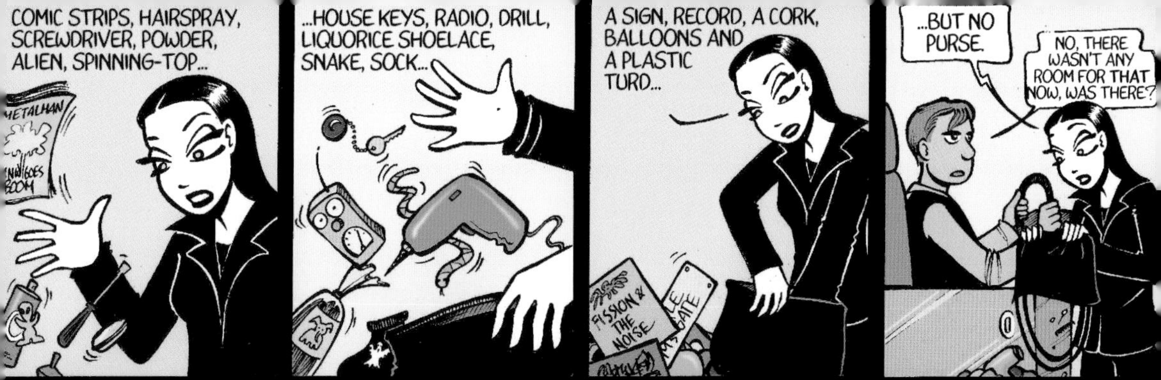
COMIC STRIPS, HAIRSPRAY, SCREWDRIVER, POWDER, ALIEN, SPINNING-TOP...
...HOUSE KEYS, RADIO, DRILL, LIQUORICE SHOELACE, SNAKE, SOCK...
A SIGN, RECORD, A CORK, BALLOONS AND A PLASTIC TURD...
...BUT NO PURSE.
NO, THERE WASN'T ANY ROOM FOR THAT NOW, WAS THERE?

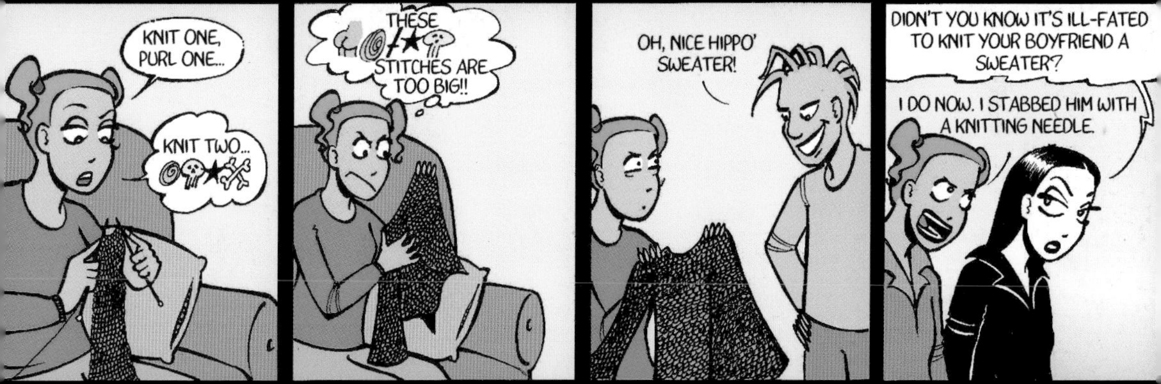
KNIT ONE, PURL ONE...
KNIT TWO...
THESE STITCHES ARE TOO BIG!!
OH, NICE HIPPO' SWEATER!
DIDN'T YOU KNOW IT'S ILL-FATED TO KNIT YOUR BOYFRIEND A SWEATER?
I DO NOW. I STABBED HIM WITH A KNITTING NEEDLE.

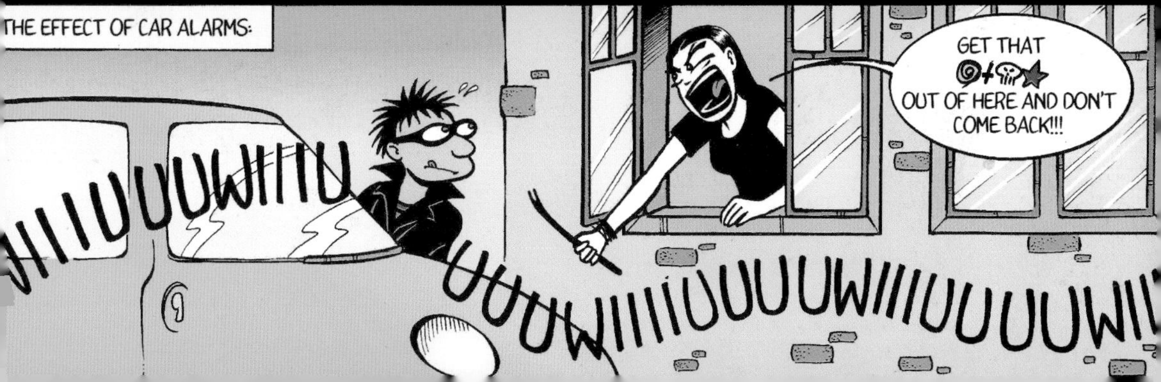
THE EFFECT OF CAR ALARMS:
GET THAT OUT OF HERE AND DON'T COME BACK!!!
WIIIUUUWIIIU
UUUWIIIIUUUUWIIIUUUUWI

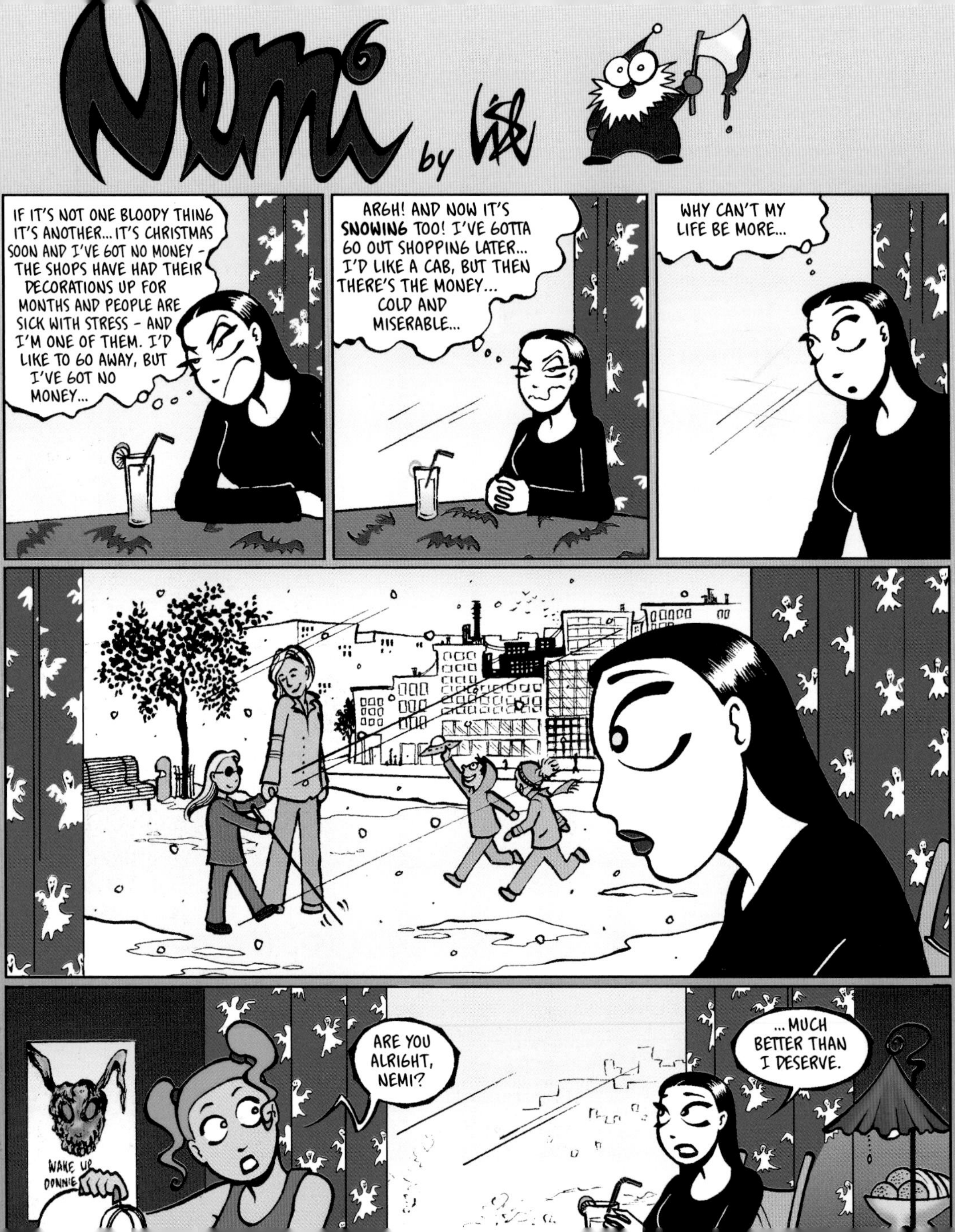
Nemi
by Lise
IF IT'S NOT ONE BLOODY THING IT'S ANOTHER... IT'S CHRISTMAS SOON AND I'VE GOT NO MONEY - THE SHOPS HAVE HAD THEIR DECORATIONS UP FOR MONTHS AND PEOPLE ARE SICK WITH STRESS - AND I'M ONE OF THEM. I'D LIKE TO GO AWAY, BUT I'VE GOT NO MONEY...
ARGH! AND NOW IT'S SNOWING TOO! I'VE GOTTA GO OUT SHOPPING LATER... I'D LIKE A CAB, BUT THEN THERE'S THE MONEY... COLD AND MISERABLE...
WHY CAN'T MY LIFE BE MORE...
WAKE UP DONNIE
ARE YOU ALRIGHT, NEMI?
...MUCH BETTER THAN I DESERVE.

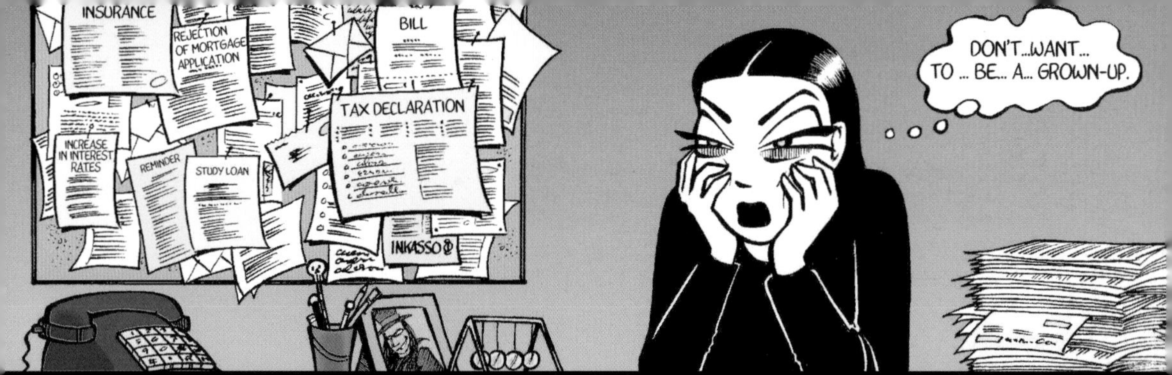
INSURANCE
REJECTION OF MORTGAGE APPLICATION
BILL
TAX DECLARATION
INCREASE IN INTEREST RATES
REMINDER
STUDY LOAN
INKASSO
DON'T...WANT... TO ... BE... A... GROWN-UP.

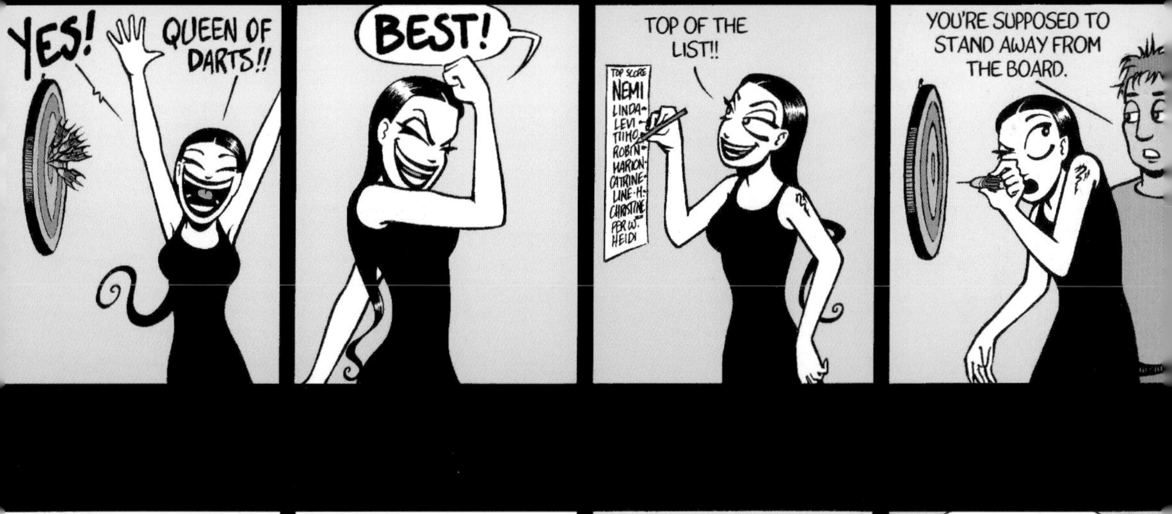
YES!
QUEEN OF DARTS!!
BEST!
TOP OF THE LIST!!
TOP SCORE
NEMI
LINDA
LEVI
TIIMO
ROBIN
MARION
CATRINE
LINE H.
CHRISTINE
PER W.
HEIDI
YOU'RE SUPPOSED TO STAND AWAY FROM THE BOARD.

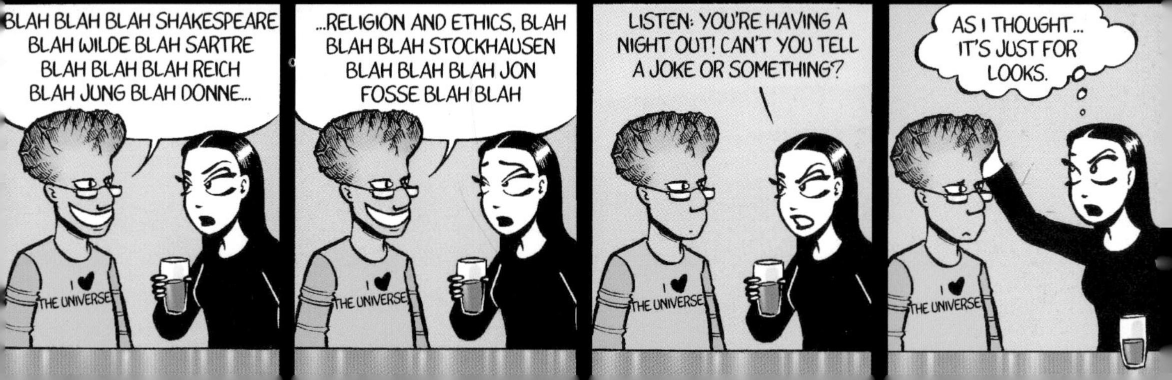
BLAH BLAH BLAH SHAKESPEARE BLAH WILDE BLAH SARTRE BLAH BLAH BLAH REICH BLAH JUNG BLAH DONNE...
...RELIGION AND ETHICS, BLAH BLAH BLAH STOCKHAUSEN BLAH BLAH BLAH JON FOSSE BLAH BLAH
I ♥ THE UNIVERSE
LISTEN: YOU'RE HAVING A NIGHT OUT! CAN'T YOU TELL A JOKE OR SOMETHING?
AS I THOUGHT... IT'S JUST FOR LOOKS.

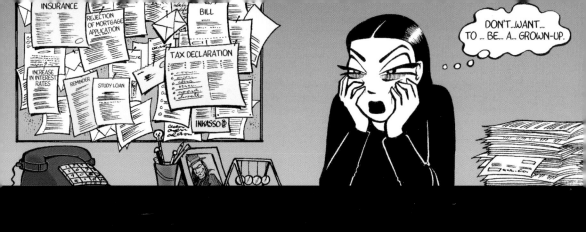

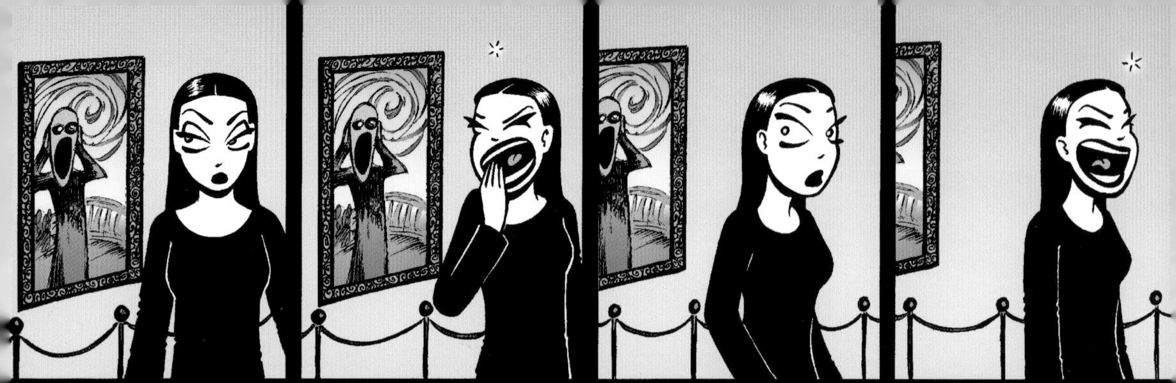

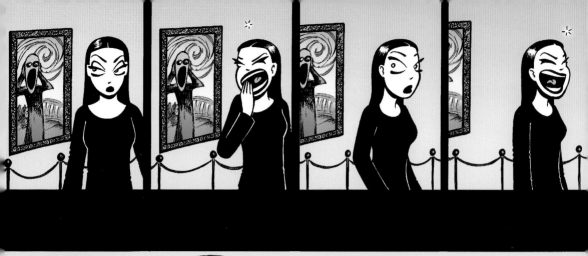

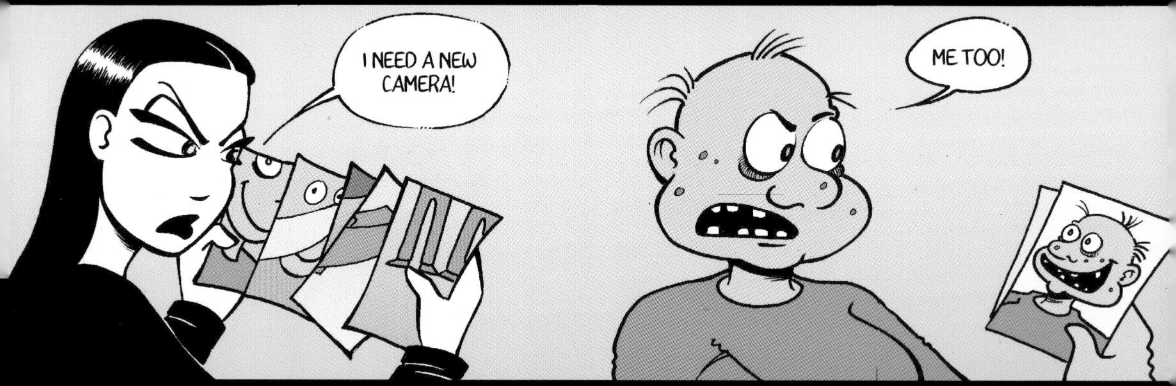
I NEED A NEW CAMERA!
ME TOO!

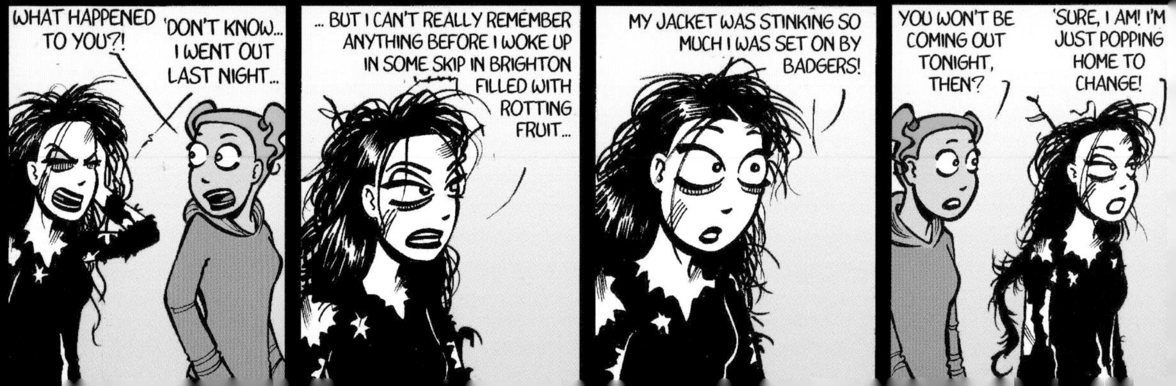
WHAT HAPPENED TO YOU?!
'DON'T KNOW... I WENT OUT LAST NIGHT...
... BUT I CAN'T REALLY REMEMBER ANYTHING BEFORE I WOKE UP IN SOME SKIP IN BRIGHTON FILLED WITH ROTTING FRUIT...
MY JACKET WAS STINKING SO MUCH I WAS SET ON BY BADGERS!
YOU WON'T BE COMING OUT TONIGHT, THEN?
'SURE, I AM! I'M JUST POPPING HOME TO CHANGE!

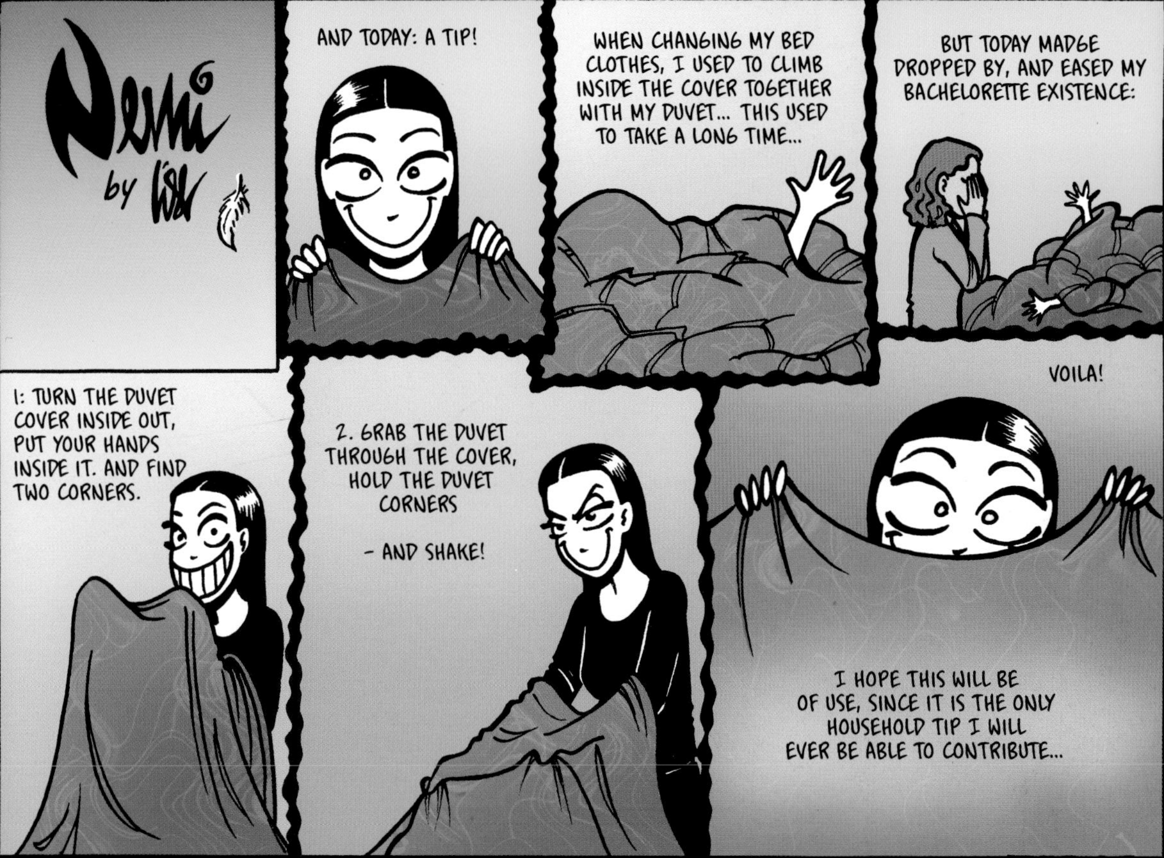
Nemi
by Lise
AND TODAY: A TIP!
WHEN CHANGING MY BED CLOTHES, I USED TO CLIMB INSIDE THE COVER TOGETHER WITH MY DUVET... THIS USED TO TAKE A LONG TIME...
BUT TODAY MADGE DROPPED BY, AND EASED MY BACHELORETTE EXISTENCE:
1: TURN THE DUVET COVER INSIDE OUT, PUT YOUR HANDS INSIDE IT. AND FIND TWO CORNERS.
2. GRAB THE DUVET THROUGH THE COVER, HOLD THE DUVET CORNERS
- AND SHAKE!
VOILA!
I HOPE THIS WILL BE OF USE, SINCE IT IS THE ONLY HOUSEHOLD TIP I WILL EVER BE ABLE TO CONTRIBUTE...

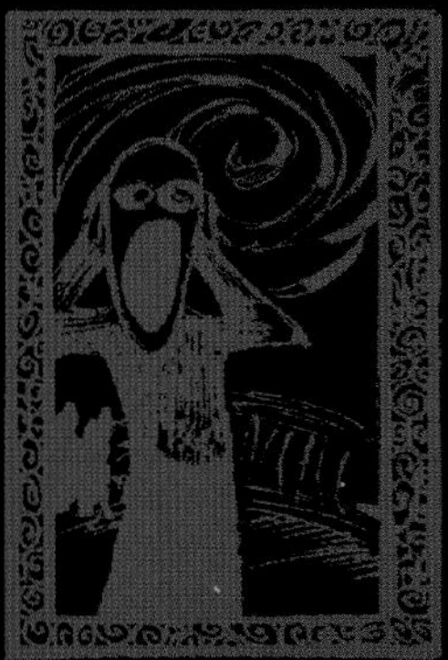

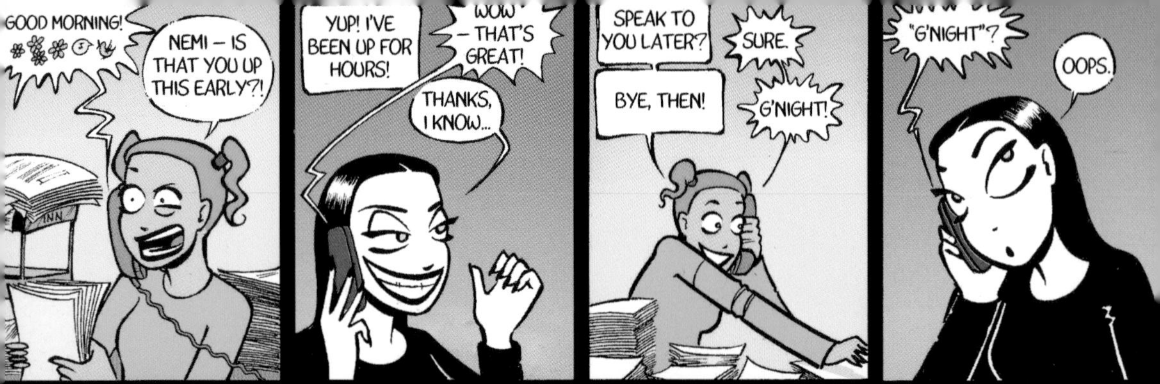
GOOD MORNING!
NEMI – IS THAT YOU UP THIS EARLY?!
YUP! I'VE BEEN UP FOR HOURS!
WOW – THAT'S GREAT!
THANKS, I KNOW...
SPEAK TO YOU LATER?
SURE.
BYE, THEN!
G'NIGHT!
"G'NIGHT"?
OOPS.

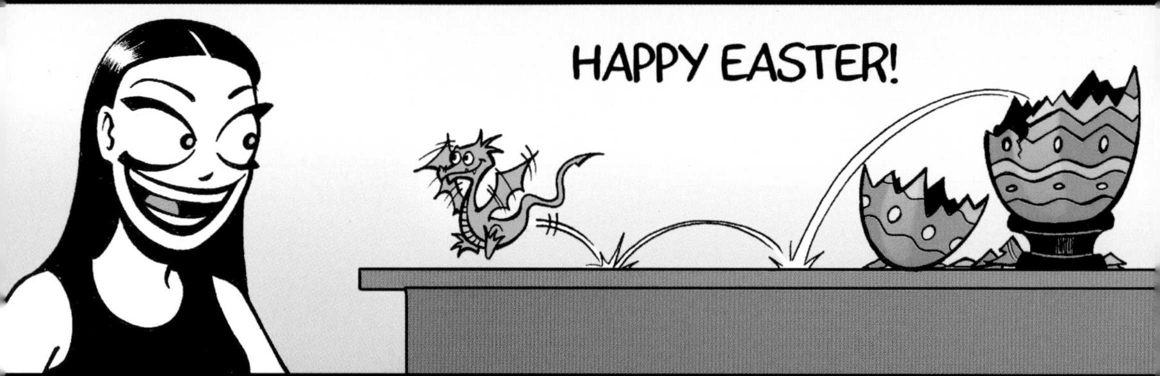
HAPPY EASTER!

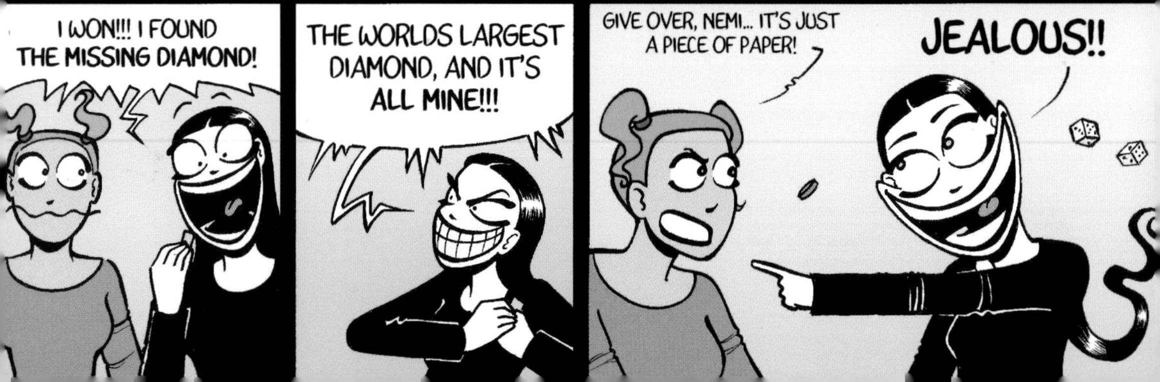
I WON!!! I FOUND THE MISSING DIAMOND!
THE WORLDS LARGEST DIAMOND, AND IT'S ALL MINE!!!
GIVE OVER, NEMI... IT'S JUST A PIECE OF PAPER!
JEALOUS!!

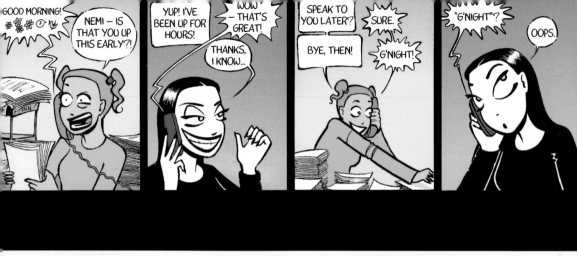

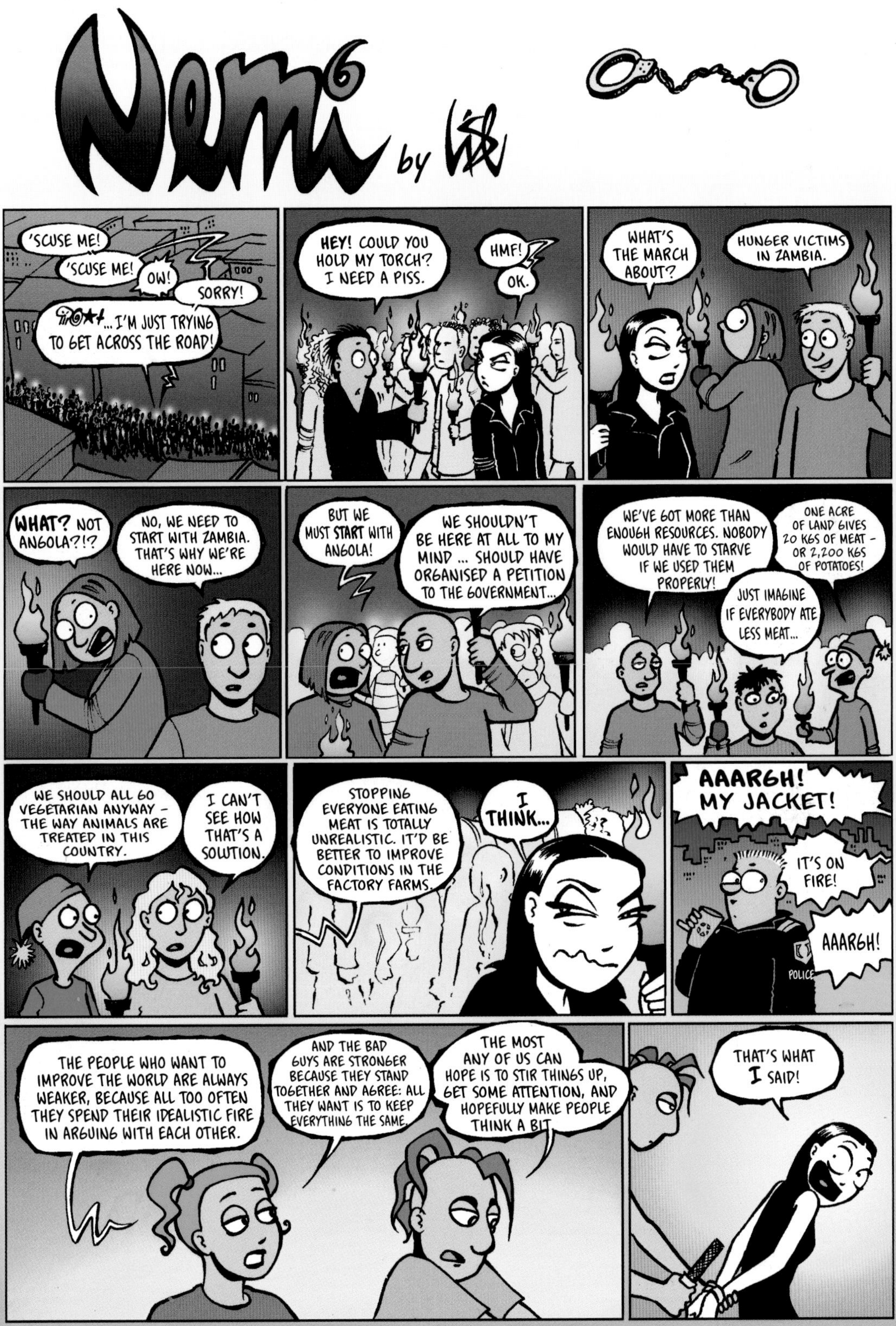
Nemi
by Lise
'SCUSE ME!
'SCUSE ME!
OW!
SORRY!
... I'M JUST TRYING TO GET ACROSS THE ROAD!
HEY! COULD YOU HOLD MY TORCH? I NEED A PISS.
HMF!
OK.
WHAT'S THE MARCH ABOUT?
HUNGER VICTIMS IN ZAMBIA.
WHAT? NOT ANGOLA?!?
NO, WE NEED TO START WITH ZAMBIA. THAT'S WHY WE'RE HERE NOW...
BUT WE MUST START WITH ANGOLA!
WE SHOULDN'T BE HERE AT ALL TO MY MIND ... SHOULD HAVE ORGANISED A PETITION TO THE GOVERNMENT...
WE'VE GOT MORE THAN ENOUGH RESOURCES. NOBODY WOULD HAVE TO STARVE IF WE USED THEM PROPERLY!
ONE ACRE OF LAND GIVES 20 KGS OF MEAT - OR 2,200 KGS OF POTATOES!
JUST IMAGINE IF EVERYBODY ATE LESS MEAT...
WE SHOULD ALL GO VEGETARIAN ANYWAY - THE WAY ANIMALS ARE TREATED IN THIS COUNTRY.
I CAN'T SEE HOW THAT'S A SOLUTION.
STOPPING EVERYONE EATING MEAT IS TOTALLY UNREALISTIC. IT'D BE BETTER TO IMPROVE CONDITIONS IN THE FACTORY FARMS.
I THINK...
AAARGH! MY JACKET!
IT'S ON FIRE!
AAARGH!
POLICE
THE PEOPLE WHO WANT TO IMPROVE THE WORLD ARE ALWAYS WEAKER, BECAUSE ALL TOO OFTEN THEY SPEND THEIR IDEALISTIC FIRE IN ARGUING WITH EACH OTHER.
AND THE BAD GUYS ARE STRONGER BECAUSE THEY STAND TOGETHER AND AGREE: ALL THEY WANT IS TO KEEP EVERYTHING THE SAME.
THE MOST ANY OF US CAN HOPE IS TO STIR THINGS UP, GET SOME ATTENTION, AND HOPEFULLY MAKE PEOPLE THINK A BIT.
THAT'S WHAT I SAID!

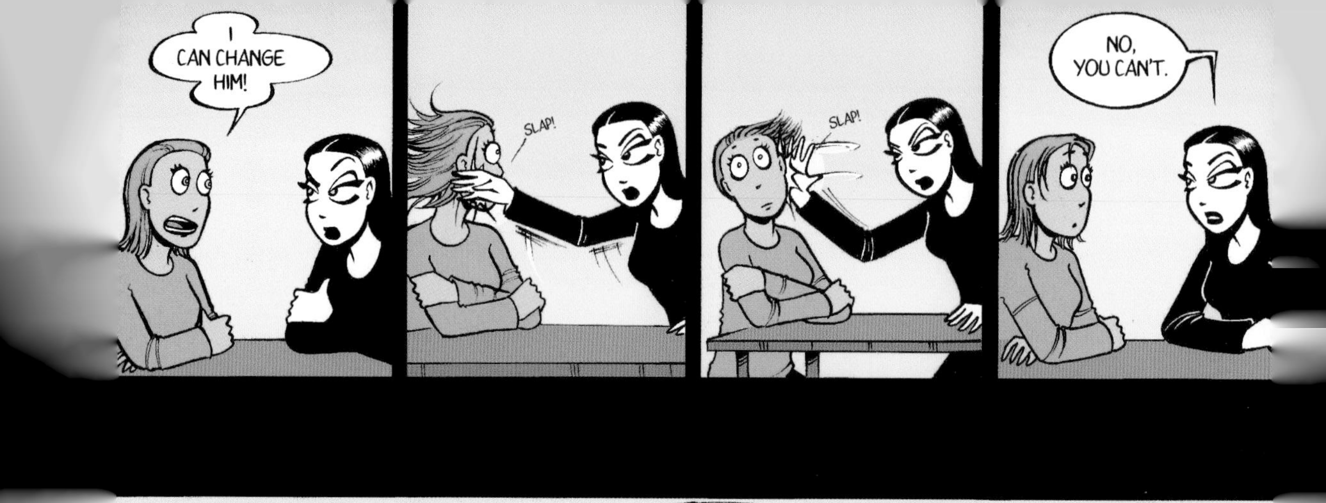
I CAN CHANGE HIM!
SLAP!
SLAP!
NO, YOU CAN'T.

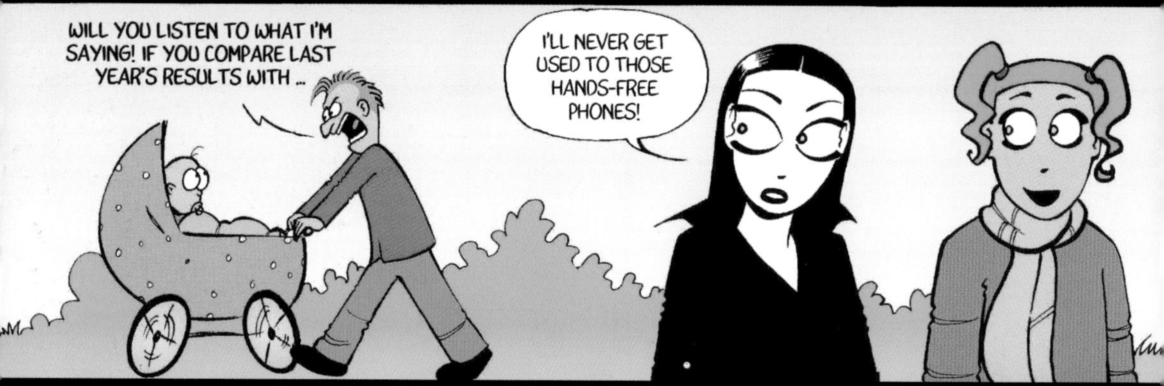
WILL YOU LISTEN TO WHAT I'M SAYING! IF YOU COMPARE LAST YEAR'S RESULTS WITH ...
I'LL NEVER GET USED TO THOSE HANDS-FREE PHONES!

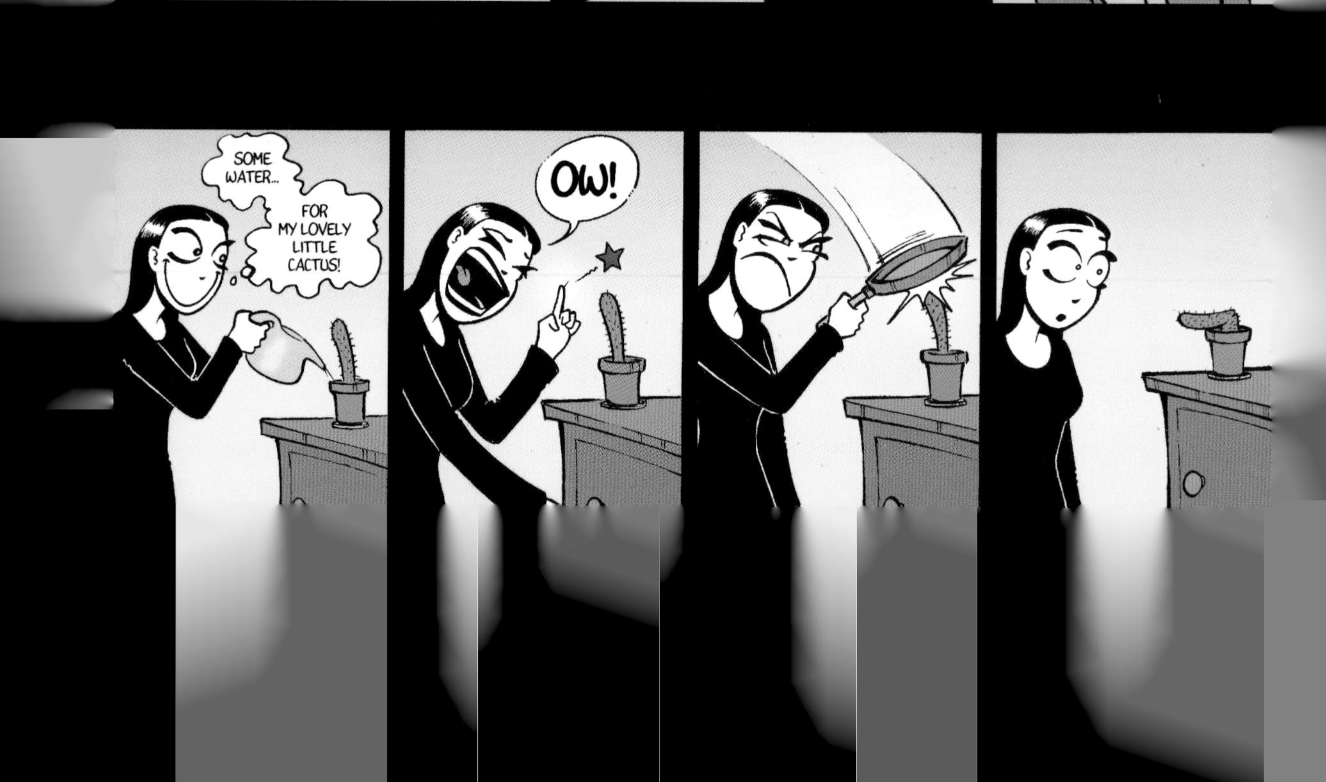
SOME WATER...
FOR MY LOVELY LITTLE CACTUS!
OW!

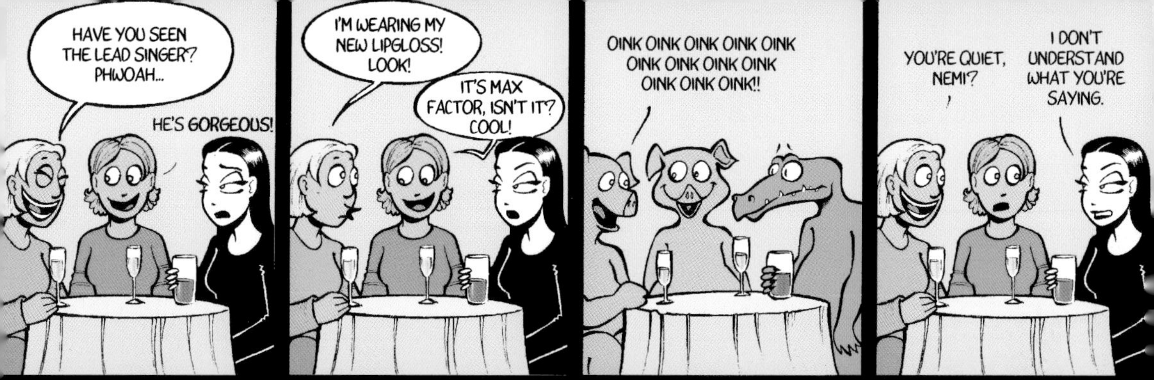
HAVE YOU SEEN THE LEAD SINGER? PHWOAH...
HE'S GORGEOUS!
I'M WEARING MY NEW LIPGLOSS! LOOK!
IT'S MAX FACTOR, ISN'T IT? COOL!
OINK OINK OINK OINK OINK OINK OINK OINK OINK OINK OINK OINK!!
YOU'RE QUIET, NEMI?
I DON'T UNDERSTAND WHAT YOU'RE SAYING.

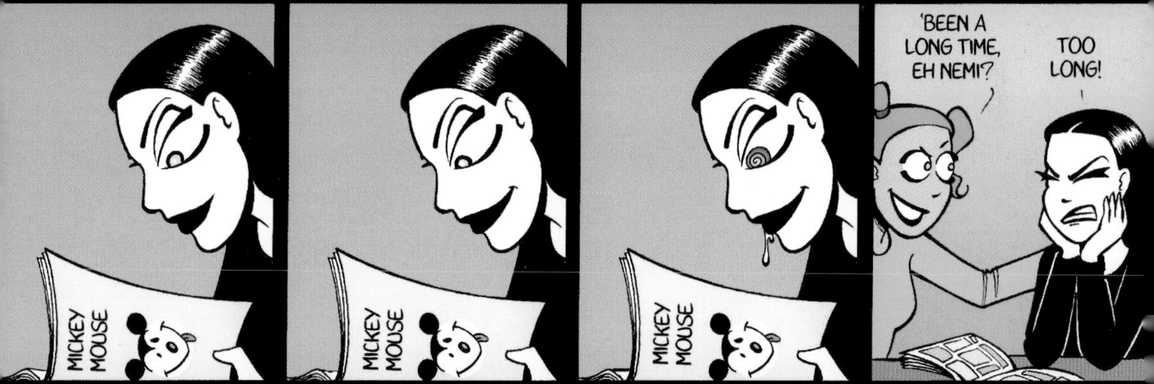
MICKEY MOUSE
MICKEY MOUSE
MICKEY MOUSE
'BEEN A LONG TIME, EH NEMI?
TOO LONG!

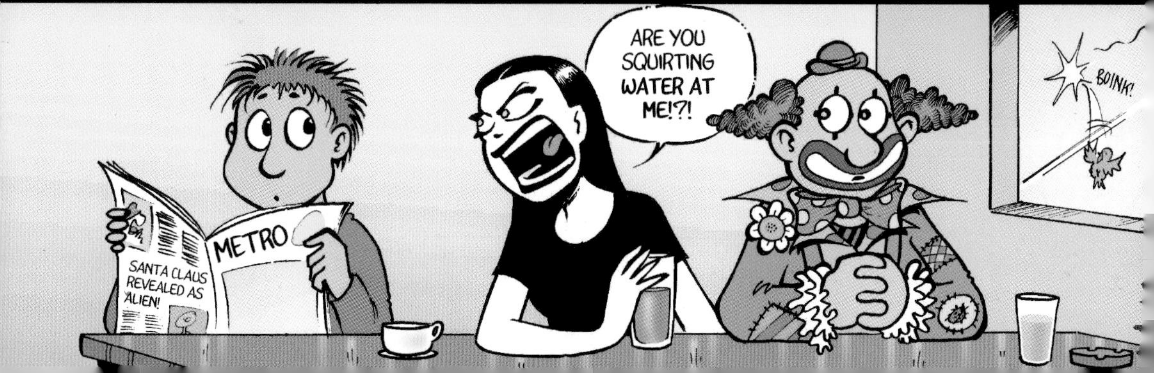
METRO
SANTA CLAUS REVEALED AS ALIEN!
ARE YOU SQUIRTING WATER AT ME!?!
BOINK!

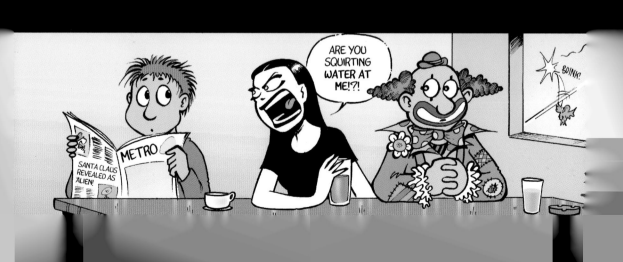

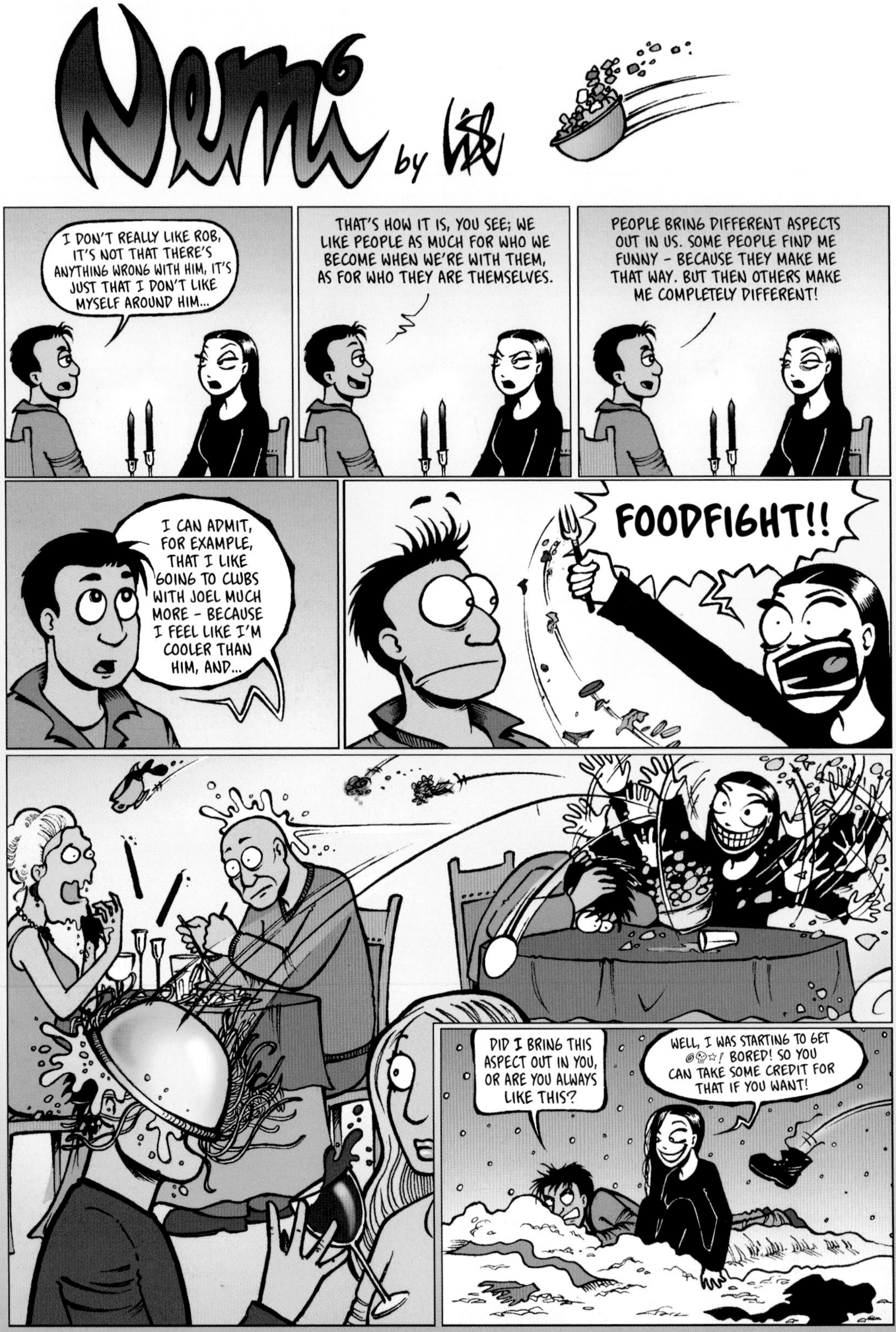

Nemi by Lise
I DON'T REALLY LIKE ROB, IT'S NOT THAT THERE'S ANYTHING WRONG WITH HIM, IT'S JUST THAT I DON'T LIKE MYSELF AROUND HIM...
THAT'S HOW IT IS, YOU SEE; WE LIKE PEOPLE AS MUCH FOR WHO WE BECOME WHEN WE'RE WITH THEM, AS FOR WHO THEY ARE THEMSELVES.
PEOPLE BRING DIFFERENT ASPECTS OUT IN US. SOME PEOPLE FIND ME FUNNY – BECAUSE THEY MAKE ME THAT WAY. BUT THEN OTHERS MAKE ME COMPLETELY DIFFERENT!
I CAN ADMIT, FOR EXAMPLE, THAT I LIKE GOING TO CLUBS WITH JOEL MUCH MORE – BECAUSE I FEEL LIKE I'M COOLER THAN HIM, AND...
FOODFIGHT!!
DID I BRING THIS ASPECT OUT IN YOU, OR ARE YOU ALWAYS LIKE THIS?
WELL, I WAS STARTING TO GET BORED! SO YOU CAN TAKE SOME CREDIT FOR THAT IF YOU WANT!

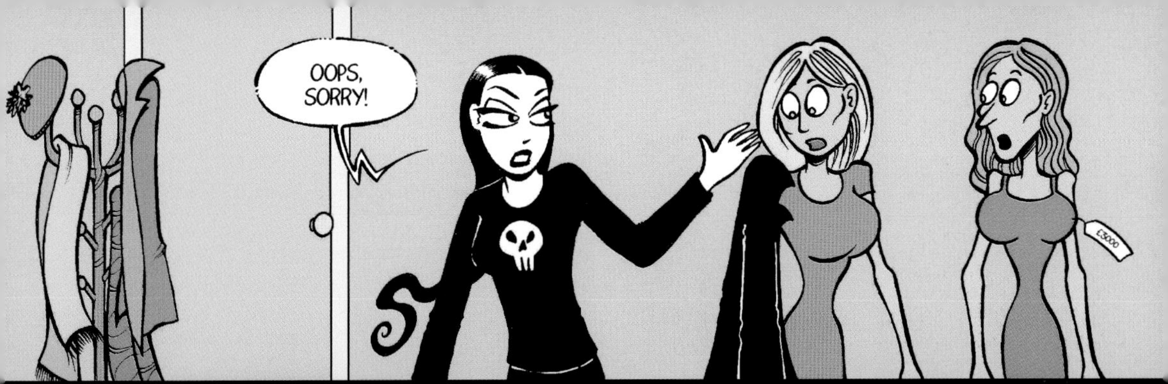
OOPS, SORRY!

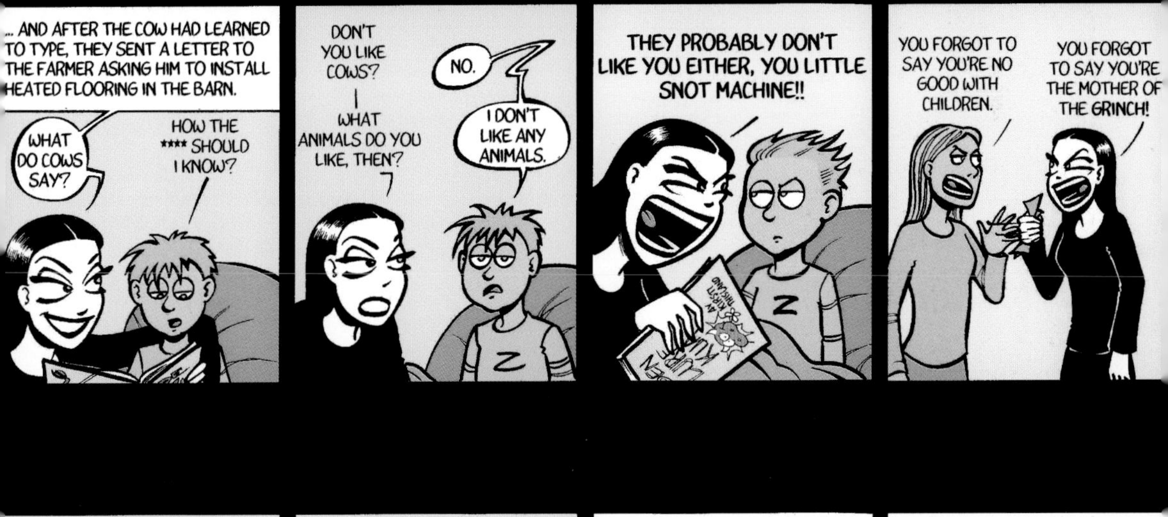
... AND AFTER THE COW HAD LEARNED TO TYPE, THEY SENT A LETTER TO THE FARMER ASKING HIM TO INSTALL HEATED FLOORING IN THE BARN.
WHAT DO COWS SAY?
HOW THE **** SHOULD I KNOW?
DON'T YOU LIKE COWS?
NO.
WHAT ANIMALS DO YOU LIKE, THEN?
I DON'T LIKE ANY ANIMALS.
THEY PROBABLY DON'T LIKE YOU EITHER, YOU LITTLE SNOT MACHINE!!
YOU FORGOT TO SAY YOU'RE NO GOOD WITH CHILDREN.
YOU FORGOT TO SAY YOU'RE THE MOTHER OF THE GRINCH!

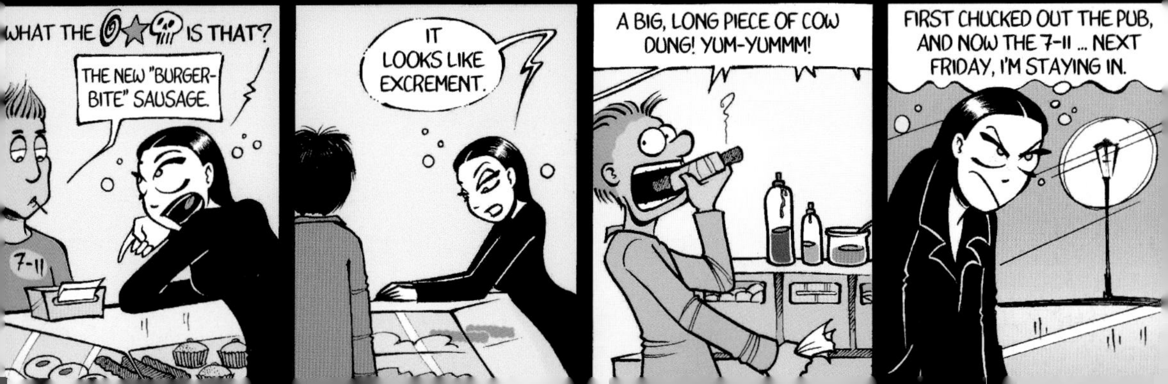
WHAT THE @☆☠ IS THAT?
THE NEW "BURGER-BITE" SAUSAGE.
7-11
IT LOOKS LIKE EXCREMENT.
A BIG, LONG PIECE OF COW DUNG! YUM-YUMMM!
FIRST CHUCKED OUT THE PUB, AND NOW THE 7-11 ... NEXT FRIDAY, I'M STAYING IN.

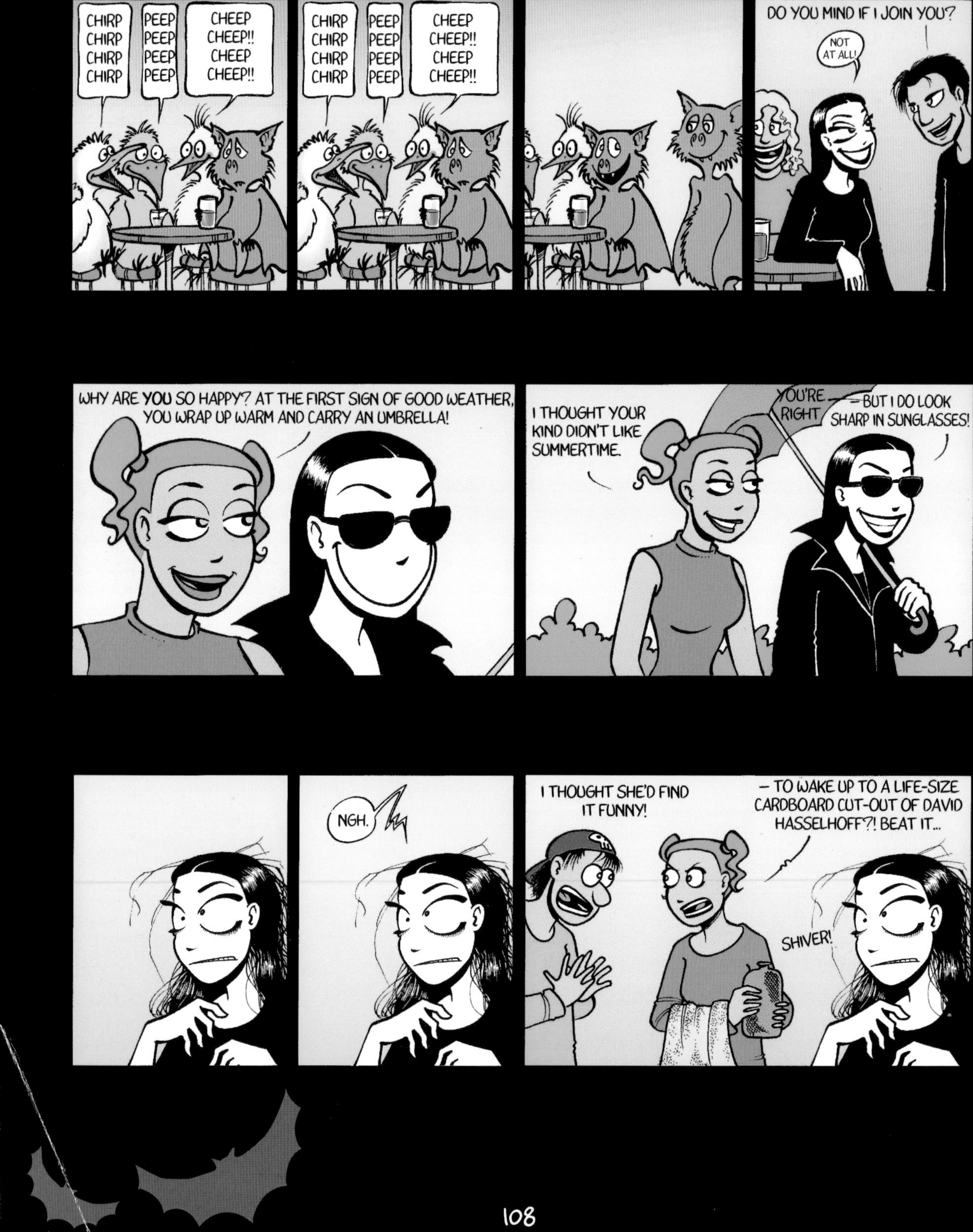
CHIRP CHIRP CHIRP CHIRP
PEEP PEEP PEEP PEEP
CHEEP CHEEP!! CHEEP CHEEP!!
CHIRP CHIRP CHIRP CHIRP
PEEP PEEP PEEP PEEP
CHEEP CHEEP!! CHEEP CHEEP!!
DO YOU MIND IF I JOIN YOU?
NOT AT ALL!
WHY ARE YOU SO HAPPY? AT THE FIRST SIGN OF GOOD WEATHER, YOU WRAP UP WARM AND CARRY AN UMBRELLA!
I THOUGHT YOUR KIND DIDN'T LIKE SUMMERTIME.
YOU'RE RIGHT
—BUT I DO LOOK SHARP IN SUNGLASSES!
NGH.
I THOUGHT SHE'D FIND IT FUNNY!
— TO WAKE UP TO A LIFE-SIZE CARDBOARD CUT-OUT OF DAVID HASSELHOFF?! BEAT IT...
SHIVER!

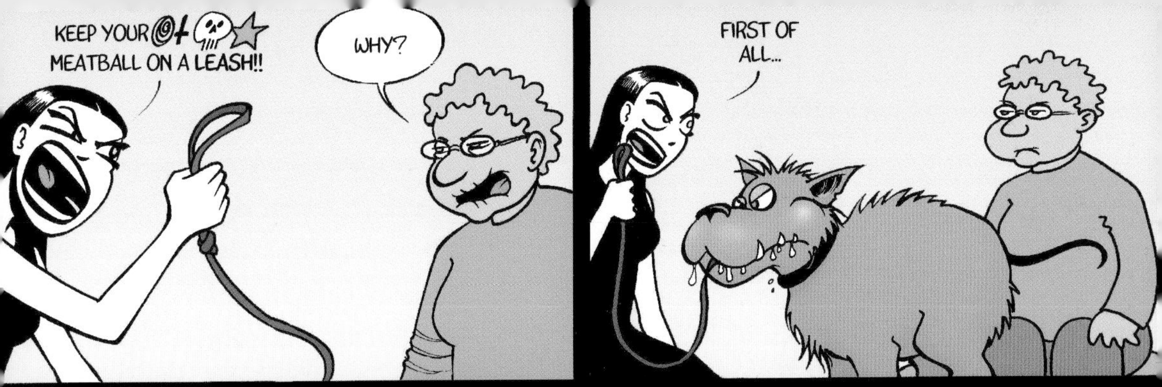

KEEP YOUR MEATBALL ON A LEASH!!
WHY?
FIRST OF ALL...

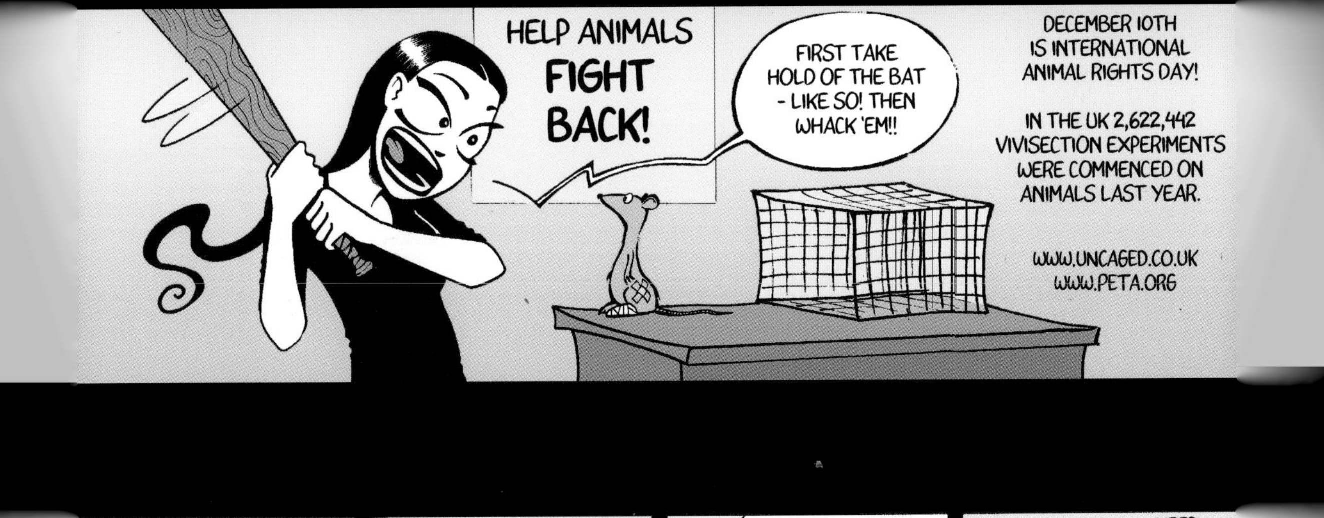

HELP ANIMALS FIGHT BACK!
FIRST TAKE HOLD OF THE BAT - LIKE SO! THEN WHACK 'EM!!
DECEMBER 10TH IS INTERNATIONAL ANIMAL RIGHTS DAY!
IN THE UK 2,622,442 VIVISECTION EXPERIMENTS WERE COMMENCED ON ANIMALS LAST YEAR.
WWW.UNCAGED.CO.UK
WWW.PETA.ORG

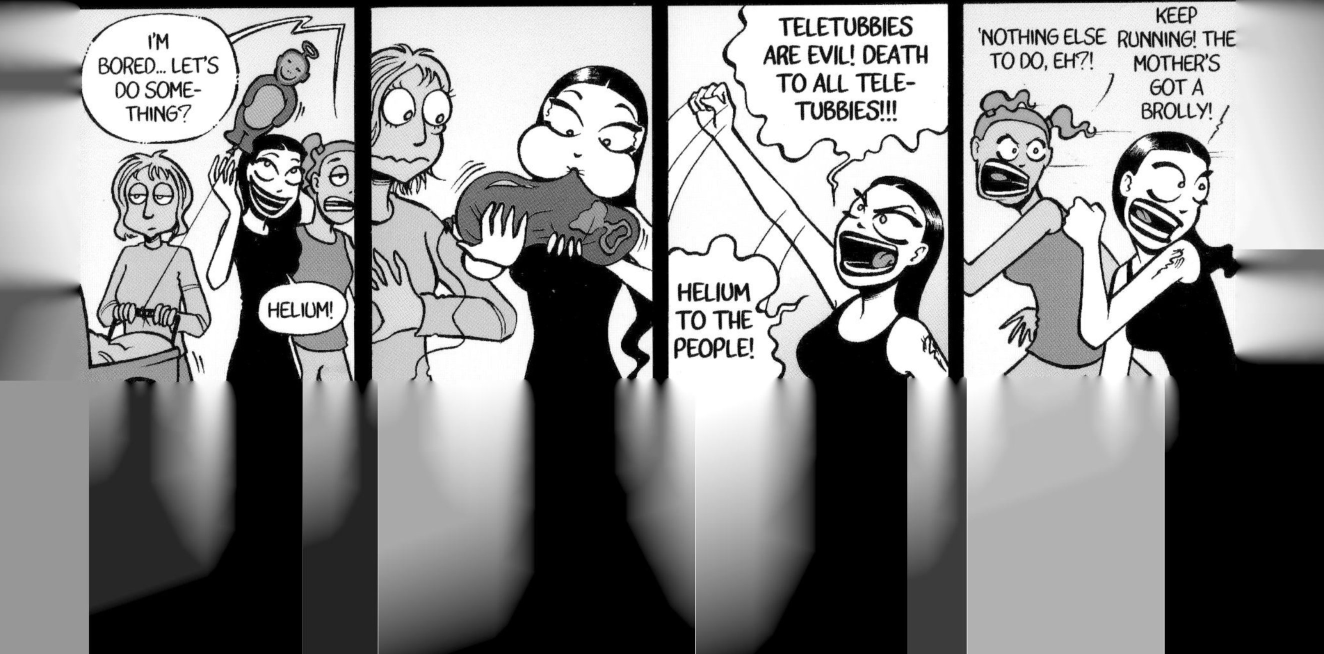

I'M BORED... LET'S DO SOME-THING?
HELIUM!
TELETUBBIES ARE EVIL! DEATH TO ALL TELE-TUBBIES!!!
HELIUM TO THE PEOPLE!
'NOTHING ELSE TO DO, EH?!
KEEP RUNNING! THE MOTHER'S GOT A BROLLY!

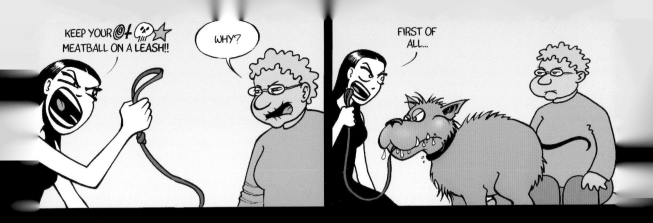

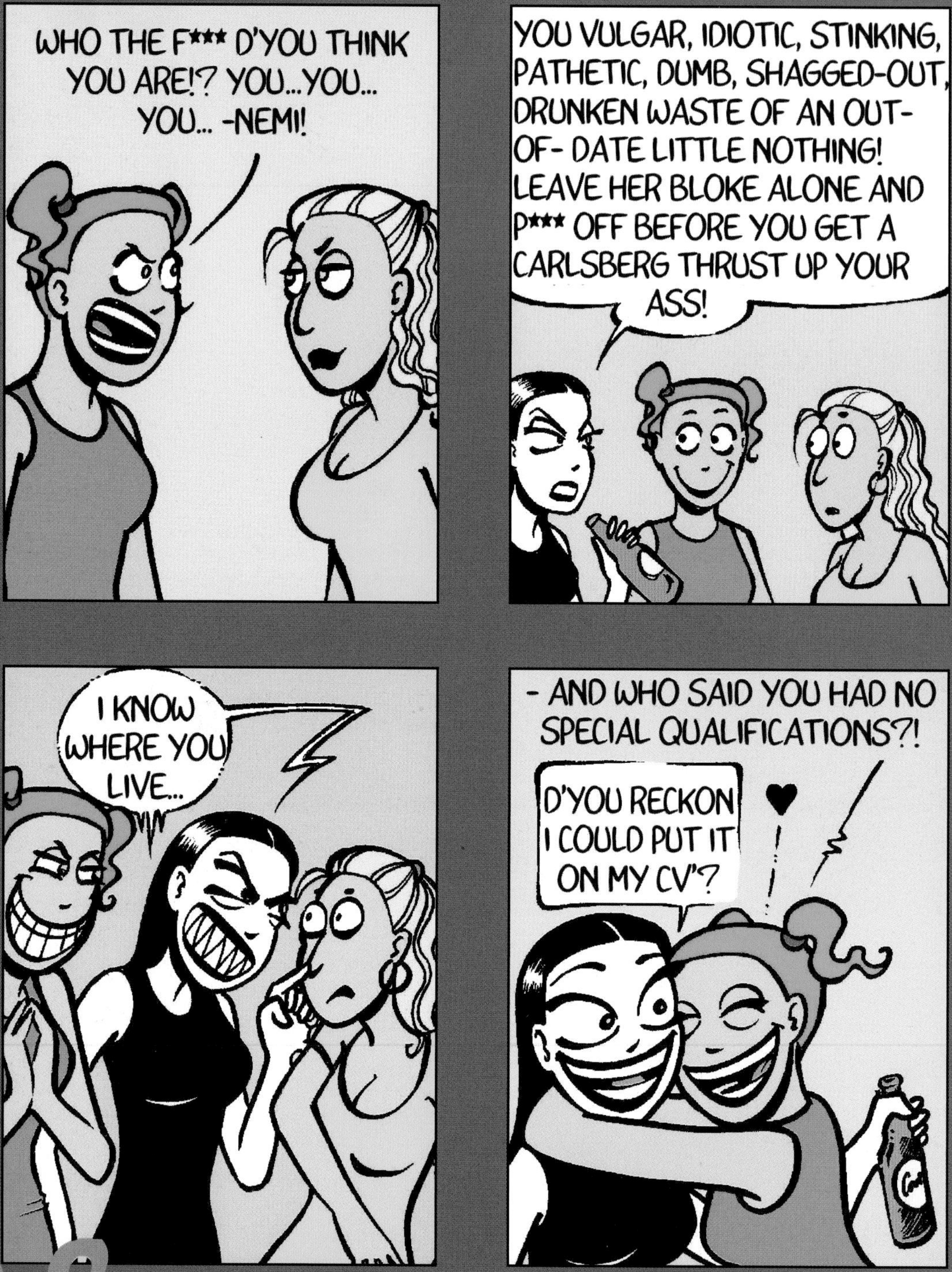
WHO THE F*** D'YOU THINK YOU ARE!? YOU...YOU... YOU... -NEMI!
YOU VULGAR, IDIOTIC, STINKING, PATHETIC, DUMB, SHAGGED-OUT, DRUNKEN WASTE OF AN OUT-OF- DATE LITTLE NOTHING! LEAVE HER BLOKE ALONE AND P*** OFF BEFORE YOU GET A CARLSBERG THRUST UP YOUR ASS!
I KNOW WHERE YOU LIVE...
- AND WHO SAID YOU HAD NO SPECIAL QUALIFICATIONS?!
D'YOU RECKON I COULD PUT IT ON MY CV'?

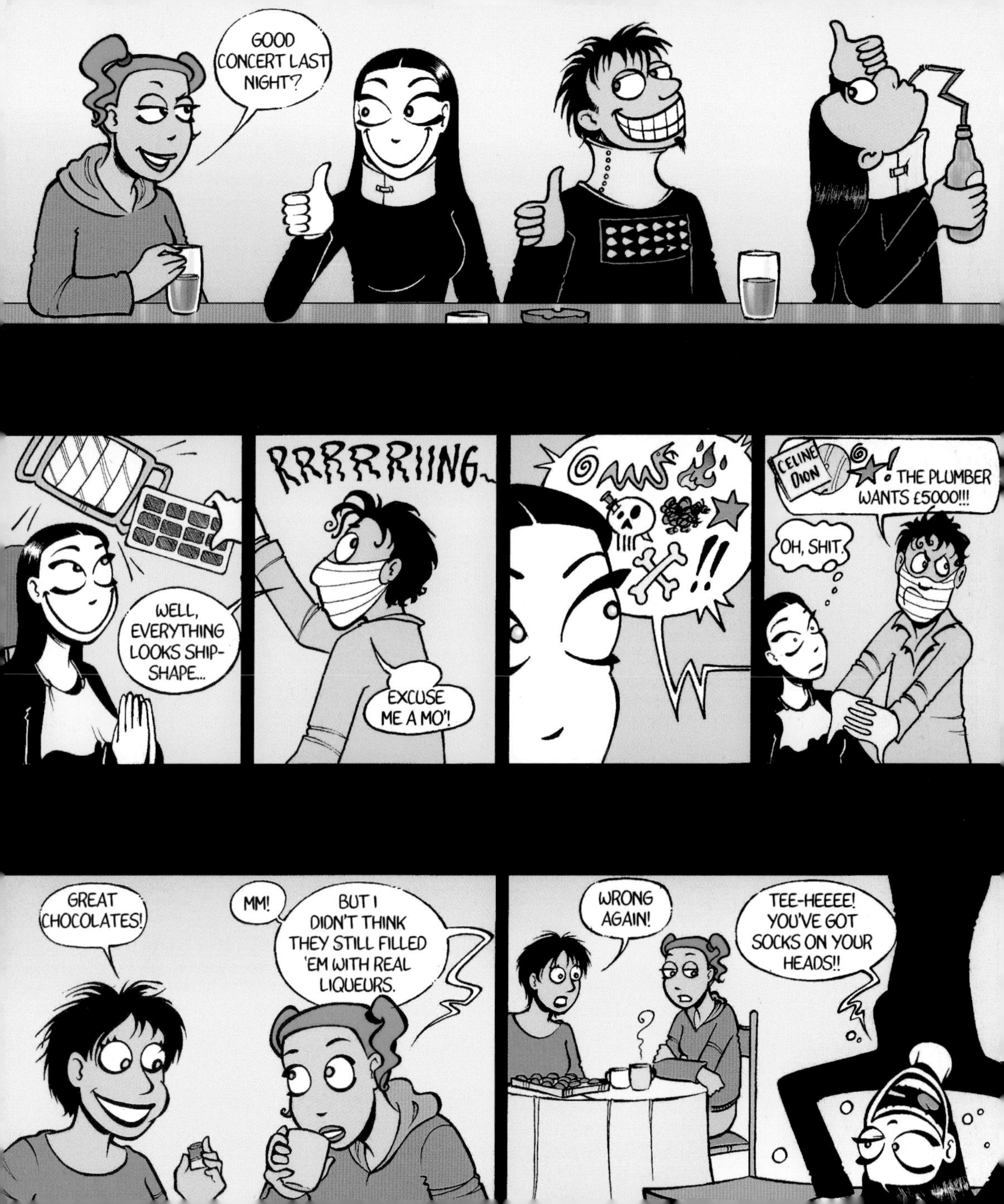
GOOD CONCERT LAST NIGHT?
WELL, EVERYTHING LOOKS SHIP-SHAPE...
RRRRRRIING
EXCUSE ME A MO'!
CELINE DION
THE PLUMBER WANTS £5000!!!
OH, SHIT.
GREAT CHOCOLATES!
MM!
BUT I DIDN'T THINK THEY STILL FILLED 'EM WITH REAL LIQUEURS.
WRONG AGAIN!
TEE-HEEEE! YOU'VE GOT SOCKS ON YOUR HEADS!!

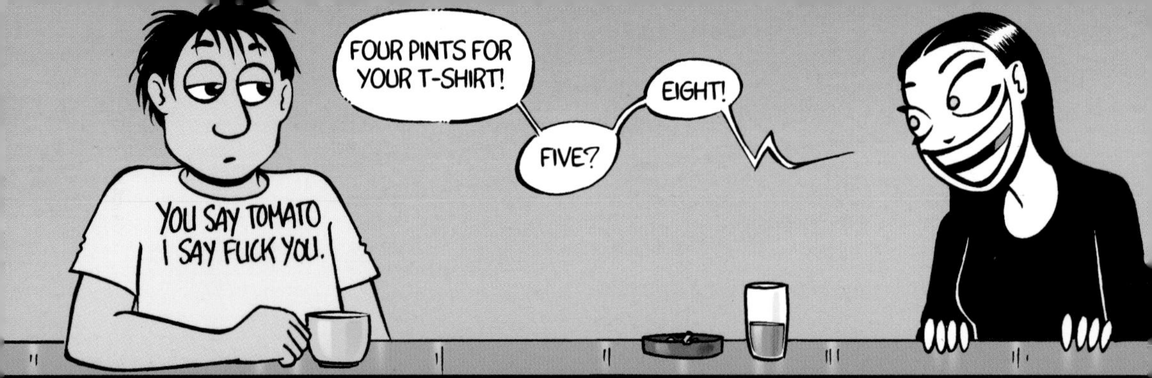
YOU SAY TOMATO
I SAY FUCK YOU.
FOUR PINTS FOR YOUR T-SHIRT!
FIVE?
EIGHT!

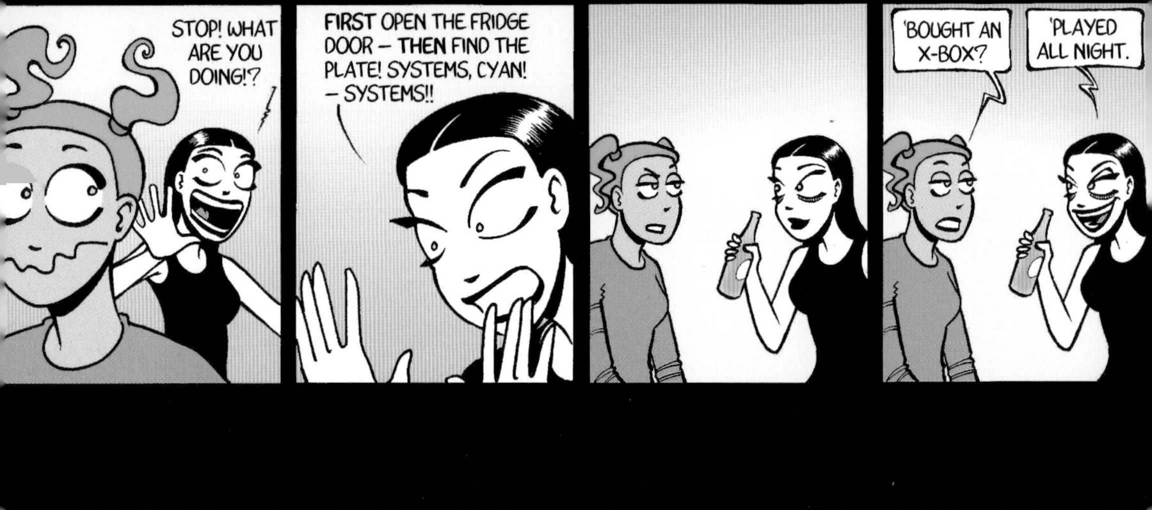
STOP! WHAT ARE YOU DOING!?
FIRST OPEN THE FRIDGE DOOR – THEN FIND THE PLATE! SYSTEMS, CYAN! – SYSTEMS!!
'BOUGHT AN X-BOX?
'PLAYED ALL NIGHT.

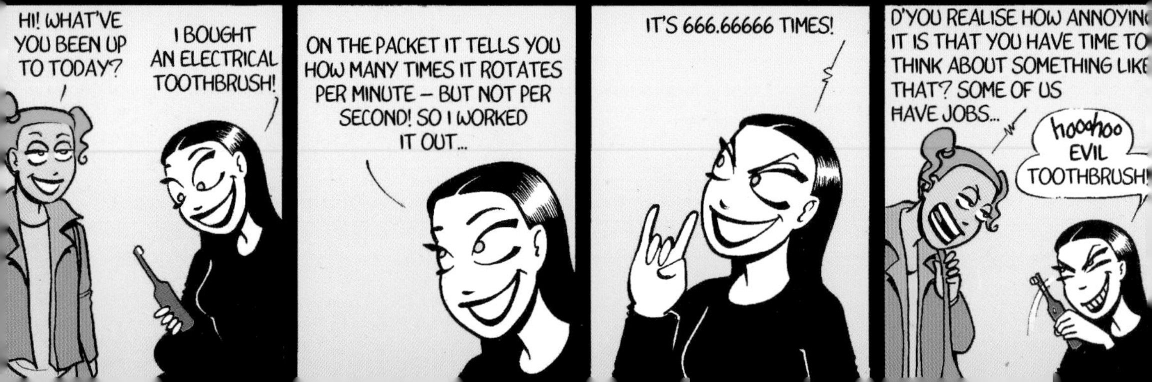
HI! WHAT'VE YOU BEEN UP TO TODAY?
I BOUGHT AN ELECTRICAL TOOTHBRUSH!
ON THE PACKET IT TELLS YOU HOW MANY TIMES IT ROTATES PER MINUTE – BUT NOT PER SECOND! SO I WORKED IT OUT...
IT'S 666.66666 TIMES!
D'YOU REALISE HOW ANNOYIN IT IS THAT YOU HAVE TIME TO THINK ABOUT SOMETHING LIKE THAT? SOME OF US HAVE JOBS...
hoohoo EVIL TOOTHBRUSH!

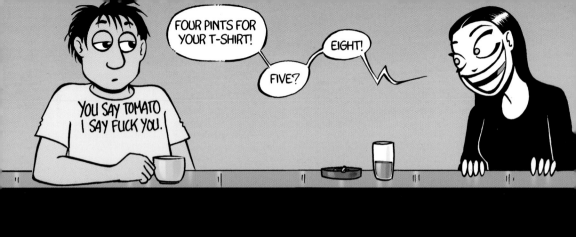

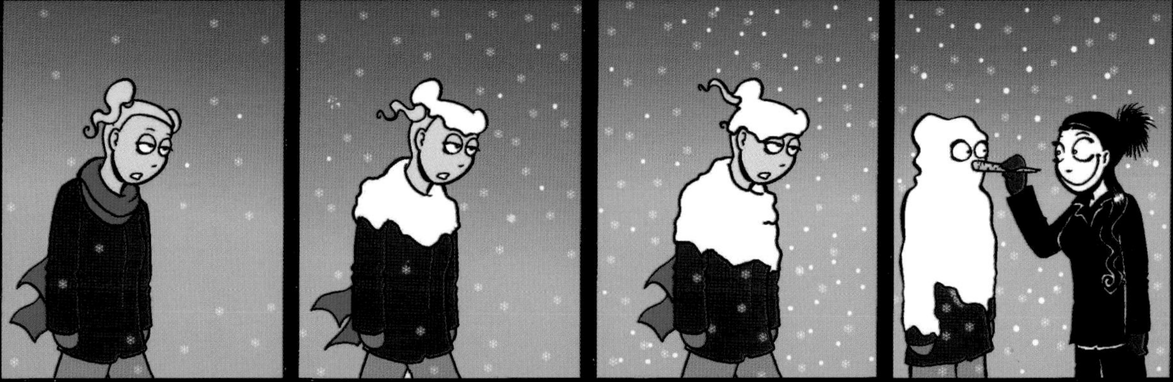

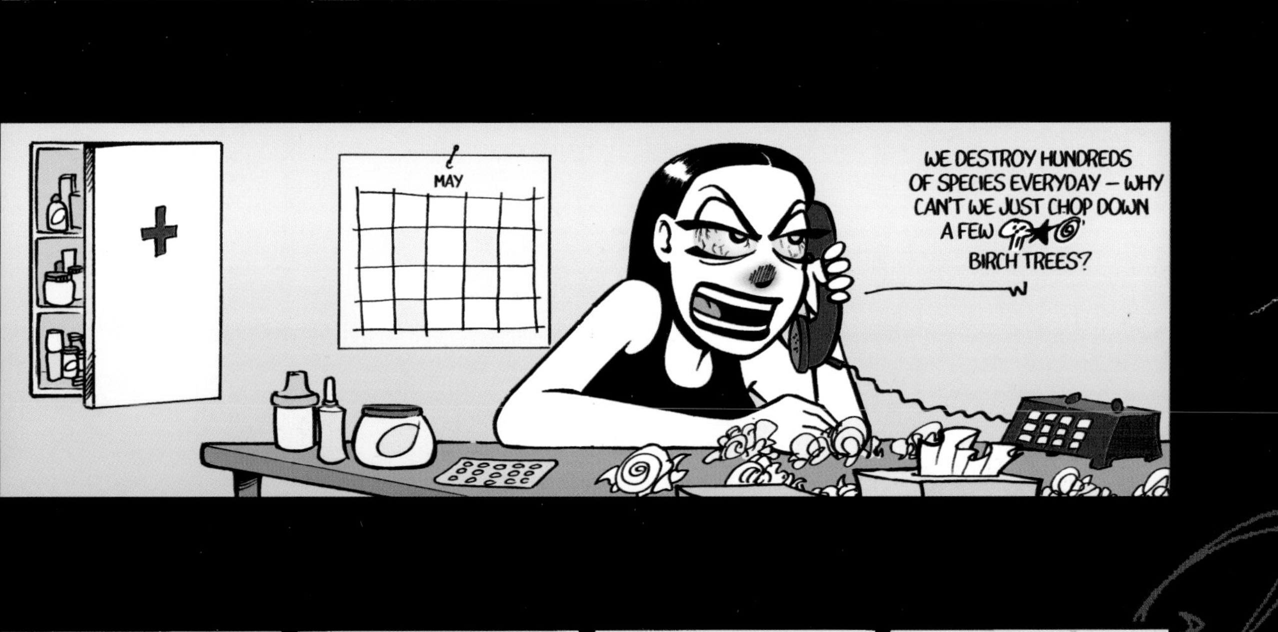
WE DESTROY HUNDREDS OF SPECIES EVERYDAY – WHY CAN'T WE JUST CHOP DOWN A FEW BIRCH TREES?

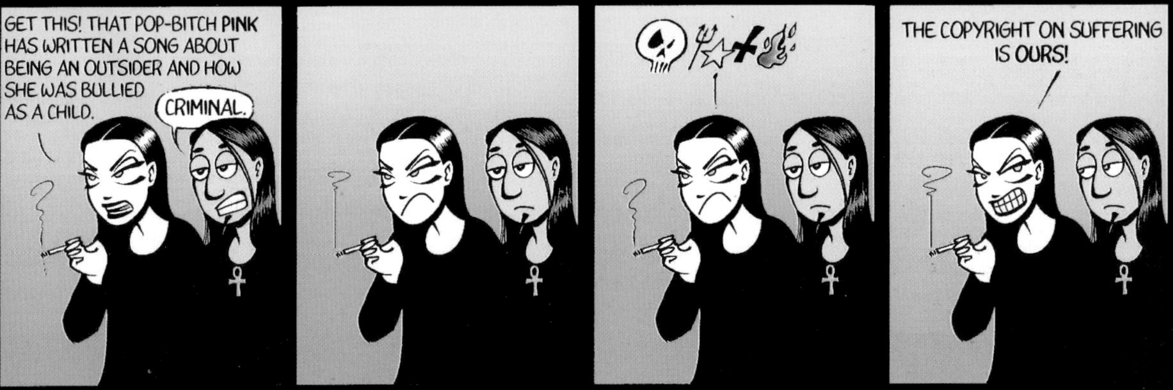
GET THIS! THAT POP-BITCH PINK HAS WRITTEN A SONG ABOUT BEING AN OUTSIDER AND HOW SHE WAS BULLIED AS A CHILD.
CRIMINAL.
THE COPYRIGHT ON SUFFERING IS OURS!

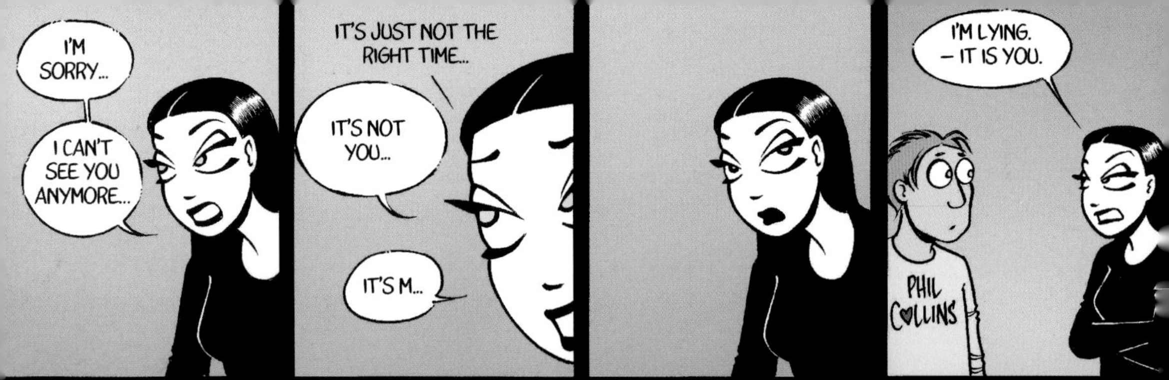
I'M SORRY...
I CAN'T SEE YOU ANYMORE...
IT'S JUST NOT THE RIGHT TIME...
IT'S NOT YOU...
IT'S M...
I'M LYING. – IT IS YOU.
PHIL COLLINS

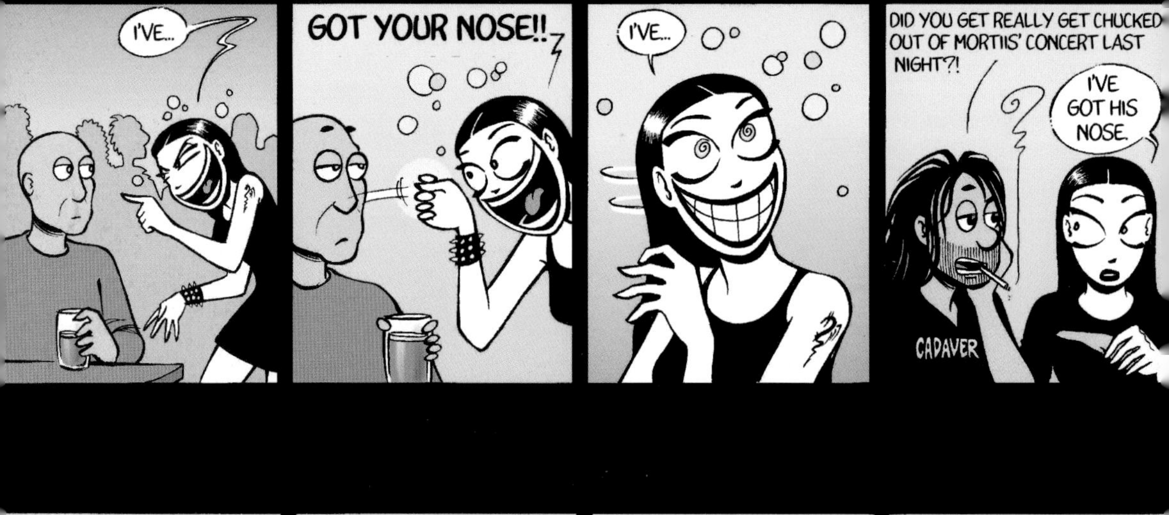
I'VE...
GOT YOUR NOSE!!
I'VE...
DID YOU GET REALLY GET CHUCKED OUT OF MORTIIS' CONCERT LAST NIGHT?!
I'VE GOT HIS NOSE.
CADAVER

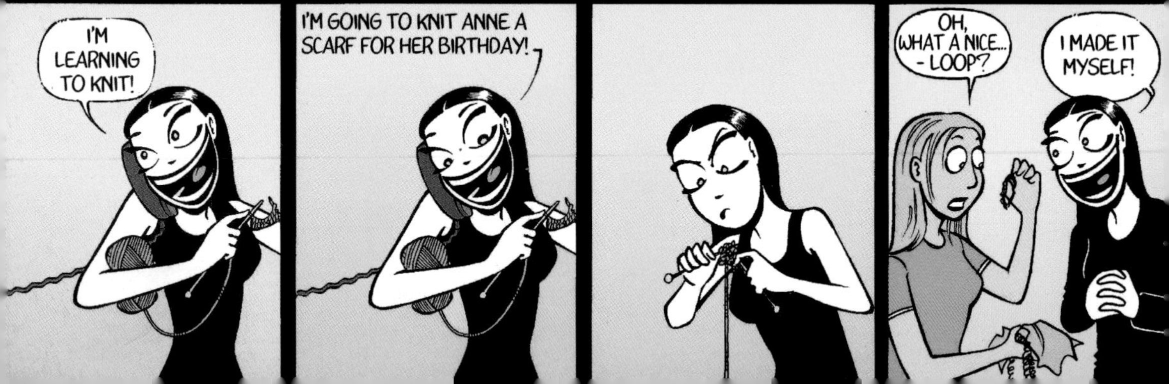
I'M LEARNING TO KNIT!
I'M GOING TO KNIT ANNE A SCARF FOR HER BIRTHDAY!
OH, WHAT A NICE... - LOOP?
I MADE IT MYSELF!

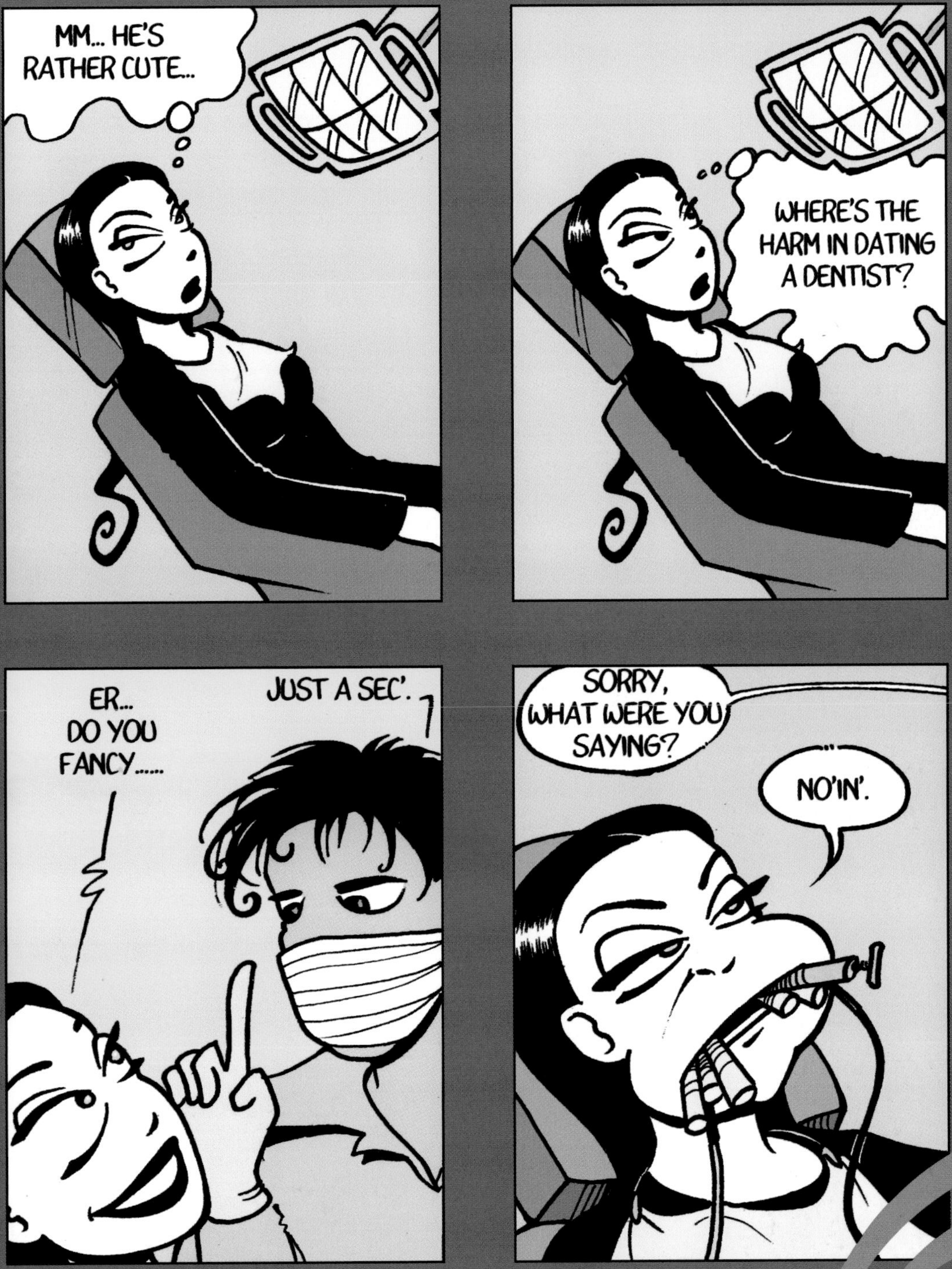
MM... HE'S RATHER CUTE...
WHERE'S THE HARM IN DATING A DENTIST?
ER... DO YOU FANCY......
JUST A SEC'.
SORRY, WHAT WERE YOU SAYING?
NO'IN'.

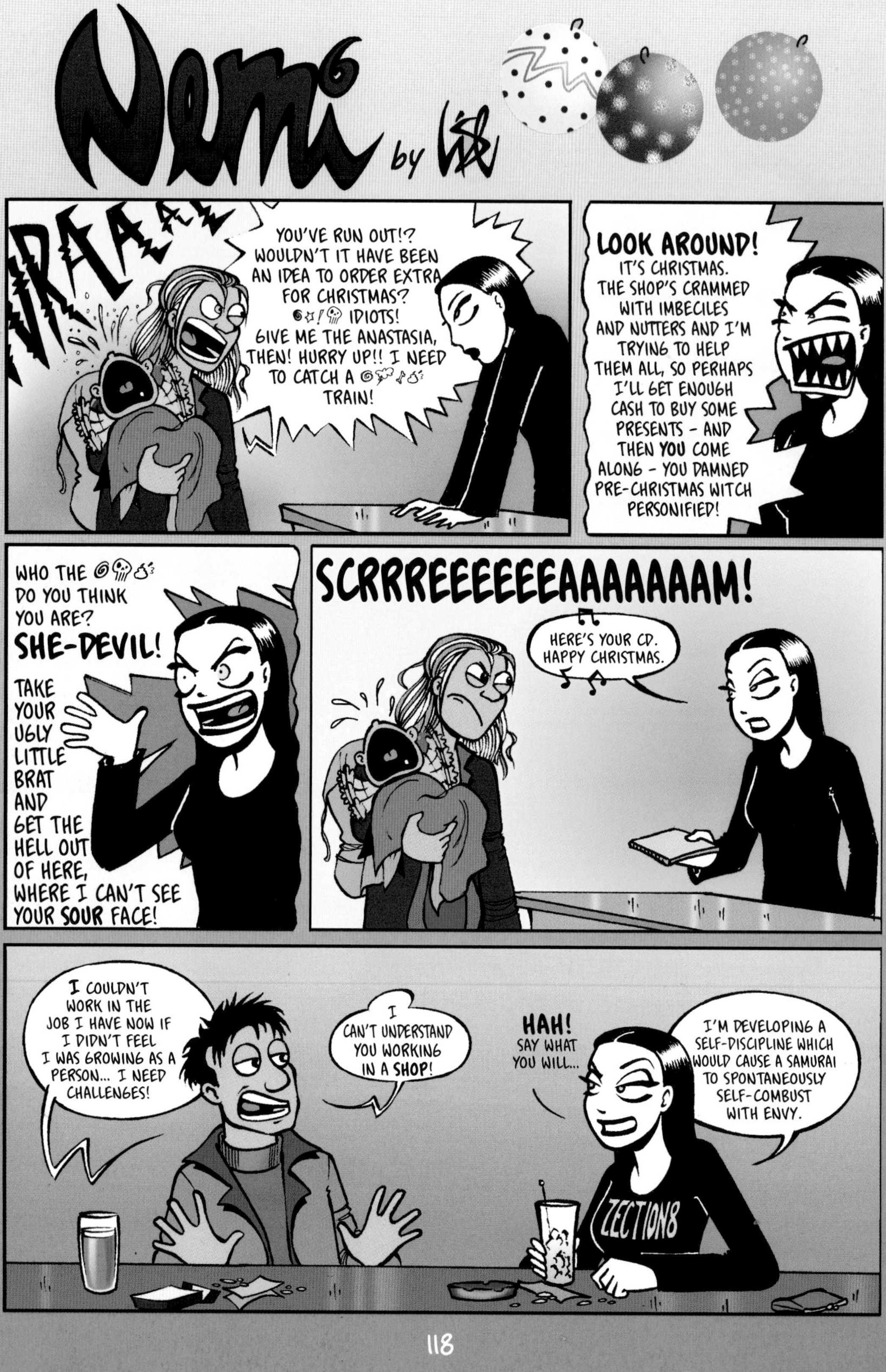
Nemi by Lise
WRAAAEE
YOU'VE RUN OUT!? WOULDN'T IT HAVE BEEN AN IDEA TO ORDER EXTRA FOR CHRISTMAS? IDIOTS! GIVE ME THE ANASTASIA, THEN! HURRY UP!! I NEED TO CATCH A TRAIN!
LOOK AROUND! IT'S CHRISTMAS. THE SHOP'S CRAMMED WITH IMBECILES AND NUTTERS AND I'M TRYING TO HELP THEM ALL, SO PERHAPS I'LL GET ENOUGH CASH TO BUY SOME PRESENTS – AND THEN YOU COME ALONG – YOU DAMNED PRE-CHRISTMAS WITCH PERSONIFIED!
WHO THE DO YOU THINK YOU ARE? SHE-DEVIL!
TAKE YOUR UGLY LITTLE BRAT AND GET THE HELL OUT OF HERE, WHERE I CAN'T SEE YOUR SOUR FACE!
SCRRREEEEEEEAAAAAAAM!
HERE'S YOUR CD. HAPPY CHRISTMAS.
I COULDN'T WORK IN THE JOB I HAVE NOW IF I DIDN'T FEEL I WAS GROWING AS A PERSON... I NEED CHALLENGES!
I CAN'T UNDERSTAND YOU WORKING IN A SHOP!
HAH! SAY WHAT YOU WILL...
I'M DEVELOPING A SELF-DISCIPLINE WHICH WOULD CAUSE A SAMURAI TO SPONTANEOUSLY SELF-COMBUST WITH ENVY.
ZECTION8

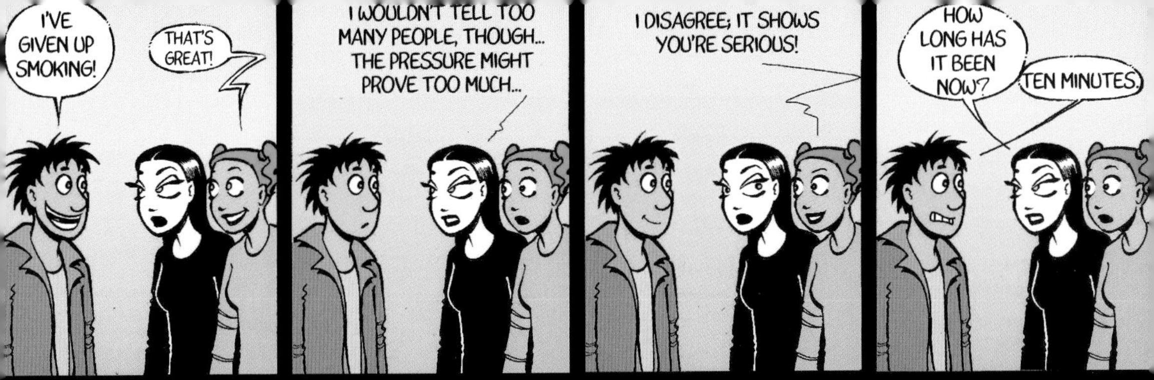
I'VE GIVEN UP SMOKING!
THAT'S GREAT!
I WOULDN'T TELL TOO MANY PEOPLE, THOUGH... THE PRESSURE MIGHT PROVE TOO MUCH...
I DISAGREE; IT SHOWS YOU'RE SERIOUS!
HOW LONG HAS IT BEEN NOW?
TEN MINUTES.

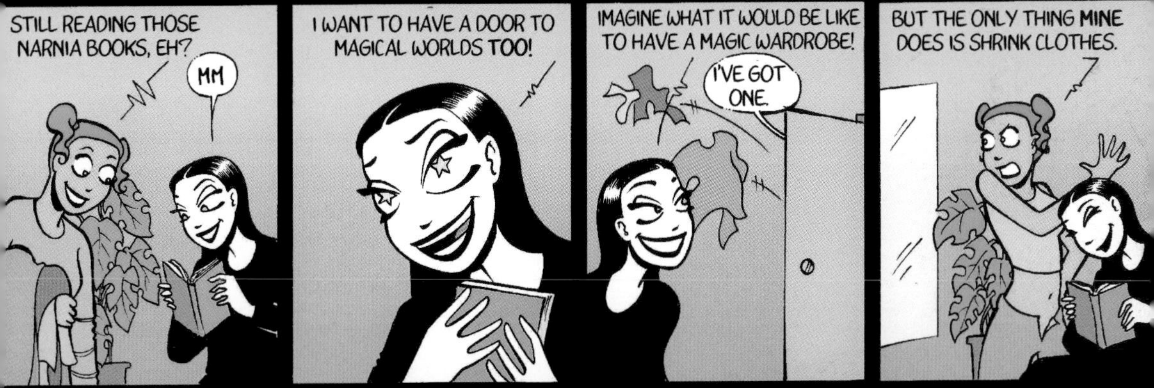
STILL READING THOSE NARNIA BOOKS, EH?
MM
I WANT TO HAVE A DOOR TO MAGICAL WORLDS TOO!
IMAGINE WHAT IT WOULD BE LIKE TO HAVE A MAGIC WARDROBE!
I'VE GOT ONE.
BUT THE ONLY THING MINE DOES IS SHRINK CLOTHES.

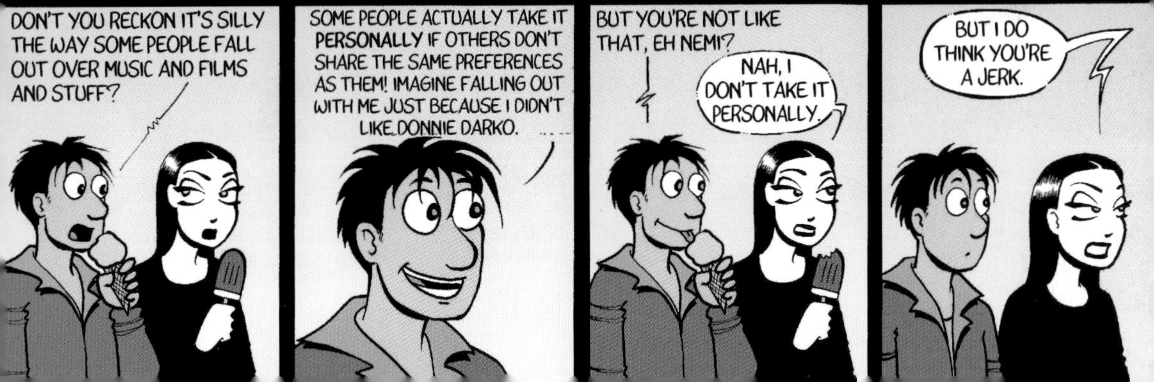
DON'T YOU RECKON IT'S SILLY THE WAY SOME PEOPLE FALL OUT OVER MUSIC AND FILMS AND STUFF?
SOME PEOPLE ACTUALLY TAKE IT PERSONALLY IF OTHERS DON'T SHARE THE SAME PREFERENCES AS THEM! IMAGINE FALLING OUT WITH ME JUST BECAUSE I DIDN'T LIKE DONNIE DARKO.
BUT YOU'RE NOT LIKE THAT, EH NEMI?
NAH, I DON'T TAKE IT PERSONALLY.
BUT I DO THINK YOU'RE A JERK.

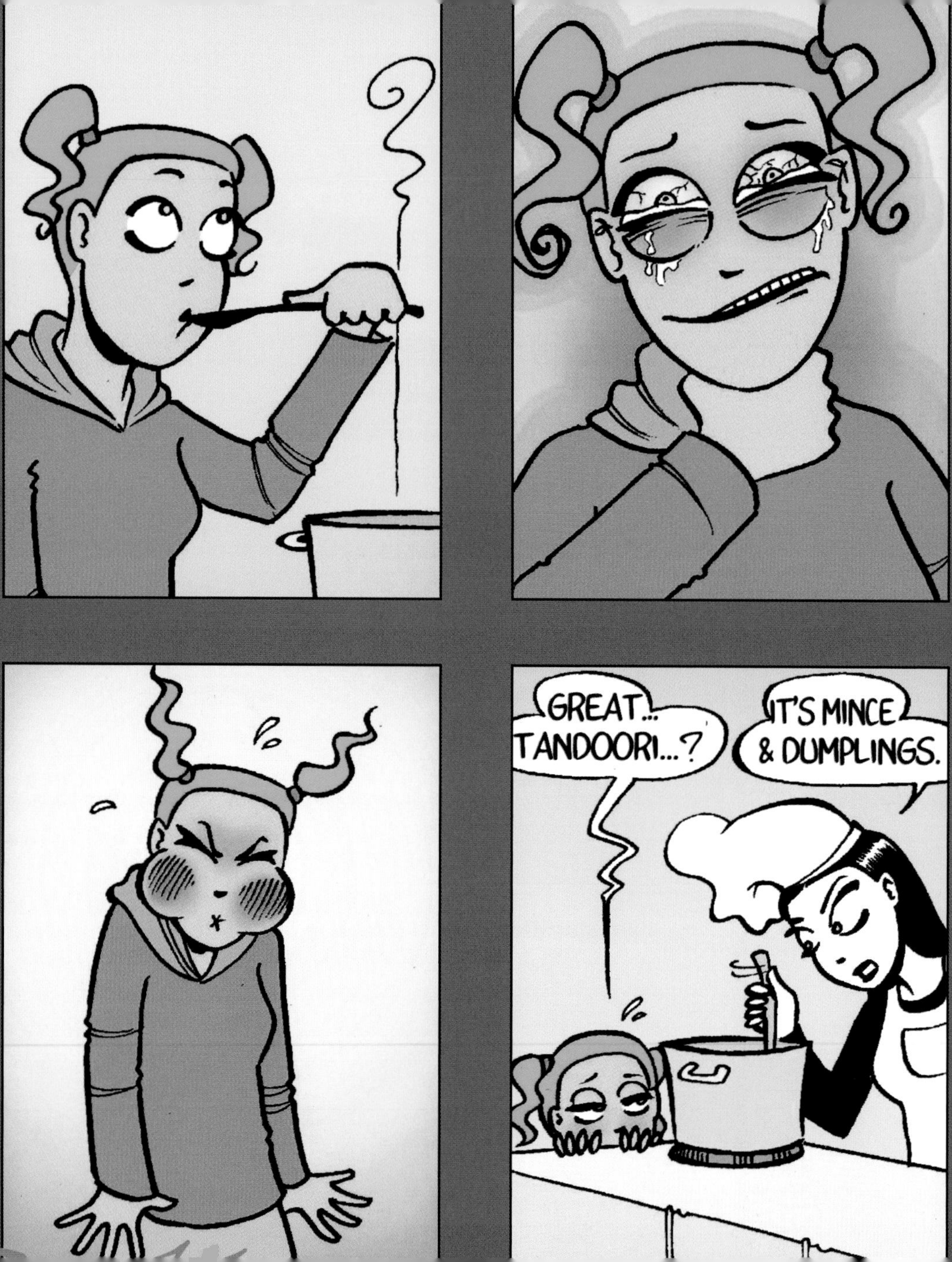
GREAT... TANDOORI...?
IT'S MINCE & DUMPLINGS.

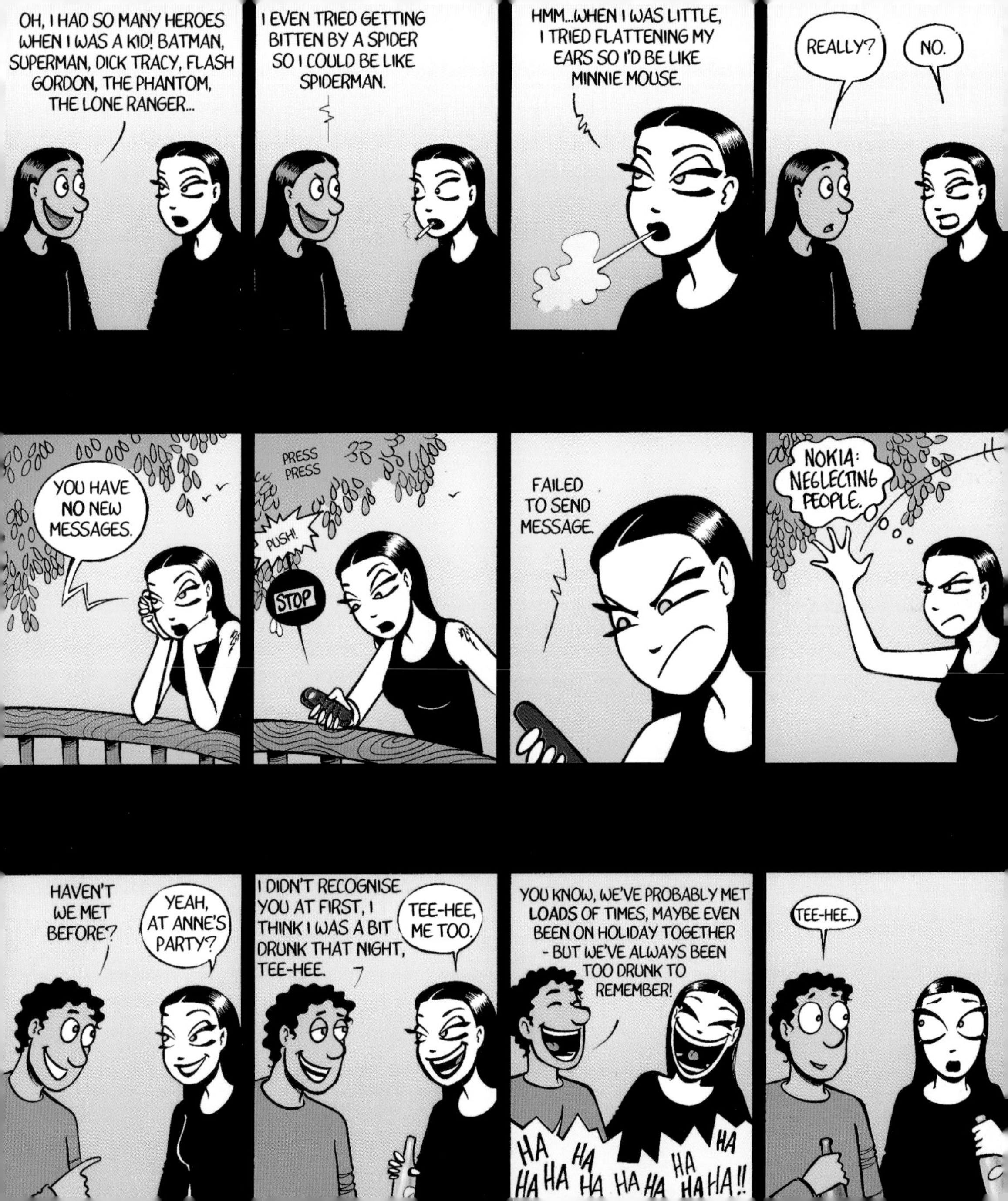
OH, I HAD SO MANY HEROES WHEN I WAS A KID! BATMAN, SUPERMAN, DICK TRACY, FLASH GORDON, THE PHANTOM, THE LONE RANGER...
I EVEN TRIED GETTING BITTEN BY A SPIDER SO I COULD BE LIKE SPIDERMAN.
HMM...WHEN I WAS LITTLE, I TRIED FLATTENING MY EARS SO I'D BE LIKE MINNIE MOUSE.
REALLY?
NO.
YOU HAVE NO NEW MESSAGES.
PRESS PRESS
PUSH!
STOP
FAILED TO SEND MESSAGE.
NOKIA: NEGLECTING PEOPLE.
HAVEN'T WE MET BEFORE?
YEAH, AT ANNE'S PARTY?
I DIDN'T RECOGNISE YOU AT FIRST, I THINK I WAS A BIT DRUNK THAT NIGHT, TEE-HEE.
TEE-HEE, ME TOO.
YOU KNOW, WE'VE PROBABLY MET LOADS OF TIMES, MAYBE EVEN BEEN ON HOLIDAY TOGETHER - BUT WE'VE ALWAYS BEEN TOO DRUNK TO REMEMBER!
HA HA HA HA HA HA HA HA HA HA HA HA HA!!
TEE-HEE...

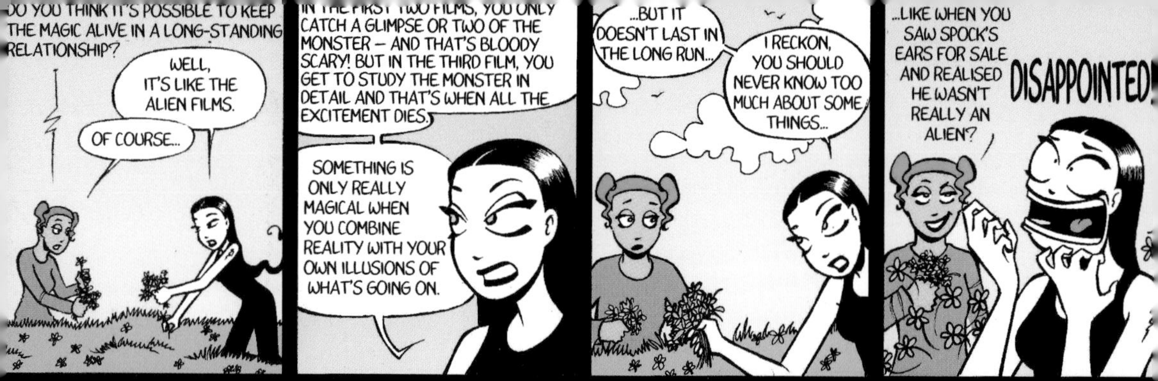
DO YOU THINK IT'S POSSIBLE TO KEEP THE MAGIC ALIVE IN A LONG-STANDING RELATIONSHIP?
WELL, IT'S LIKE THE ALIEN FILMS.
OF COURSE...
IN THE FIRST TWO FILMS, YOU ONLY CATCH A GLIMPSE OR TWO OF THE MONSTER – AND THAT'S BLOODY SCARY! BUT IN THE THIRD FILM, YOU GET TO STUDY THE MONSTER IN DETAIL AND THAT'S WHEN ALL THE EXCITEMENT DIES.
SOMETHING IS ONLY REALLY MAGICAL WHEN YOU COMBINE REALITY WITH YOUR OWN ILLUSIONS OF WHAT'S GOING ON.
...BUT IT DOESN'T LAST IN THE LONG RUN...
I RECKON, YOU SHOULD NEVER KNOW TOO MUCH ABOUT SOME THINGS...
...LIKE WHEN YOU SAW SPOCK'S EARS FOR SALE AND REALISED HE WASN'T REALLY AN ALIEN?
DISAPPOINTED!

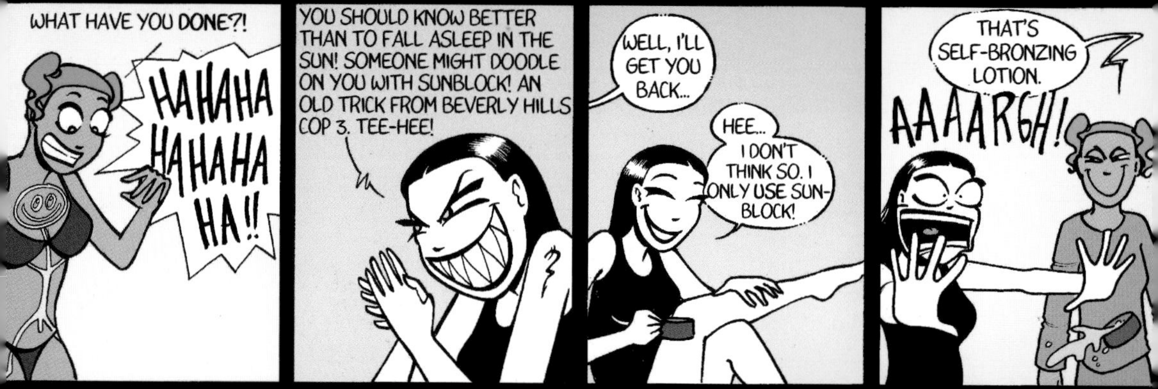
WHAT HAVE YOU DONE?!
HAHAHA HAHAHA HA!!
YOU SHOULD KNOW BETTER THAN TO FALL ASLEEP IN THE SUN! SOMEONE MIGHT DOODLE ON YOU WITH SUNBLOCK! AN OLD TRICK FROM BEVERLY HILLS COP 3. TEE-HEE!
WELL, I'LL GET YOU BACK...
HEE... I DON'T THINK SO. I ONLY USE SUN-BLOCK!
THAT'S SELF-BRONZING LOTION.
AAAARGH!

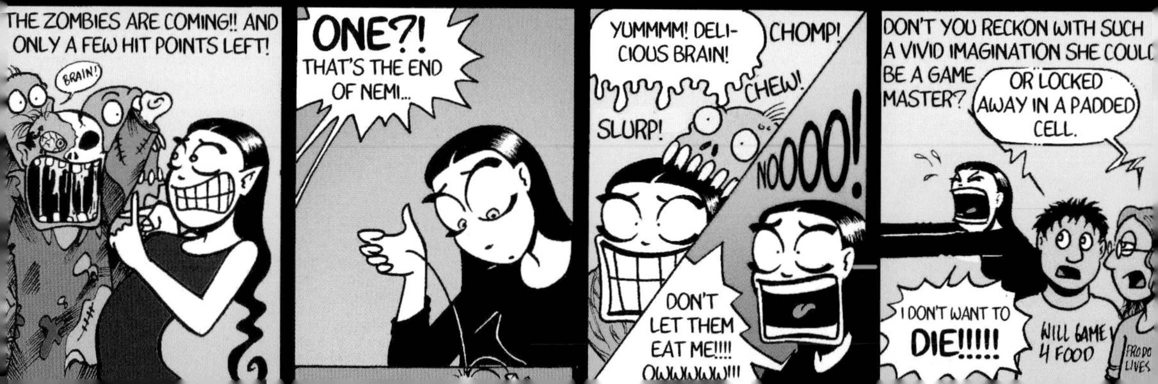
THE ZOMBIES ARE COMING!! AND ONLY A FEW HIT POINTS LEFT!
BRAIN!
ONE?!
THAT'S THE END OF NEMI...
YUMMMM! DELI-CIOUS BRAIN!
CHOMP!
CHEW!
SLURP!
NOOOO!
DON'T LET THEM EAT ME!!!!
DON'T YOU RECKON WITH SUCH A VIVID IMAGINATION SHE COULD BE A GAME MASTER?
OR LOCKED AWAY IN A PADDED CELL.
I DON'T WANT TO DIE!!!!!
WILL GAME 4 FOOD
FRODO LIVES

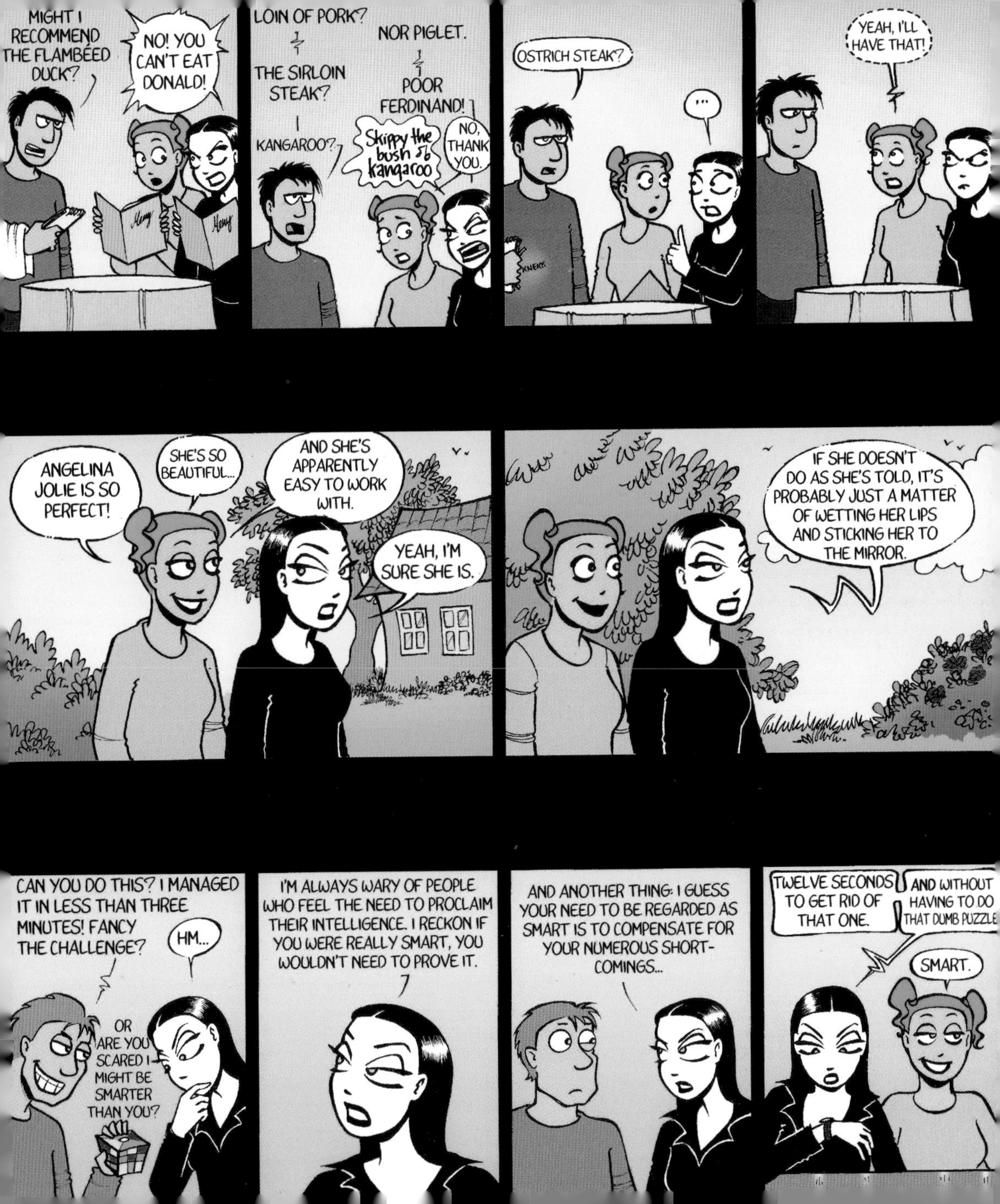
MIGHT I RECOMMEND THE FLAMBÉED DUCK?
NO! YOU CAN'T EAT DONALD!
LOIN OF PORK?
NOR PIGLET.
THE SIRLOIN STEAK?
POOR FERDINAND!
KANGAROO?
Skippy the bush kangaroo
NO, THANK YOU.
OSTRICH STEAK?
...
YEAH, I'LL HAVE THAT!
ANGELINA JOLIE IS SO PERFECT!
SHE'S SO BEAUTIFUL...
AND SHE'S APPARENTLY EASY TO WORK WITH.
YEAH, I'M SURE SHE IS.
IF SHE DOESN'T DO AS SHE'S TOLD, IT'S PROBABLY JUST A MATTER OF WETTING HER LIPS AND STICKING HER TO THE MIRROR.
CAN YOU DO THIS? I MANAGED IT IN LESS THAN THREE MINUTES! FANCY THE CHALLENGE?
HM...
OR ARE YOU SCARED I MIGHT BE SMARTER THAN YOU?
I'M ALWAYS WARY OF PEOPLE WHO FEEL THE NEED TO PROCLAIM THEIR INTELLIGENCE. I RECKON IF YOU WERE REALLY SMART, YOU WOULDN'T NEED TO PROVE IT.
AND ANOTHER THING: I GUESS YOUR NEED TO BE REGARDED AS SMART IS TO COMPENSATE FOR YOUR NUMEROUS SHORT-COMINGS...
TWELVE SECONDS TO GET RID OF THAT ONE.
AND WITHOUT HAVING TO DO THAT DUMB PUZZLE
SMART.

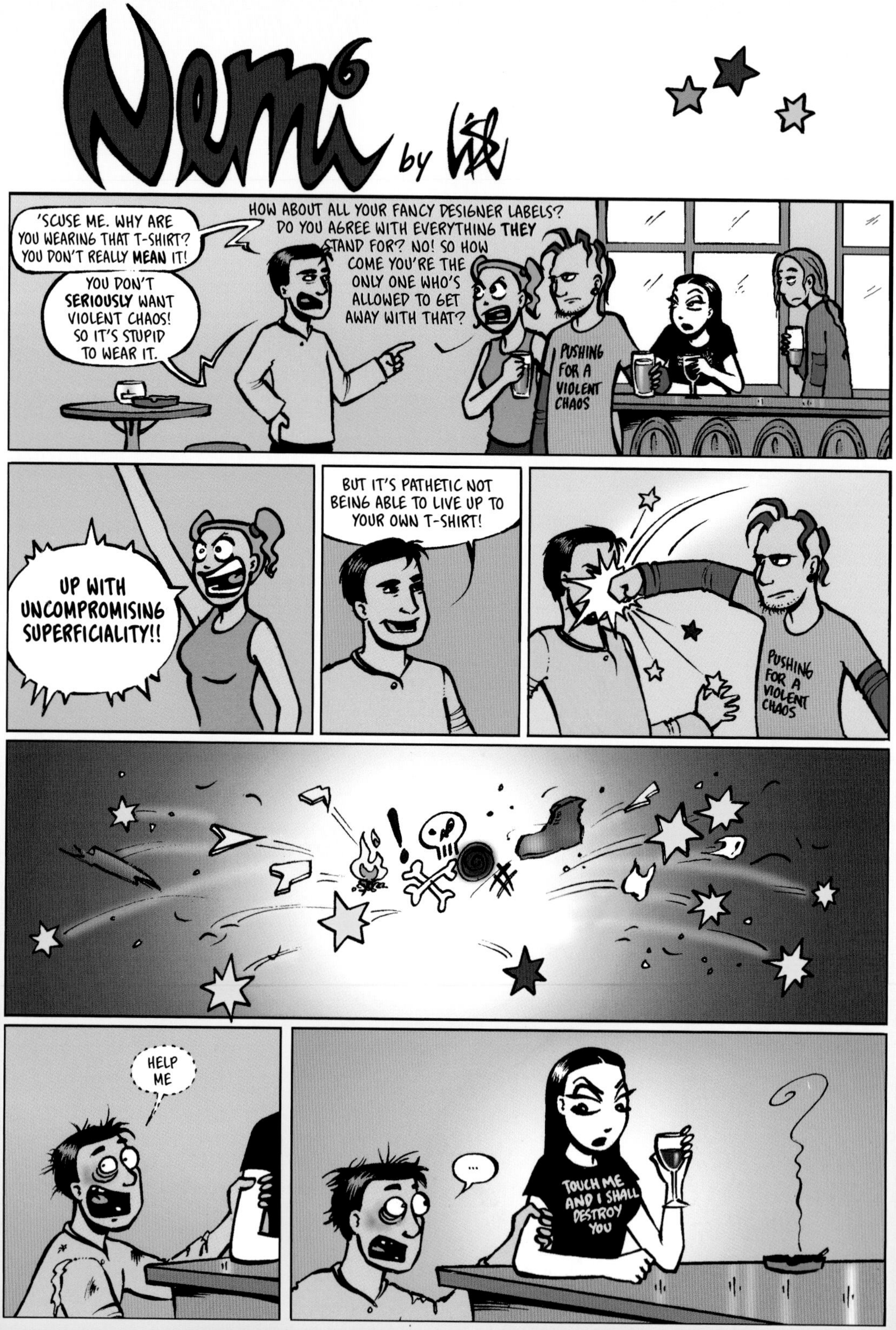
Nemi by Lise
'SCUSE ME. WHY ARE YOU WEARING THAT T-SHIRT? YOU DON'T REALLY MEAN IT!
YOU DON'T SERIOUSLY WANT VIOLENT CHAOS! SO IT'S STUPID TO WEAR IT.
HOW ABOUT ALL YOUR FANCY DESIGNER LABELS? DO YOU AGREE WITH EVERYTHING THEY STAND FOR? NO! SO HOW COME YOU'RE THE ONLY ONE WHO'S ALLOWED TO GET AWAY WITH THAT?
PUSHING FOR A VIOLENT CHAOS
UP WITH UNCOMPROMISING SUPERFICIALITY!!
BUT IT'S PATHETIC NOT BEING ABLE TO LIVE UP TO YOUR OWN T-SHIRT!
PUSHING FOR A VIOLENT CHAOS
!
HELP ME
...
TOUCH ME AND I SHALL DESTROY YOU

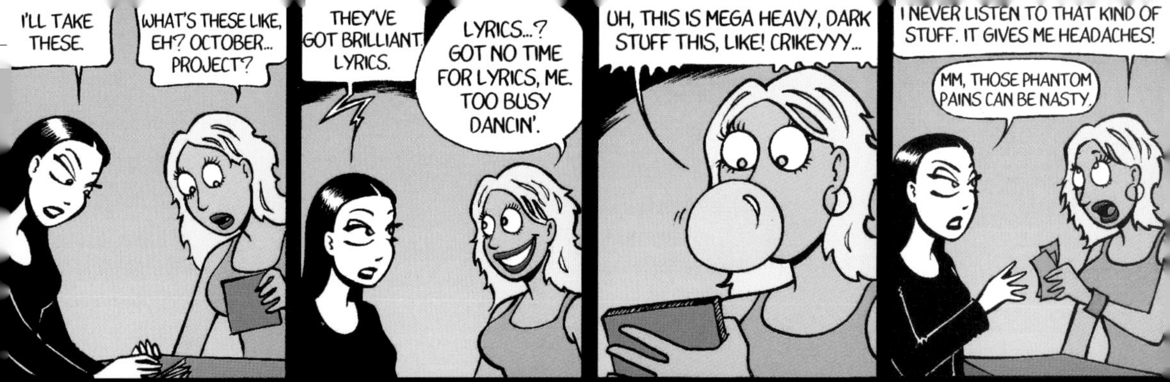
I'LL TAKE THESE.
WHAT'S THESE LIKE, EH? OCTOBER... PROJECT?
THEY'VE GOT BRILLIANT LYRICS.
LYRICS...? GOT NO TIME FOR LYRICS, ME. TOO BUSY DANCIN'.
UH, THIS IS MEGA HEAVY, DARK STUFF THIS, LIKE! CRIKEYYY...
I NEVER LISTEN TO THAT KIND OF STUFF. IT GIVES ME HEADACHES!
MM, THOSE PHANTOM PAINS CAN BE NASTY.

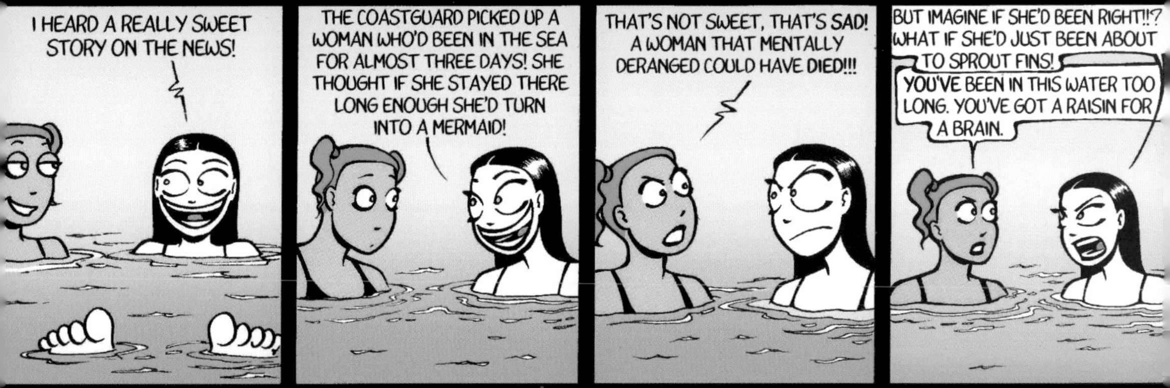
I HEARD A REALLY SWEET STORY ON THE NEWS!
THE COASTGUARD PICKED UP A WOMAN WHO'D BEEN IN THE SEA FOR ALMOST THREE DAYS! SHE THOUGHT IF SHE STAYED THERE LONG ENOUGH SHE'D TURN INTO A MERMAID!
THAT'S NOT SWEET, THAT'S SAD! A WOMAN THAT MENTALLY DERANGED COULD HAVE DIED!!!
BUT IMAGINE IF SHE'D BEEN RIGHT!!? WHAT IF SHE'D JUST BEEN ABOUT TO SPROUT FINS!
YOU'VE BEEN IN THIS WATER TOO LONG. YOU'VE GOT A RAISIN FOR A BRAIN.

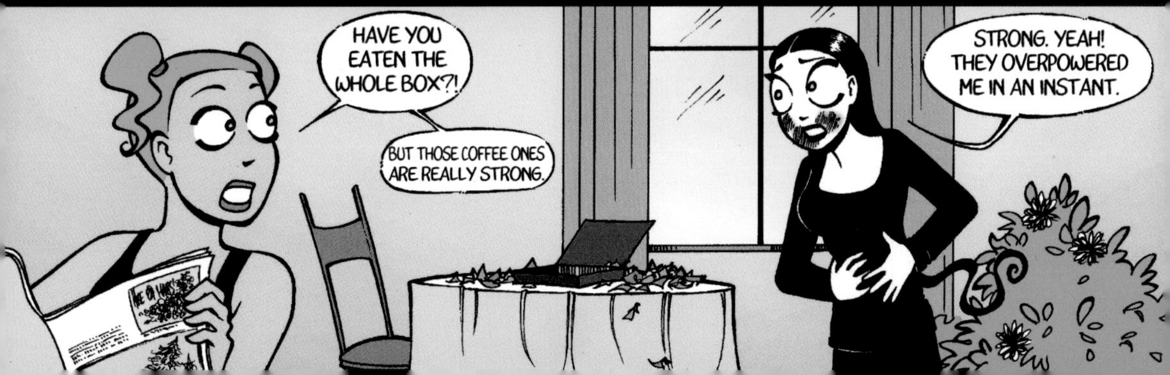
HAVE YOU EATEN THE WHOLE BOX?!
BUT THOSE COFFEE ONES ARE REALLY STRONG.
STRONG. YEAH! THEY OVERPOWERED ME IN AN INSTANT.

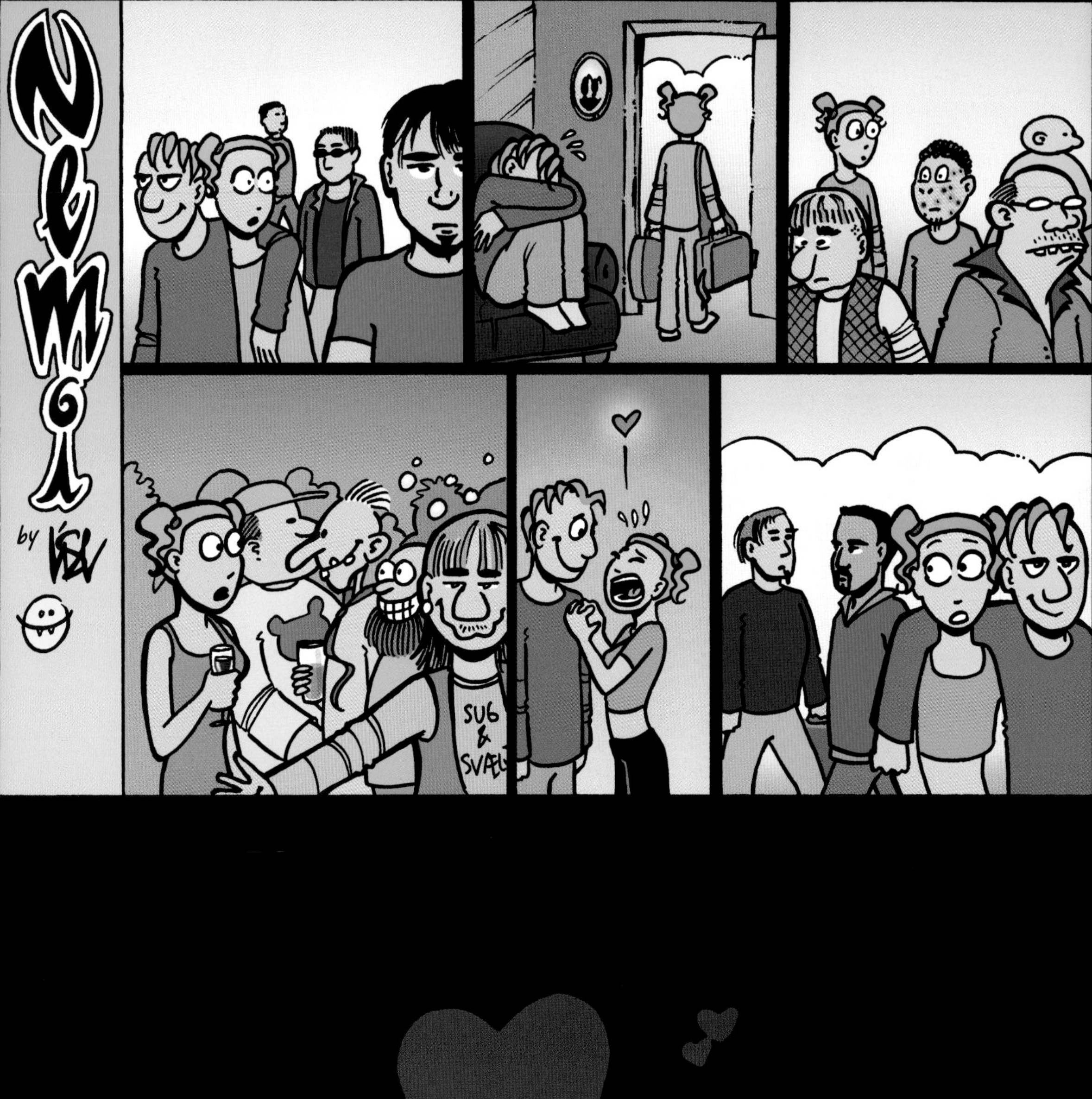
Nemi
by
SUG
&
SVÆL

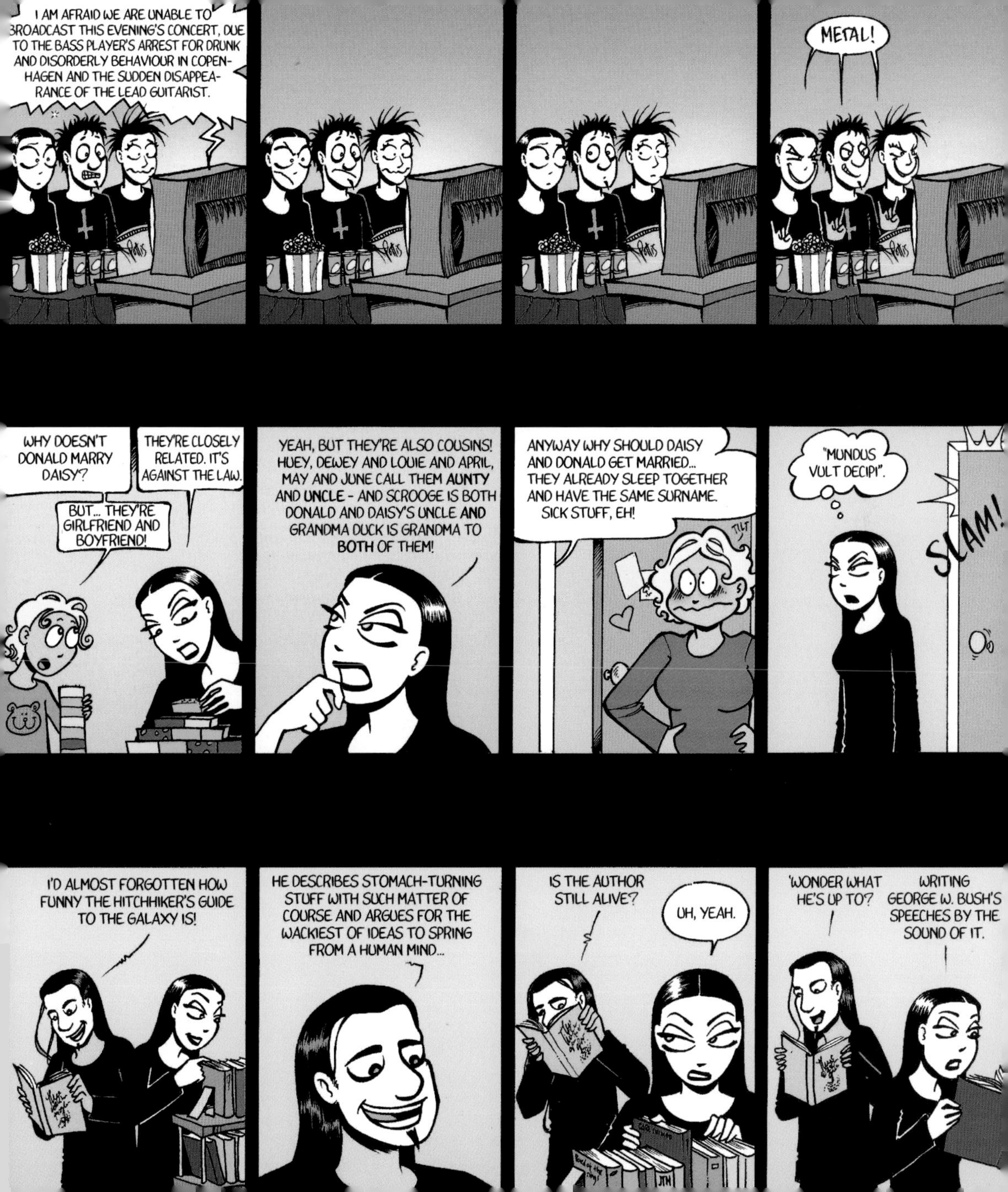

I AM AFRAID WE ARE UNABLE TO BROADCAST THIS EVENING'S CONCERT, DUE TO THE BASS PLAYER'S ARREST FOR DRUNK AND DISORDERLY BEHAVIOUR IN COPENHAGEN AND THE SUDDEN DISAPPEARANCE OF THE LEAD GUITARIST.
METAL!
WHY DOESN'T DONALD MARRY DAISY?
THEY'RE CLOSELY RELATED. IT'S AGAINST THE LAW.
BUT... THEY'RE GIRLFRIEND AND BOYFRIEND!
YEAH, BUT THEY'RE ALSO COUSINS! HUEY, DEWEY AND LOUIE AND APRIL, MAY AND JUNE CALL THEM AUNTY AND UNCLE - AND SCROOGE IS BOTH DONALD AND DAISY'S UNCLE AND GRANDMA DUCK IS GRANDMA TO BOTH OF THEM!
ANYWAY WHY SHOULD DAISY AND DONALD GET MARRIED... THEY ALREADY SLEEP TOGETHER AND HAVE THE SAME SURNAME. SICK STUFF, EH!
TILT
"MUNDUS VULT DECIPI".
SLAM!
I'D ALMOST FORGOTTEN HOW FUNNY THE HITCHHIKER'S GUIDE TO THE GALAXY IS!
HE DESCRIBES STOMACH-TURNING STUFF WITH SUCH MATTER OF COURSE AND ARGUES FOR THE WACKIEST OF IDEAS TO SPRING FROM A HUMAN MIND...
IS THE AUTHOR STILL ALIVE?
UH, YEAH.
'WONDER WHAT HE'S UP TO?
WRITING GEORGE W. BUSH'S SPEECHES BY THE SOUND OF IT.

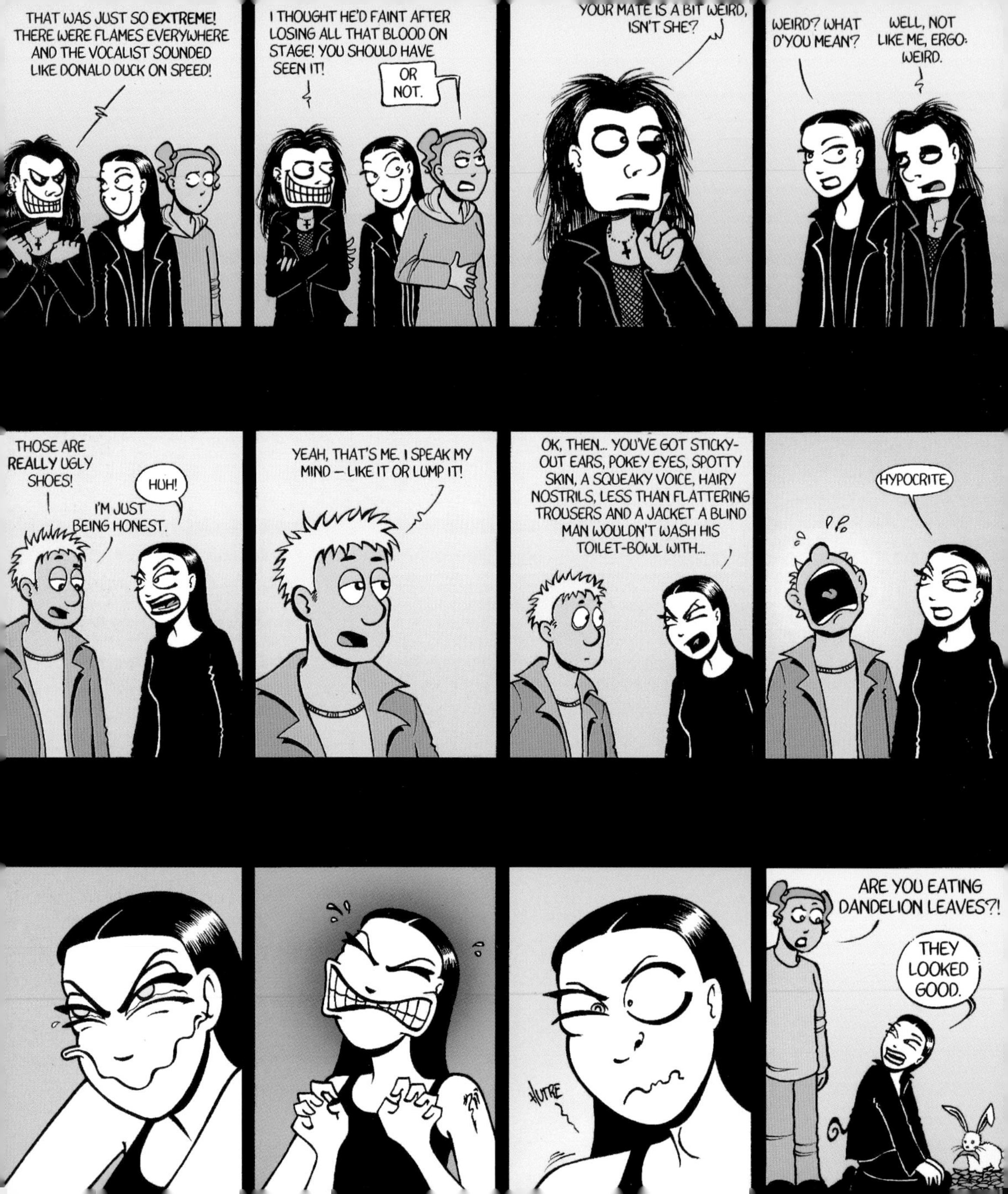

THAT WAS JUST SO EXTREME! THERE WERE FLAMES EVERYWHERE AND THE VOCALIST SOUNDED LIKE DONALD DUCK ON SPEED!
I THOUGHT HE'D FAINT AFTER LOSING ALL THAT BLOOD ON STAGE! YOU SHOULD HAVE SEEN IT!
OR NOT.
YOUR MATE IS A BIT WEIRD, ISN'T SHE?
WEIRD? WHAT D'YOU MEAN?
WELL, NOT LIKE ME, ERGO: WEIRD.
THOSE ARE REALLY UGLY SHOES!
HUH!
I'M JUST BEING HONEST.
YEAH, THAT'S ME. I SPEAK MY MIND – LIKE IT OR LUMP IT!
OK, THEN... YOU'VE GOT STICKY-OUT EARS, POKEY EYES, SPOTTY SKIN, A SQUEAKY VOICE, HAIRY NOSTRILS, LESS THAN FLATTERING TROUSERS AND A JACKET A BLIND MAN WOULDN'T WASH HIS TOILET-BOWL WITH...
HYPOCRITE.
ARE YOU EATING DANDELION LEAVES?!
THEY LOOKED GOOD.

Nemi by Lise
BANG BANG BANG
AAAAA
AAAAAAAA
BWAAAAAARGHA!
SHRIEK!
GAH! COUGH
BLAM!
YOU DO KNOW THE LOCAL KIDS CHARGE PEOPLE FOR VIEWINGS OF YOUR MORNING FACE?
SHUT UP!

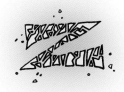

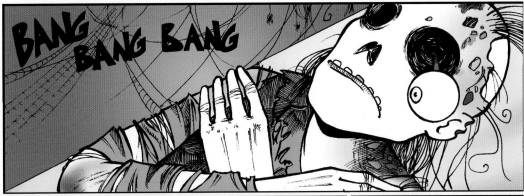

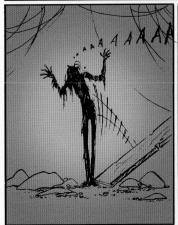

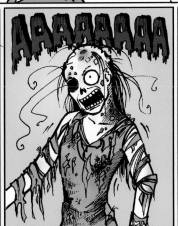

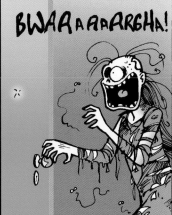

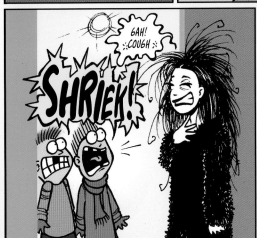

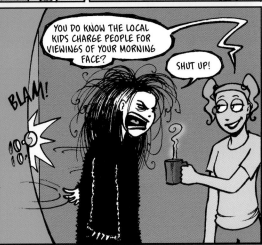

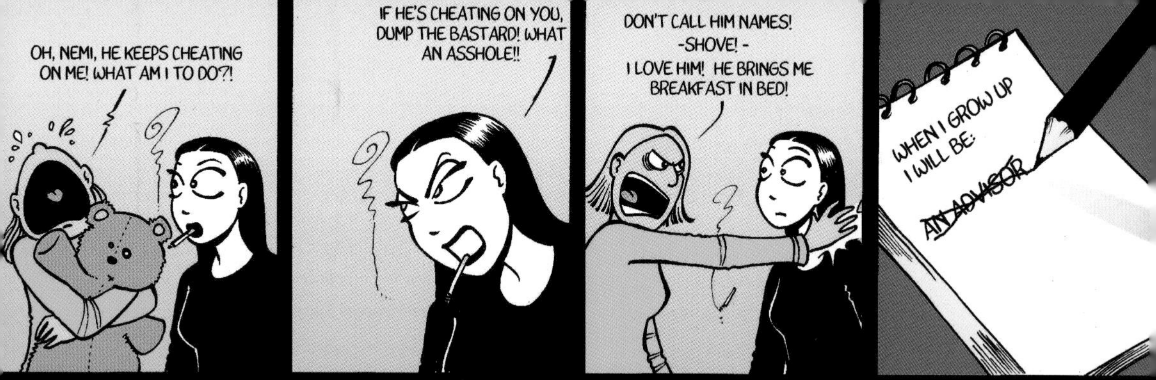
OH, NEMI, HE KEEPS CHEATING ON ME! WHAT AM I TO DO?!
IF HE'S CHEATING ON YOU, DUMP THE BASTARD! WHAT AN ASSHOLE!!
DON'T CALL HIM NAMES!
-SHOVE! -
I LOVE HIM! HE BRINGS ME BREAKFAST IN BED!
WHEN I GROW UP I WILL BE:
AN ADVISOR

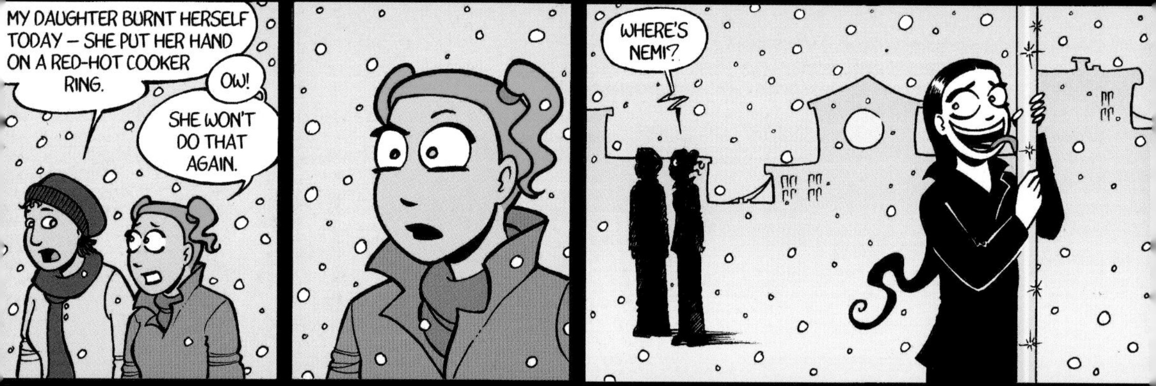
MY DAUGHTER BURNT HERSELF TODAY – SHE PUT HER HAND ON A RED-HOT COOKER RING.
OW!
SHE WON'T DO THAT AGAIN.
WHERE'S NEMI?

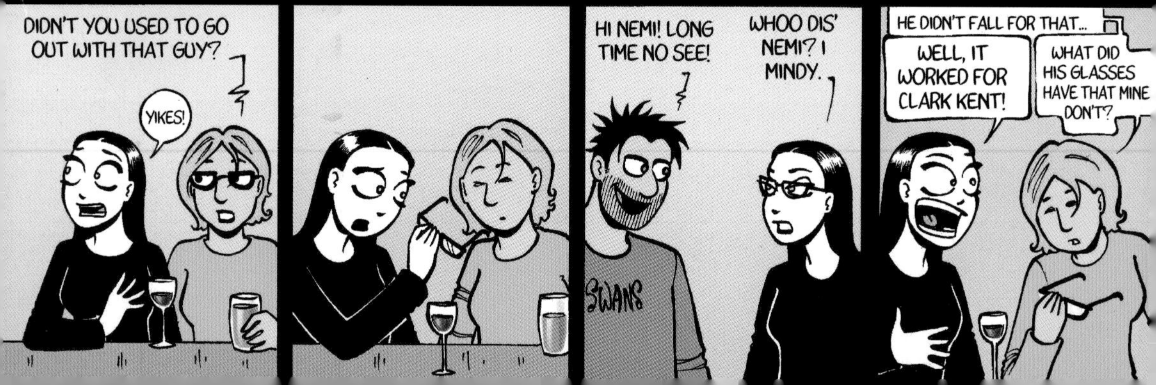
DIDN'T YOU USED TO GO OUT WITH THAT GUY?
YIKES!
HI NEMI! LONG TIME NO SEE!
WHOO DIS' NEMI? I MINDY.
SWANS
HE DIDN'T FALL FOR THAT...
WELL, IT WORKED FOR CLARK KENT!
WHAT DID HIS GLASSES HAVE THAT MINE DON'T?

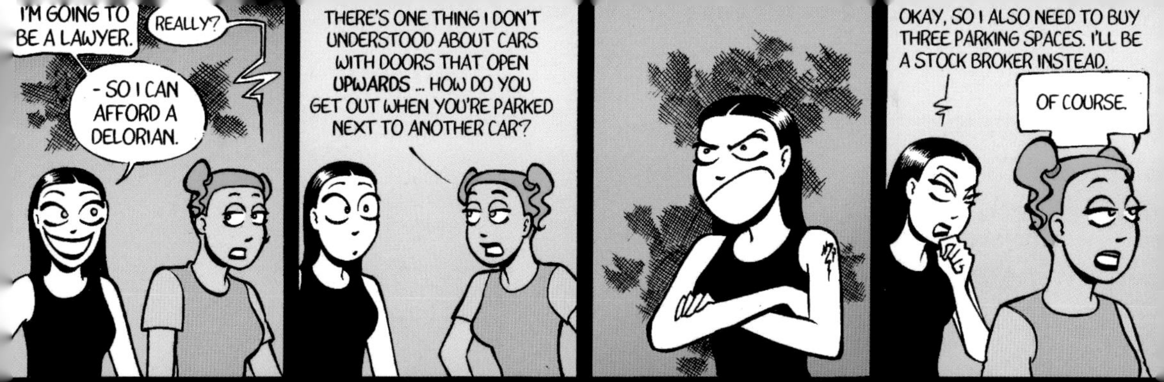
I'M GOING TO BE A LAWYER.
REALLY?
- SO I CAN AFFORD A DELORIAN.
THERE'S ONE THING I DON'T UNDERSTOOD ABOUT CARS WITH DOORS THAT OPEN **UPWARDS** ... HOW DO YOU GET OUT WHEN YOU'RE PARKED NEXT TO ANOTHER CAR?
OKAY, SO I ALSO NEED TO BUY THREE PARKING SPACES. I'LL BE A STOCK BROKER INSTEAD.
OF COURSE.

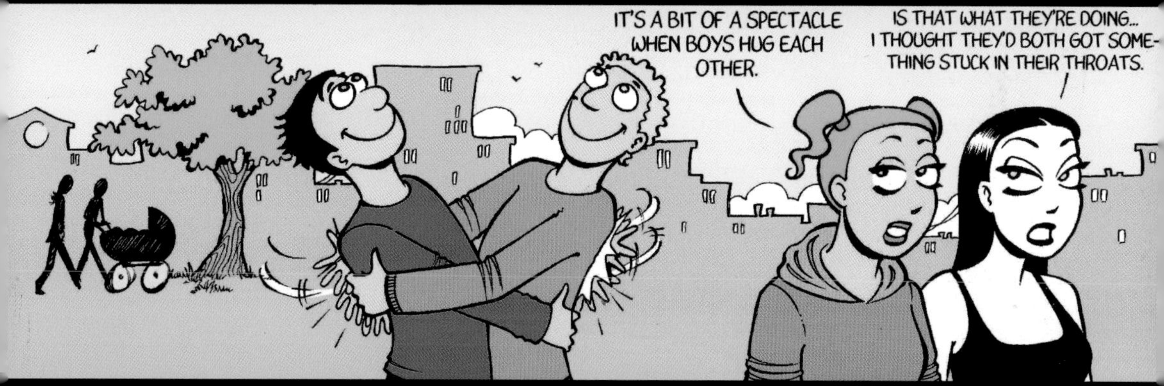
IT'S A BIT OF A SPECTACLE WHEN BOYS HUG EACH OTHER.
IS THAT WHAT THEY'RE DOING... I THOUGHT THEY'D BOTH GOT SOMETHING STUCK IN THEIR THROATS.

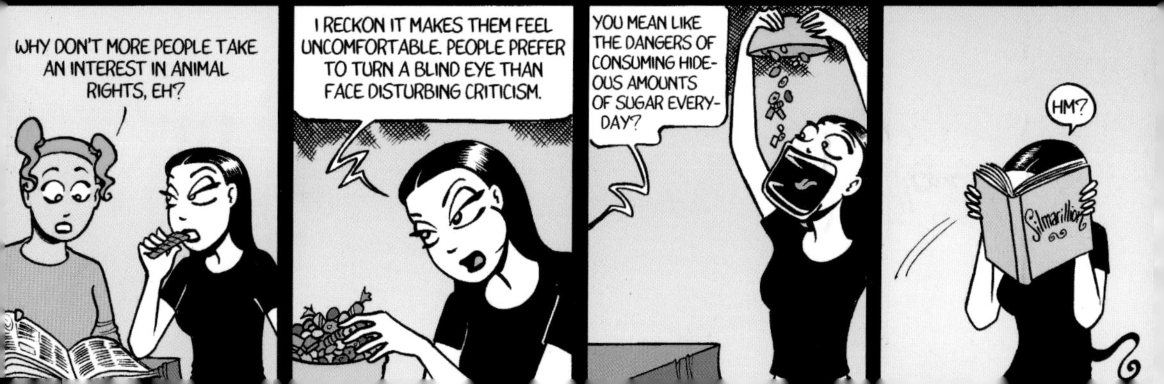
WHY DON'T MORE PEOPLE TAKE AN INTEREST IN ANIMAL RIGHTS, EH?
I RECKON IT MAKES THEM FEEL UNCOMFORTABLE. PEOPLE PREFER TO TURN A BLIND EYE THAN FACE DISTURBING CRITICISM.
YOU MEAN LIKE THE DANGERS OF CONSUMING HIDEOUS AMOUNTS OF SUGAR EVERYDAY?
HM?
Silmarillion

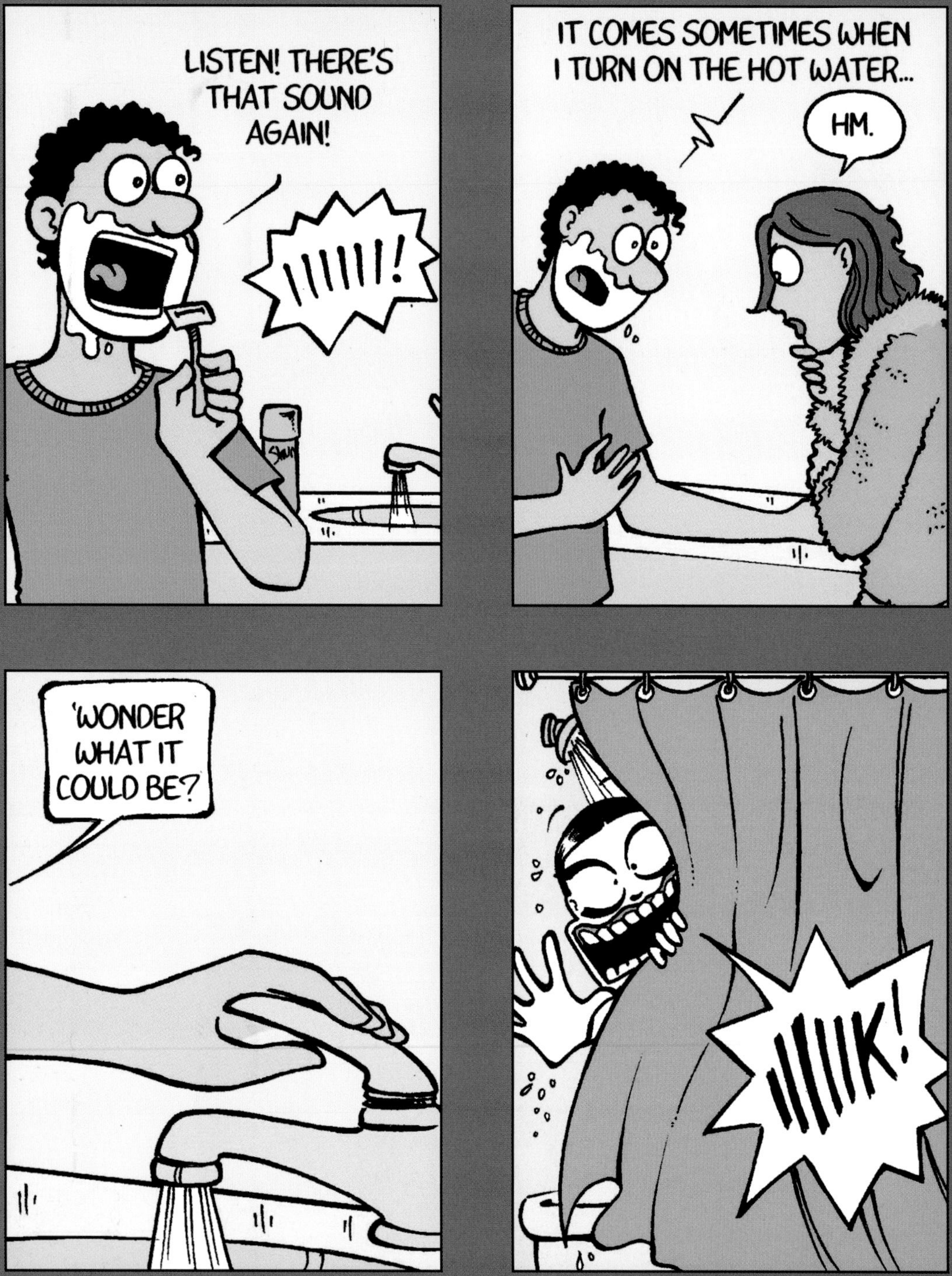
LISTEN! THERE'S THAT SOUND AGAIN!
!!!!!!!
IT COMES SOMETIMES WHEN I TURN ON THE HOT WATER...
HM.
'WONDER WHAT IT COULD BE?
!!!!!K!

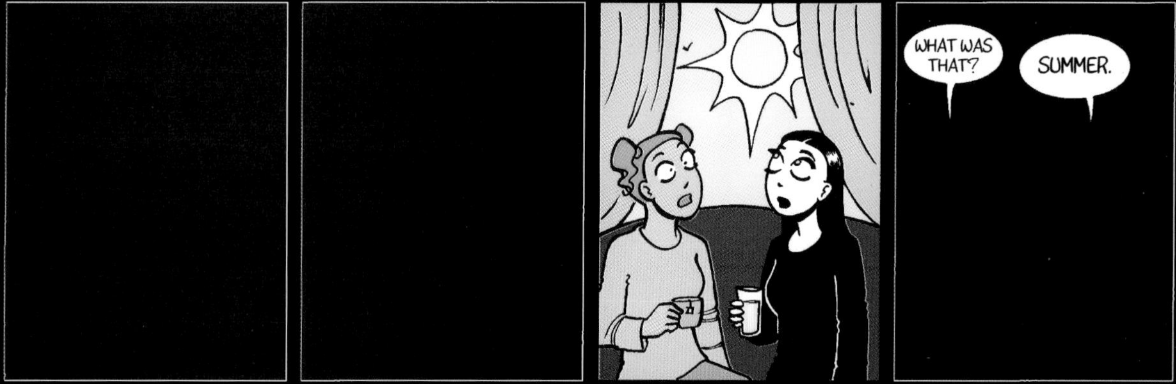
WHAT WAS THAT?
SUMMER.

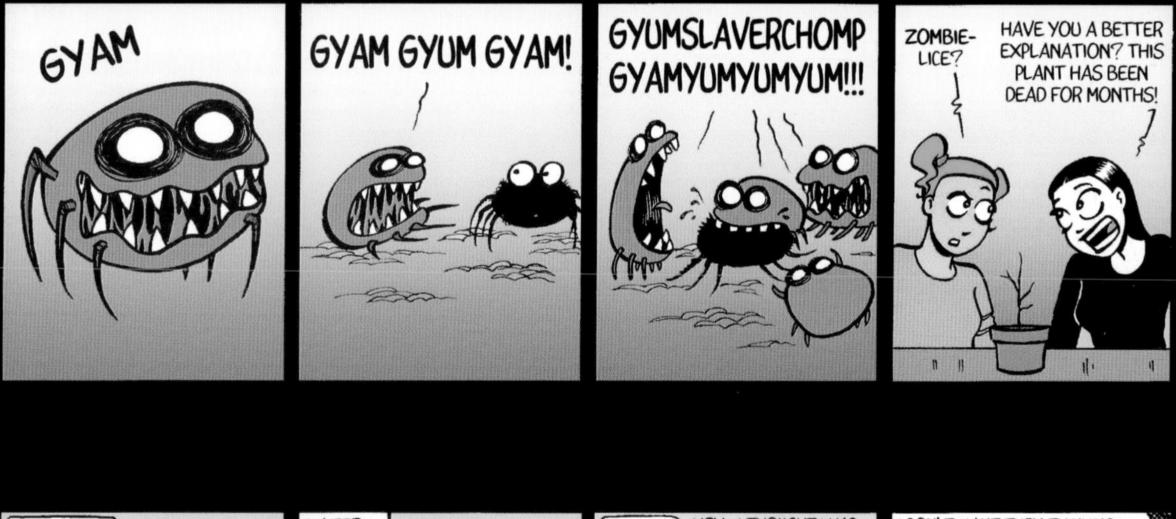
GYAM
GYAM GYUM GYAM!
GYUMSLAVERCHOMP GYAMYUMYUMYUM!!!
ZOMBIE-LICE?
HAVE YOU A BETTER EXPLANATION? THIS PLANT HAS BEEN DEAD FOR MONTHS!

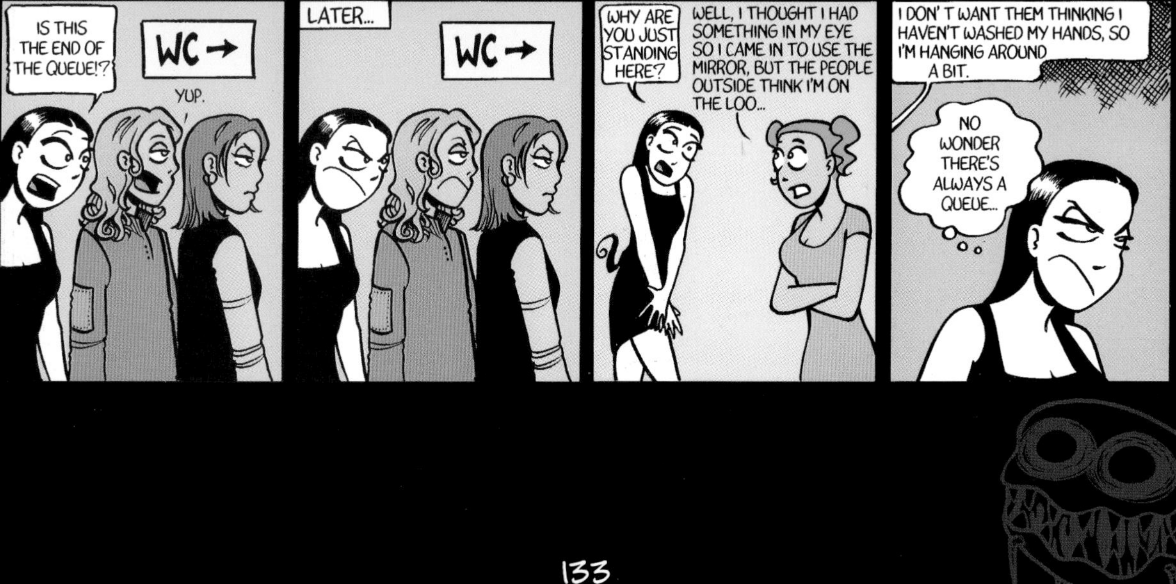
IS THIS THE END OF THE QUEUE!?
WC →
YUP.
LATER...
WC →
WHY ARE YOU JUST STANDING HERE?
WELL, I THOUGHT I HAD SOMETHING IN MY EYE SO I CAME IN TO USE THE MIRROR, BUT THE PEOPLE OUTSIDE THINK I'M ON THE LOO...
I DON'T WANT THEM THINKING I HAVEN'T WASHED MY HANDS, SO I'M HANGING AROUND A BIT.
NO WONDER THERE'S ALWAYS A QUEUE...

Panel 1: AAAGH! THERE'S AN ENORMOUS SPIDER IN YOUR HALLWAY!

Panel 2: DON'T KILL IT!

Panel 3: NEMI, YOU CAN NEVER KILL ANYTHING...

Panel 4: EVER.

Panel 5: COMING OUT TONIGHT? / I'M SORRY, I CAN'T. I'VE NO CLEAN CLOTHES!

Panel 6: OH, GO ON, YOU PROMISED! / SERIOUSLY, I HAVEN'T DONE ANY LAUNDRY FOR AGES!

Panel 7: I MIGHT HAVE SOME WEIRD STUFF AT THE BACK OF MY WARDROBE... / WEAR THAT! I'LL FIND A PLACE WHERE YOU WON'T STAND OUT!

Panel 8: GOOD LUCK.

Panel 9: I RECKON ALL THE FUN OF MEETING NEW PEOPLE HAS GONE... IT USED TO BE GREAT, BUT...

Panel 10: NOW IT'S ALMOST TEDIOUS. YOU SEEM TO KNOW A PERSON BEFORE THEY'VE OPENED THEIR MOUTH.

Panel 11: ANYONE YOU MEET NOW IS SOMEONE YOU'VE MET BEFORE – IF YOU KNOW WHAT I MEAN? / HM.

Panel 12: THERE ARE ALWAYS EXCEPTIONS, THOUGH...

 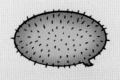

HAVE YOU SEEN LATEST?

EH?

DON'T YOU LIKE?

I'VE ASKED TOM TO TURN THE MUSIC DOWN. IT'S IMPOSSIBLE TO HEAR WHAT ANYONE'S SAYING IN HERE...

I KNOW.

I TOLD HIM, I SAID... "YOU'RE MAD", I SAID. MAD, MAD, MAD.

YUCK! DON'T WALK THERE. THERE'S PUKE ON THE FLOOR!

OY! LOOK AT THEM TITS!

YOU LOOKED AT HER! ADMIT IT: YOU LOOKED AT HER. YES YOU DID!

I THOUGHT IT WAS SOMEONE I KNEW.

HE MUST HAVE EATEN SOME WEIRD STUFF. LOOK. GREEN BITS!

YOU'RE DEAD.

YOU ⊙☆✏ TART! ARE YOU DANCING WITH THAT SHITE! ☆✳♪

RATS TALES

I KNOW I HELD FOUR FINGERS UP, BUT I WANTED A BAG OF CRISPS.

WOW! LOOK AT THE ARSE ON HIM!

...NINA'S BLOKE'S GONE, AND WE WANT YOU TO COME HOME WITH US.

BABY. C'MON. GISSA CUDDLE.

COME ON, GIRL! LET'S HAVE A QUICK SHAG IN THE TOILET...!

ENOUGH!

TURN THE ☠🔥🦴 SOUND UP AGAIN!

135

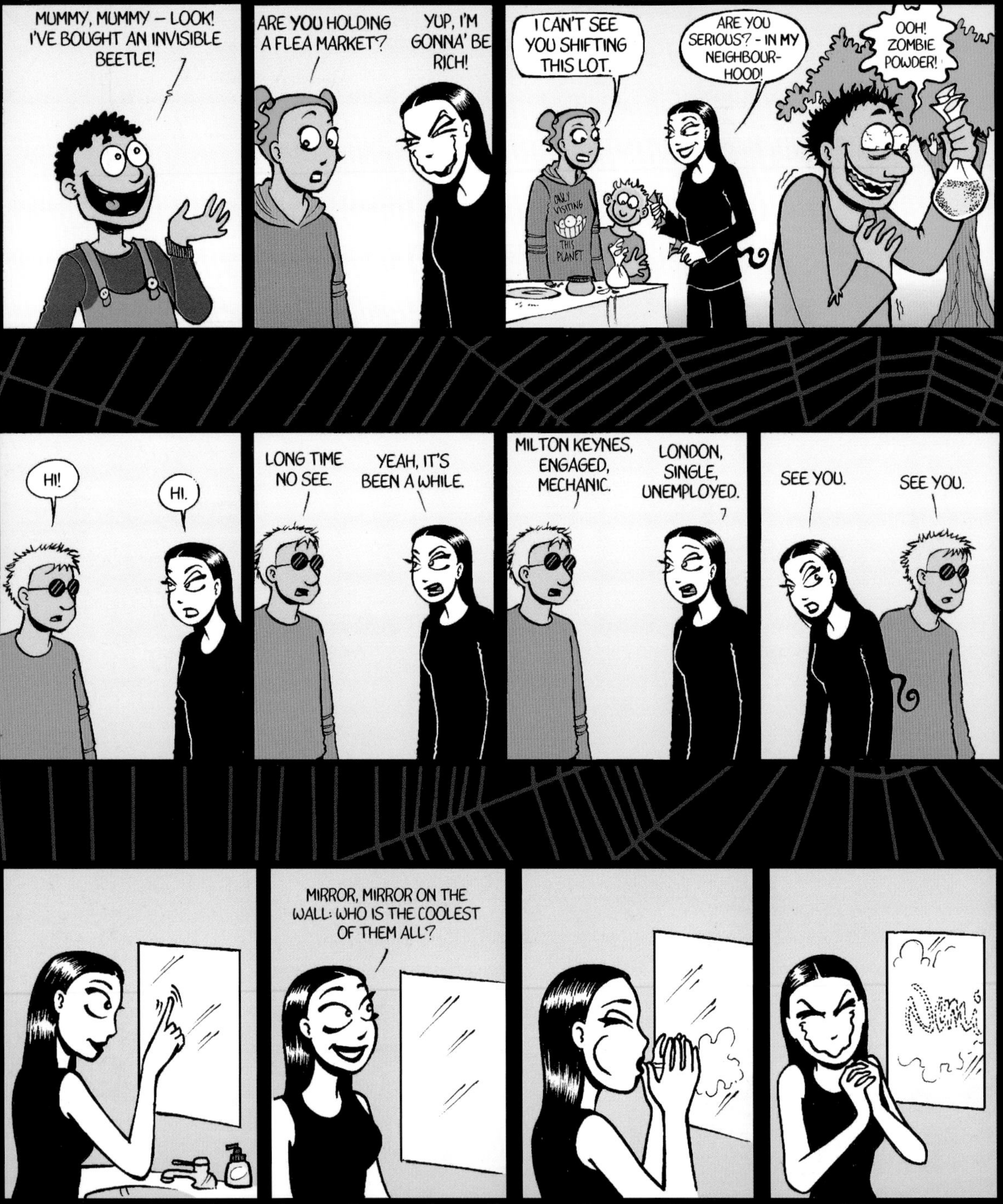
MUMMY, MUMMY — LOOK! I'VE BOUGHT AN INVISIBLE BEETLE!
ARE YOU HOLDING A FLEA MARKET?
YUP, I'M GONNA' BE RICH!
I CAN'T SEE YOU SHIFTING THIS LOT.
ARE YOU SERIOUS? - IN MY NEIGHBOURHOOD!
ONLY VISITING THIS PLANET
OOH! ZOMBIE POWDER!
HI!
HI.
LONG TIME NO SEE.
YEAH, IT'S BEEN A WHILE.
MILTON KEYNES, ENGAGED, MECHANIC.
LONDON, SINGLE, UNEMPLOYED.
SEE YOU.
SEE YOU.
MIRROR, MIRROR ON THE WALL: WHO IS THE COOLEST OF THEM ALL?

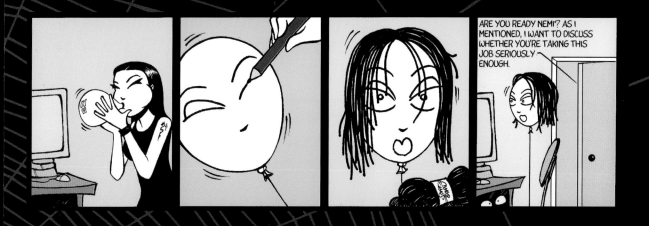

ARE YOU READY NEMI? AS I MENTIONED, I WANT TO DISCUSS WHETHER YOU'RE TAKING THIS JOB SERIOUSLY ENOUGH.

ARE THERE REALLY MORE TRAFFIC ACCIDENTS IN BRITAIN'S BACKWATERS?

I BELIEVE SO.

SEAHORSES ARE SO LOVELY!

MM. THEY ARE MONO-GAMOUS CREATURES TOO.

EVERY MORNING THEY DO A LITTLE DANCE TO SHOW HOW MUCH THEY LOVE EACH OTHER!

I WANT US TO BE LIKE SEA-HORSES!

KINKY!

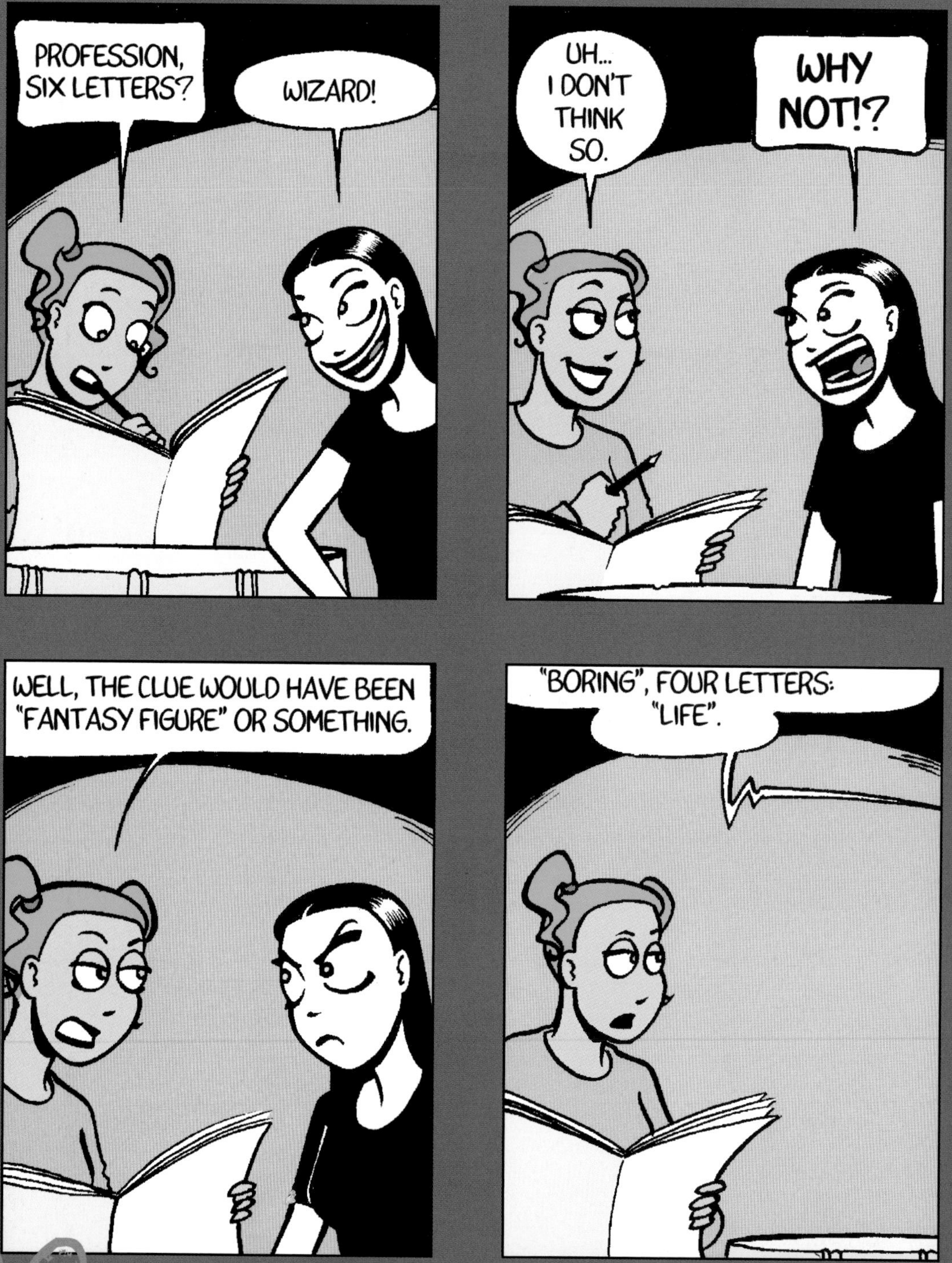
PROFESSION, SIX LETTERS?
WIZARD!
UH... I DON'T THINK SO.
WHY NOT!?
WELL, THE CLUE WOULD HAVE BEEN "FANTASY FIGURE" OR SOMETHING.
"BORING", FOUR LETTERS: "LIFE".

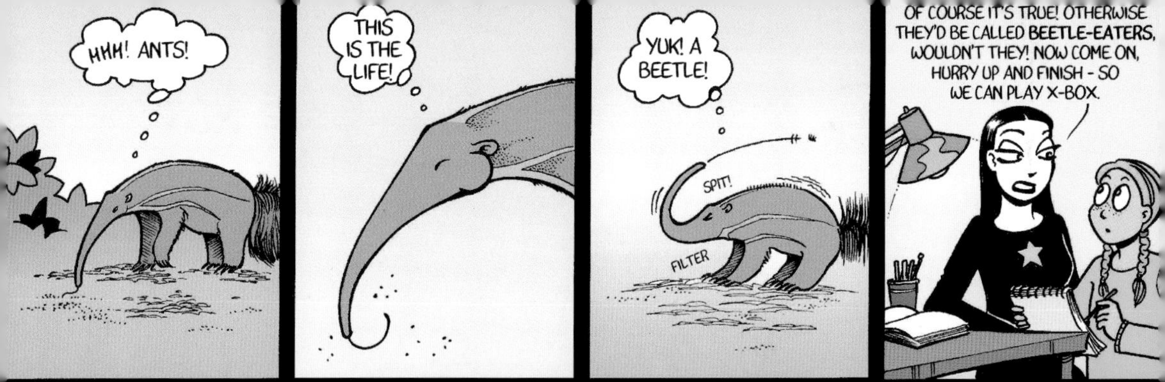
HMM! ANTS!
THIS IS THE LIFE!
YUK! A BEETLE!
SPIT!
FILTER
OF COURSE IT'S TRUE! OTHERWISE THEY'D BE CALLED **BEETLE-EATERS**, WOULDN'T THEY! NOW COME ON, HURRY UP AND FINISH - SO WE CAN PLAY X-BOX.

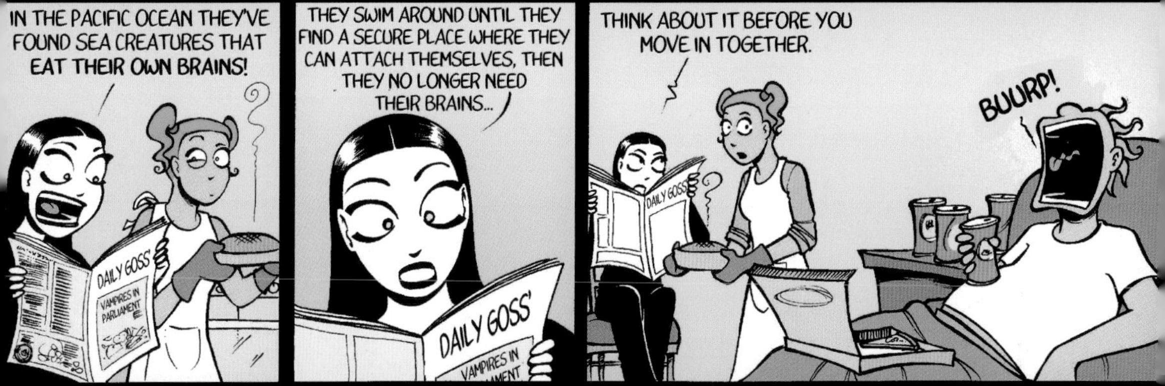
IN THE PACIFIC OCEAN THEY'VE FOUND SEA CREATURES THAT **EAT THEIR OWN BRAINS!**
DAILY GOSS'
VAMPIRES IN PARLIAMENT
THEY SWIM AROUND UNTIL THEY FIND A SECURE PLACE WHERE THEY CAN ATTACH THEMSELVES, THEN THEY NO LONGER NEED THEIR BRAINS...
DAILY GOSS'
THINK ABOUT IT BEFORE YOU MOVE IN TOGETHER.
DAILY GOSS'
BUURP!

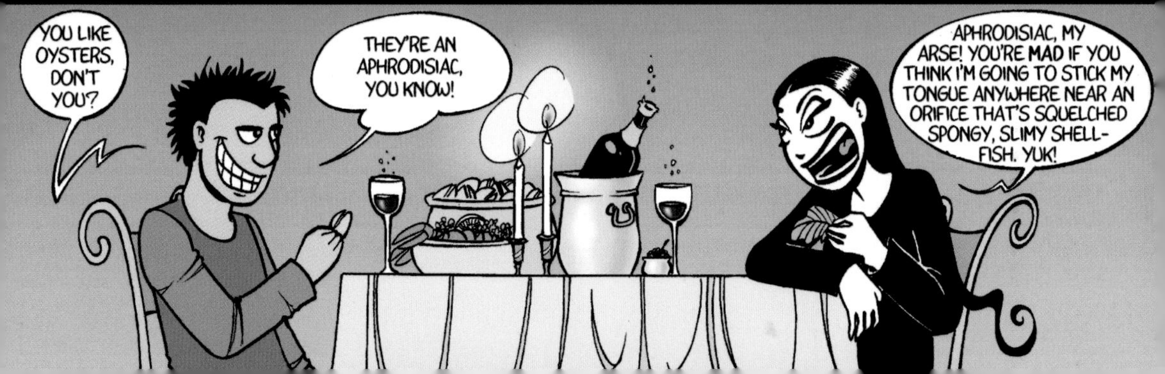
YOU LIKE OYSTERS, DON'T YOU?
THEY'RE AN APHRODISIAC, YOU KNOW!
APHRODISIAC, MY ARSE! YOU'RE **MAD** IF YOU THINK I'M GOING TO STICK MY TONGUE ANYWHERE NEAR AN ORIFICE THAT'S SQUELCHED SPONGY, SLIMY SHELL-FISH. YUK!

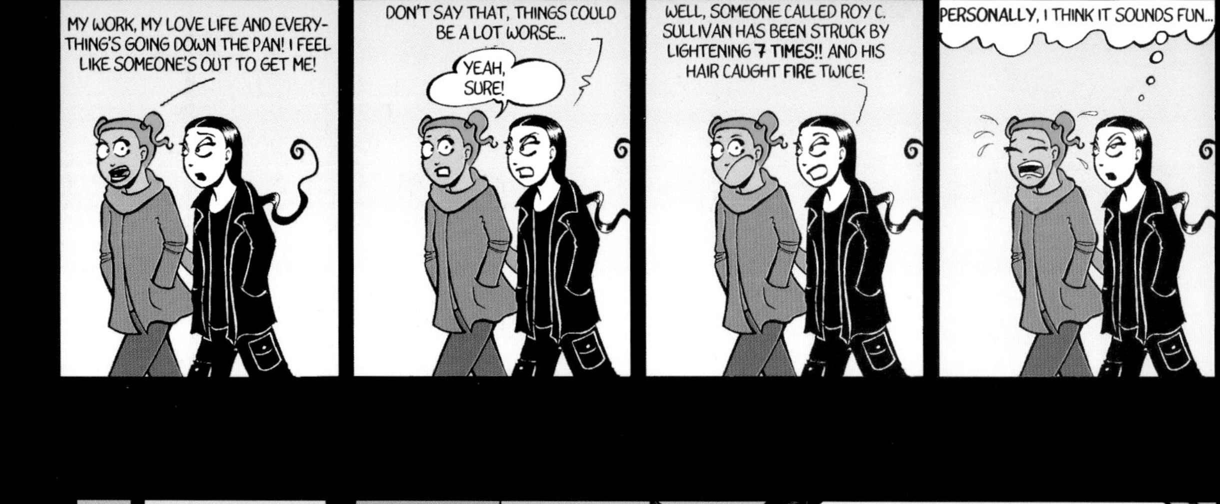
MY WORK, MY LOVE LIFE AND EVERY-THING'S GOING DOWN THE PAN! I FEEL LIKE SOMEONE'S OUT TO GET ME!
DON'T SAY THAT, THINGS COULD BE A LOT WORSE...
YEAH, SURE!
WELL, SOMEONE CALLED ROY C. SULLIVAN HAS BEEN STRUCK BY LIGHTENING 7 TIMES!! AND HIS HAIR CAUGHT FIRE TWICE!
PERSONALLY, I THINK IT SOUNDS FUN...

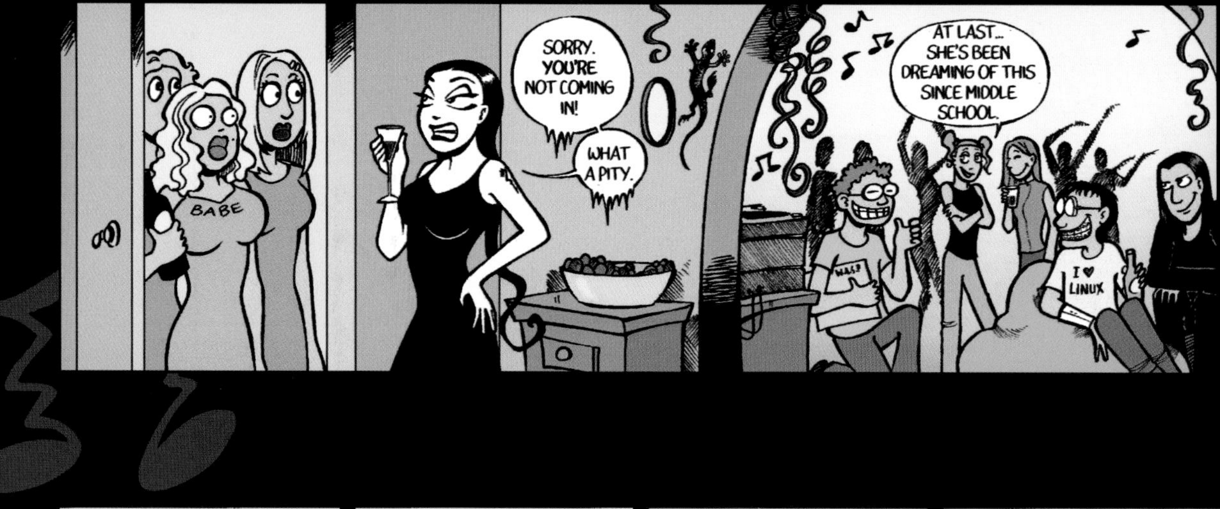
BABE
SORRY. YOU'RE NOT COMING IN!
WHAT A PITY.
AT LAST... SHE'S BEEN DREAMING OF THIS SINCE MIDDLE SCHOOL.
I ♥ LINUX

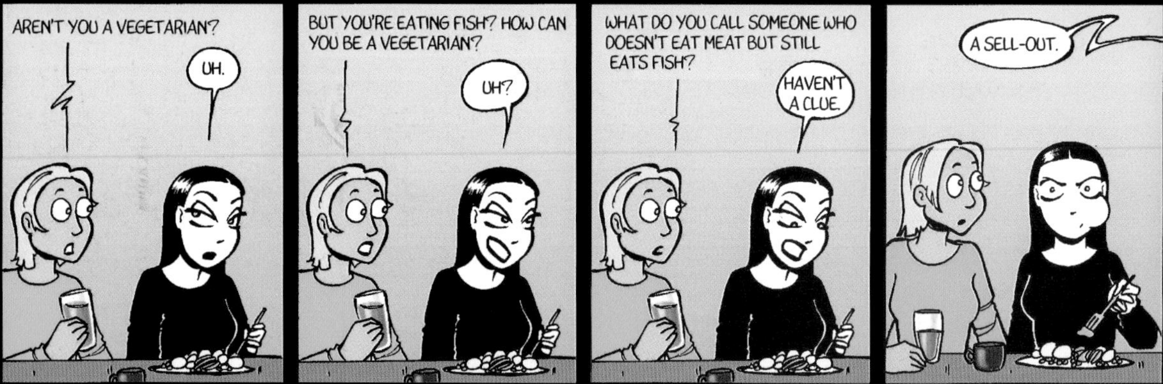
AREN'T YOU A VEGETARIAN?
UH.
BUT YOU'RE EATING FISH? HOW CAN YOU BE A VEGETARIAN?
UH?
WHAT DO YOU CALL SOMEONE WHO DOESN'T EAT MEAT BUT STILL EATS FISH?
HAVEN'T A CLUE.
A SELL-OUT.

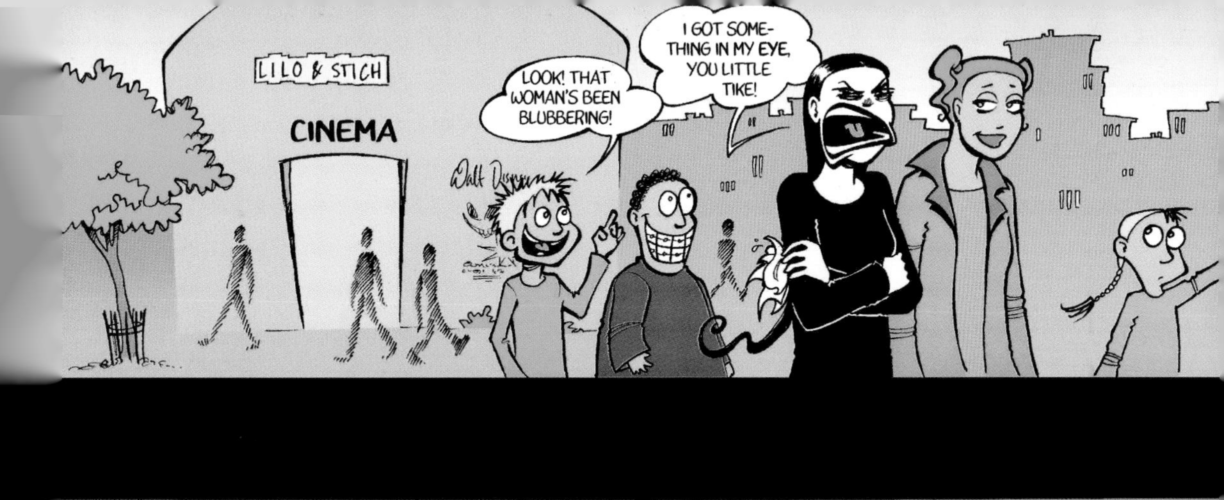
LILO & STICH
CINEMA
LOOK! THAT WOMAN'S BEEN BLUBBERING!
I GOT SOME-THING IN MY EYE, YOU LITTLE TIKE!

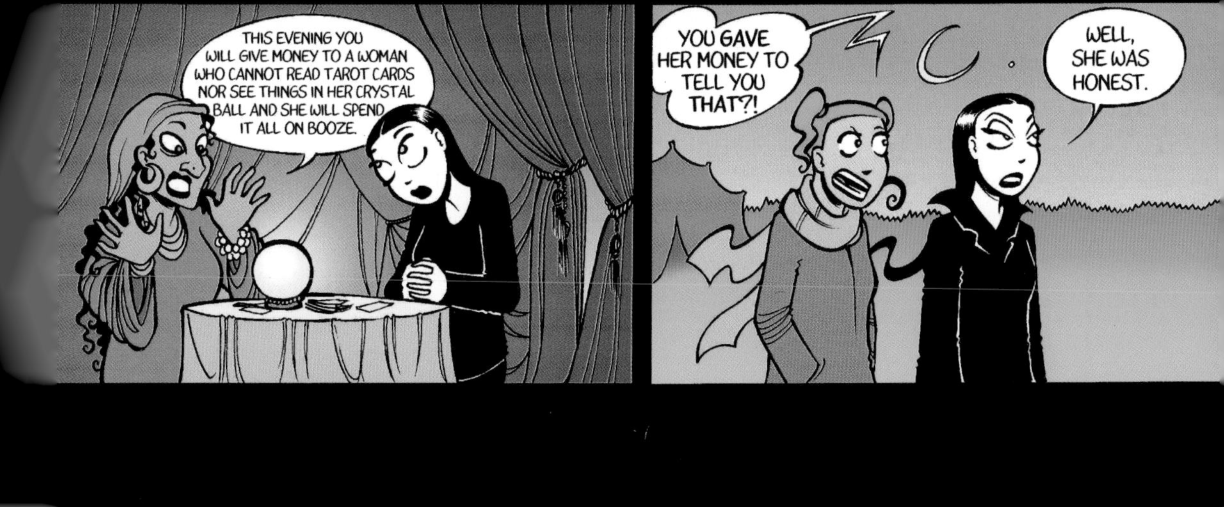
THIS EVENING YOU WILL GIVE MONEY TO A WOMAN WHO CANNOT READ TAROT CARDS NOR SEE THINGS IN HER CRYSTAL BALL AND SHE WILL SPEND IT ALL ON BOOZE.
YOU GAVE HER MONEY TO TELL YOU THAT?!
WELL, SHE WAS HONEST.

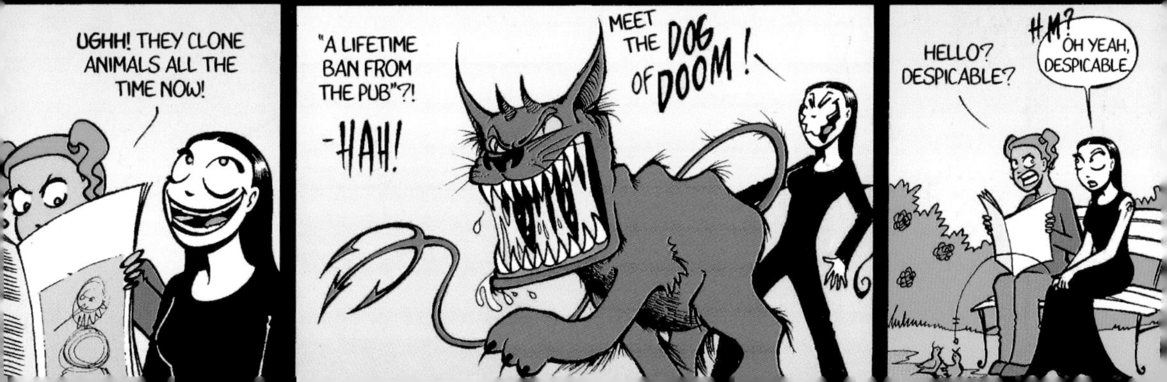
UGHH! THEY CLONE ANIMALS ALL THE TIME NOW!
"A LIFETIME BAN FROM THE PUB"?!
-HAH!
MEET THE DOG OF DOOM!
HELLO? DESPICABLE?
HM?
OH YEAH, DESPICABLE.

A CHAT WITH
LISE MYHRE

How did you get into producing comic strips?

I had been working as a freelance illustrator for a while when a friend tipped me about this comic strip competition. I have always loved to read comics, but up until then never considered making my own. I gave it a try, and didn't do too well, but it got me started — and I discovered I really enjoyed it.

When did Nemi first appear?

Nemi was my first attempt to draw a human being; my other characters up until then had all been rats, crocodiles or snakes... Nemi first appeared as a guest comic in *The Far Side Gallery* in 1997.

Where did you get your inspiration for the character?

I guess I set out to find an imaginary friend. It's important that we have things in common and that I like her, considering how many hours a day we spend together!

Was there a particular reason for making Nemi a goth?

Goths are fun to draw. Lots of ink. But it's also a scene I know and love — and I wanted to write about things I knew from experience.

Why did you name her 'Nemi Montoya'?

Nemi after a supposedly-enchanted lake in Italy, and Montoya after a character in one of my all-time favourite movies, *The Princess Bride*. "My name is Inigo Montoya. You killed my father. Prepare to die." (Yes, I know the rest of the lines by heart too. Being a movie-geek is another thing I share with Nemi.)

Do you have any particular influences or heroes?

A Swedish guy, Charlie Christensen, inspired